ISBN 978-1-331-98976-9
PIBN 10226838

1 MONTH OF FREE READING

at

www.ForgottenBooks.com

By purchasing this book you are eligible for one month membership to ForgottenBooks.com, giving you unlimited access to our entire collection of over 1,000,000 titles via our web site and mobile apps.

To claim your free month visit:

www.forgottenbooks.com/free226838

English
Français
Deutsche
Italiano
Español
Português

www.forgottenbooks.com

Mythology Photography **Fiction**
Fishing Christianity **Art** Cooking
Essays Buddhism Freemasonry
Medicine **Biology** Music **Ancient**
Egypt Evolution Carpentry Physics
Dance Geology **Mathematics** Fitness
Shakespeare **Folklore** Yoga Marketing
Confidence Immortality Biographies
Poetry **Psychology** Witchcraft
Electronics Chemistry History **Law**
Accounting **Philosophy** Anthropology
Alchemy Drama Quantum Mechanics
Atheism Sexual Health **Ancient History**
Entrepreneurship Languages Sport
Paleontology Needlework Islam
Metaphysics Investment Archaeology
Parenting Statistics Criminology
Motivational

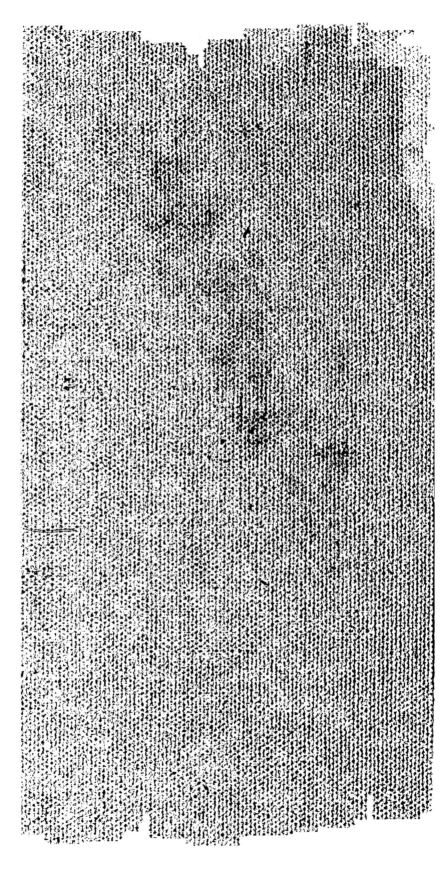

CRITICAL REFLECTIONS

O N

POETRY

A N D

PAINTING.

Written in FRENCH

By M. l'Abbé Du Bos, Member and perpetual
Secretary of the FRENCH ACADEMY.

Tranſlated into ENGLISH by

THOMAS NUGENT, Gent.

*From the fifth Edition reviſed, correƐted, and
inlarged by the Author.*

Ut piƐura poeſis erit. ———

HOR. de arte poet.

VOL. II.

═══════════════

LONDON:
Printed for JOHN NOURSE, at the *Lamb*, oppoſite
Katherine-Street in the *Strand.*
MDCCXLVIII.

THE
CONTENTS.

C H A P. I.
OF Genius in general.   *Page* 1

C H A P. II.
Of the Genius which forms painters and poets.   10

C H A P. III.
That the impulse of genius determines men to be painters or poets.   18

C H A P. IV.
Objection against the preceding proposition, and answer to the objection.   26

C H A P. V.
Of the studies and progress of painters and poets.   32

C H A P. VI.
Of artists without genius.   42

C H A P. VII.
That Genius's are limited.   49

A 2   CHAP.

The CONTENTS.

CHAP. VIII.

Of plagiaries : What it is they differ in from thofe, who improve their ftudies to the beft advantage. page 56

CHAP. IX.

Of the obftacles which retard the progrefs of young artifts. 67

CHAP. X.

Of the time requifite for men of genius to attain to that degree of merit of which they are capable. 82

CHAP. XI.

Of works fuitable to men of genius, and of artifts who counterfeit other people's manner. 90

CHAP. XII.

Of illuftrious ages, and of the fhare which moral caufes have in the progrefs of arts. 95

CHAP. XIII.

That phyfical caufes have probably had alfo a fhare in the furprizing progrefs of arts and fciences. 107

First REFLECTION: *That there are countries and times in which arts and fciences do not flourifh, notwithftanding the vigorous concurrence of moral caufes in their favor.* 110

Second REFLECTION. *That the arts attain to their higheft degree of elevation by a fudden progrefs, and that the effects of moral caufes cannot carry them to that point of perfection, to which they feem to have fpontaneoufly rifen.* 128

Third

The CONTENTS.

Third REFLECTION. *That eminent painters have been always cotemporaries with the great poets of their own country.* page 164

CHAP. XIV.

How it is possible for physical causes to influence the fate of illustrious ages. Of the power of air over human bodies. 176

CHAP. XV.

The power of the air over our bodies proved by the different characters of nations. 186

CHAP. XVI.

Objection drawn from the character of the Romans and the Dutch. Answer to this objection. 204

CHAP. XVII.

Of the extent of climates fitter for the arts and sciences, than others. And of the changes which these climates are subject to. 213

CHAP. XVIII.

That we must attribute the diversity of the air of different countries, to the nature of the emanations of the earth which vary according to the difference of countries. 217

CHAP. XIX.

That the difference we observe in the genius of people of the same country in different ages, must be attributed to the variations of the air. 224

CHAP.

The CONTENTS.

CHAP. XX.

Of the difference of manners and inclinations in people of the same country in different ages. page 230

CHAP. XXI.

Of the manner in which the reputation of poets and painters is established. 235

CHAP. XXII.

That the public judges right of poems and pictures in general. Of the sense we have to distinguish the merit of these works. 237

CHAP. XXIII.

That the way of discussion is not so proper for distinguishing the merit of poems and pictures, as that of sense. 250

CHAP. XXIV.

Objection against the solidity of the public judgments, and answer to this objection. 259

CHAP. XXV.

Of the judgment of people of the profession. 267

CHAP. XXVI.

That the public judgments prevail at length over the decisions of artists. 273

CHAP. XXVII.

That there is a greater regard due to the judgments of painters, than to those of poets. Of the art of discovering the hand of painters. 279

CHAP.

The CONTENTS.

CHAP. XXVIII.

Of the time when poems and pictures are appraised to their full value. page 283

CHAP. XXIX.

That there are some countries in which the value of works is sooner known, than in others. 288

CHAP. XXX.

Objection drawn from good works which have been disapproved at first by the public ; as also from bad ones that have been commended. Answer to this objection. 298

CHAP. XXXI.

That the public judgment is not recalled, but is every day more strongly confirmed. 307

CHAP. XXXII.

That, in spite of critics, the reputation of our admired poets will always increase. 314

CHAP. XXXIII.

That the veneration and respect for the excellent authors of antiquity will always continue. Whether it be true that we reason better than the ancients. 329

CHAP. XXXIV.

That the reputation of a system of philosophy may be ruined. And that this cannot happen to a poem. 353

CHAP.

The CONTENTS.

CHAP. XXXV.

Of the idea which men have of the writings of the ancients, when they do not underſtand the originals.

page 370

CHAP. XXXVI.

Of the errors which perſons are liable to, who judge of a poem by a tranſlation, or by the remarks of critics.

386

CHAP. XXXVII.

Of the defeᴄts we imagine we ſee in the poems of the ancients.

388

CHAP. XXXVIII.

That the remarks of critics on particular poems do not give people a diſreliſh of them ; and that when they lay them aſide, 'tis only in order to read better performances of the ſame kind.

400

CHAP. XXXIX.

That there are profeſſions, in which ſucceſs depends more upon genius, than upon the ſuccour which may be received from art ; and others on the contrary, in which it depends more upon art than genius. We ought not to infer, that one age ſurpaſſes another in the profeſſions of the firſt kind, becauſe it excels them in the ſecond.

403

CRITICAL

CRITICAL REFLECTIONS

ON

POETRY *and* PAINTING.

PART II.

CHAP. I.

Of Genius in general.

THE fublimity of poetry and painting confifts in moving and pleafing, as that of eloquence in perfuading. 'Tis not fufficient (fays Horace in a legiflative ftyle, in order to add more weight to his decifion,) that your verfes be elegant, they muft alfo be capable of moving the heart, and of infpiring it with fuch fentiments as they intend to excite.

Non fatis eft pulchra effe poemata, dulcia funto,
Et quocunque volent animum auditoris agunto.
HOR. de arte.

'Tis not enough, that plays are neatly wrought,
Exactly form'd, and of an even plot,
They must be taking too, surprize, and seize,
And force our souls which way the writers please.
                                        CREECH.

Horace would have addressed himself in the same manner to painters.

'Tis impossible for either a poem, or picture, to produce this effect, unless they have some other merit besides that of the regularity and elegance of execution. The best drawn picture imaginable, or a poem disposed in the most regular manner, and written with the greatest accuracy of style, may prove frigid and tiresom. In order to render a work affecting, the elegance of design and the truth of coloring, if a picture; and the richness of verfification, if a poem, ought to be employed in displaying such objects as are naturally capable of moving and pleasing [a].

If the heroes of a tragic poet do not engage me by their characters and adventures, the play grows tiresom, though it be written with the greatest purity of style, and the exactest conformity to the rules of the stage. But if the poet relates such adventures, and exhibits such situations and characters, as are equally interesting as those of Pyrrhus and Paulina, his poem calls forth my tears, and obliges me to acknowledge the artist as a divine performer, who has so great a command over my heart.

[a] *Ars enim cum a natura profecta sit, nisi natura moveat & delectet, nihil sane egisse videatur.* CIC. lib. 3. de Oratore.

Ille

Ille per extensum funem mihi posse videtur
Ire poeta, meum qui pectus inaniter angit,
Irritat, mulcet, falsis terroribus implet.

HOR. ep. 1. l. 2.

I fairly grant those poets wit, that rule
My passions as they please, disturb my soul ;
And then by a short turn my thoughts relieve :
Whose lively fiction makes me laugh or grieve ;
Whose well-wrought scenes nat'ral and just appear;
I see the place, and fancy I am there.

CREECH.

The resemblance therefore between the ideas, which the poet draws from his own genius, and those which men are supposed to have in the situation in which he represents his personages, the pathetic likewise of the images he has formed before he took either pen or pencil in hand, constitute the chief merit of poems and pictures. 'Tis by the design and the invention of ideas and images, proper for moving us, and employed in the executive part, that we distinguish the great artist from the plain workman, who frequently excels the former in execution. The best versifiers are not the greatest poets, as the most regular designers are far from being the greatest painters.

The works of eminent masters are seldom long examined, before we find that they considered the regularity and graces of execution not as the ultimate end of their art, but only as means for displaying beauties of a much superior nature.

They conform to rules, in order to gain our minds by a continued probability ; a probability capable of making us forget, that 'tis a mere fiction which

B 2

softens

softens our hearts. They display the beauties of execution, to prevent us in favor of their perfonages by external elegance, or the charms of language. They chufe to fix our fenfes on fuch objects, as are defigned to move our fouls. This is the end an orator propofes to himfelf, when he fubmits to the precepts of grammar and rhetoric : his principal aim is not to be commended for the correctnefs and elegance of his compofition, things that have no perfuafive virtue ; but to bring us over to his opinion by the force of his arguments, or by the pathetic of thofe images, which his invention furnifhes, and whereof his art fupplies him only with the oeconomical management.

Now a perfon muft be born with a genius, to know how to invent ; but to be able to invent well, requires a long and unwearied application. A man who invents ill, and executes without judgment, does not, as Quintilian [*] obferves when fpeaking of invention, even fo much as merit the name of an inventer. The rules which have been hitherto reduced to method, are guides that point out the way only at a diftance ; and 'tis merely by the help of experience, that men of a happy genius learn from thence, how to make a practical application of the concife maxims of thofe laws and their general precepts. Obferve always the pathetic (fay thefe rules) and never let your fpectators or auditors grow heavy or tired. Fine maxims indeed ! but a perfon born without a genius underftands nothing of the nature of the precept they contain ; and even the greateft

[*] *Ego porro nec inveniffe quidem credo eum qui non judicavit.* QUINT. Inft. orat. l. 3. c. 3.

genius

genius does not learn in a day's time to make a proper application of them. 'Tis fit therefore we treat here of the genius and studies requisite to form painters and poets.

If our artists happen to want that divine enthusiasm, which renders painters poets, and poets painters, if they have not, as Monsieur Perrault expresses it [a],

> *Ce feu, cette divine flâme,*
> *L'esprit de notre esprit, & l'ame de notre ame.*

> *That fire, that flame divine,*
> *Soul of our souls, and substance of our minds.*

they must continue all their lives in the low rank of journeymen, who are paid for their daily hire, but are far from deserving the consideration and rewards which polite nations owe to illustrious artists. They belong to that class of men, of whom Cicero says [b], that *they are paid for their work, not for their skill.* What little they know of their profession, they have learnt by rote, just as one might learn any other mechanic business. Men of the most ordinary capacities may become indifferent painters and poets.

Genius is an aptitude, which man has received from nature to perform well and easily, that which others can do but indifferently, and with a great deal of pains. We learn to execute things for which we have a genius, with as much facility as we speak our own mother-tongue.

A man born with a genius for commanding an army, and capable of becoming a great general by

---

[a] *Epistle on genius to Monsieur de Fontenelle.*
[b] *Quorum opera, non quorum artes emuntur.* Cic. de offic. l. 1.

         the

the help of experience, is one whose organical conformation is such, that his valor is no obstruction to his presence of mind, and his presence of mind makes no abatement of his valor. He is a man endowed with a sound judgment and lively imagination, who preserves the free use of these two faculties in the ebullition of blood, that succeeds immediately after the chillness, which the first view of great perils throws into human breasts ; in the same manner as heat follows cold in the accesses of an ague. In the midst of the ardor which makes him forget his danger, he sees, he deliberates, and resolves, as if he were tranquil and serene in his tent. He discovers therefore in an instant a wrong motion made by the enemy, which other officers much older than himself would have looked at a long time, before they could have discovered the motive or defect.

Such a disposition of mind, as I have here spoke of, cannot be acquired by art ; it can be possessed only by a person, who has brought it with him into the world. The apprehension of death intimidates those who are not animated at the sight of the enemy ; and those who are too much animated, lose that presence of mind so necessary for discerning distinctly what passes, and discovering justly what is most expedient. Let a man have ever so great abilities in cool blood, he can never be a good general, if the sight of the enemy renders him, either fiery, or timorous. Hence such numbers of people who reason so well on military affairs in their closets, perform so indifferently in the field. Hence such multitudes of men spend their whole lives in the art of war, without attaining the capacity of commanding.

I am

I am not ignorant that honor and emulation frequently induce men, who are naturally timorous, to take the fame fteps, and ufe the fame external demonftrations, as thofe who are born brave. In like manner men of the greateft impetuofity and fire obey their officers, when they are forbidden to advance where their ardor leads them. But men have not the fame command over their imaginations, as over their limbs. Wherefore, tho' military difcipline may be capable of reftraining the impetuous within their ranks, and of making the timorous ftand to their pofts ; yet it cannot prevent the inward confufion of either of them, nor with-hold the fouls of the former from advancing, or the hearts of the latter from retiring. Neither of them are any longer capable of having that liberty of mind and imagination in danger, which even the Romans themfelves commended in Hannibal [a]. This is what we call being every where prefent during the time of action.

What has been here faid of the art of war, may be equally applied to all other profeffions. The adminiftration of great concerns, the art of putting people to thofe employments for which they are naturally formed, the ftudy of phyfic, and even gaming itfelf, all require a genius. Nature has thought fit to make a diftribution of her talents amongft men, in order to render them neceffary to one another ; the wants of men being the very firft link of fociety. She has therefore pitched upon particular perlons to give them an aptitude to perform rightly fome things, which fhe has rendered impoffible to others ; and

[a] *Plurimum confilii inter ipfa pericula.* Livius l. 2.

the

the latter have a facility granted them for other things, which facility has been refused the former. Some have a fublime and extenfive genius in a particular fphere, while others have received the talent of application in the fame fphere; a talent fo neceffary for managing the execution. If the latter ftand in need of the former to direct them, the former want likewife the latter to execute their directions. Nature indeed has made an unequal diftribution of her bleflings amongft her children, yet fhe has difinherited none, and a man divefted of all kind of abilities is as great a phænomenon as an univerfal genius. It has been obferved by the moft celebrated mafter that ever appeared in the art of inftructing children [a], that men void of all abilities are as rare to be met with as monfters.

Providence feems even to have rendered peculiar talents and inclinations more common amongft fome people than others, in order to introduce that mutual dependence between different nations, which fhe has fo carefully eftablifhed between individuals. Thofe wants which engage individuals to form focieties, induce alfo nations to fettle a mutual correfpondence. It has been therefore the Divine will, that nations fhould be obliged to make an exchange of talents and induftry with one another, in the fame manner as they exchange the different products of their countries, to the end that they fhould have recourfe to each other, for the very fame motive which induces individuals to enter into fociety in order to

* *Hebetes vero & indociles non magis fecundum natures hominis eduntur, quàm prodigiofa corpora & monftris infignia.* QUINT. l. I. cap. I.

form

form one body of people; which is, the want of being well, or the defire of being better.

From the diverfity of genius the difference of inclination arifes in men, whom nature has had the precaution of leading to the employments for which fhe defigns them, with more or lefs impetuofity, in proportion to the greater or leffer number of obftacles they have to furmount, in order to render themfelves capable of anfwering this vocation. Thus the inclinations of men are fo very different, only by reafon that they all follow the fame mover, that is, the impulfe of their genius.

Caftor gaudet equis, ovo prognatus eodem,
Pugnis, quot capitum vivunt totidem ftudiorum
Millia.   HOR. fat. 1. l. 2.

Pollux on foot, on horfeback Caftor fights ;
As many men, fo many their delights. CREECH.

" Whence arifes this difference? Go and inquire,
" *fays the fame philofopher*, of the genius of each
" perfon, which alone is able to anfwer your quef-
" tion : every individual has his particular genius
" different from that of others, and in fome there is
" as great a difference as between black and white."

Scit genius natale comes qui temperat aftrum
Naturæ Deus humanæ, mortalis in unum
Quodque caput, vultu mutabilis, albus & ater.
          HOR. ep. 2. l. 2.

That genius only knows, that's wont to wait
On birth day ftars, the guider of our fate,
Our nature's God, that doth his influence fhed,
Eafy to any fhape, or good, or bad. CREECH.

                              This

This is what renders some poets pleasing, even when they trespass against rules, whilst others are disagreable, notwithstanding their strict regularity. The character, which men bring with them into the world, causes some, as Quintilian observes [a], to please us even with their failings, whilst others displease us in spite of their good qualities.

My subject will not permit me to expatiate any longer on the difference of genius in men and nations. Those who are desirous of further instruction on this article, and of improving the natural instinct which teaches us the knowledge of mankind, may read *the examen of minds by* Huarté, *and the portraiture of the characters of men, ages, and nations by* Barclay. A person may profit very much by the perusal of these works, tho' they do not merit the intire confidence of the reader ; but my business is to treat only of the genius which forms painters and poets.

CHAP. II.

Of the genius which forms painters and poets.

THE genius of these arts consists, as I apprehend, in a happy arrangement of the organs of the brain, in a just conformation of each of these organs, as also in the quality of blood which disposes it to ferment during exercise, so as to furnish a plenty of spirits to the springs employed in the functions

a *In quibusdam virtutes non habent gratiam, in quibusdam vitia ipsa delectant.* QUINT. Inst. l. 11. c. 3.

of

of the imagination. In fact, the exceffive laffitude and wafting of fpirits, which attend a long application of mind, are fufficient to evince, that the fatigues of the imagination confiderably exhauft the ftrength of the body. I have fuppofed here, that the compofer's blood is heated ; for indeed painters and poets cannot invent in cool blood ; nay 'tis evident they muft be wrapt into a kind of enthufiafm when they produce their ideas. Ariftotle mentions a poet, who never compofed fo well, as when his poetic fury hurried him into a kind of frenzy. The admirable pictures we have in Taffo of Armida and Clorinda, were drawn at the expence of a difpofition he had to real madnefs, into which he fell before he died. Apollo has his drunkennefs as well as Bacchus. *Do you imagine,* fays Cicero [a], *that Pacuvius wrote in cool blood ? No, it was impoffible. He muft have been infpired with a kind of fury, to be able to write fuch admirable verfes.*

But the very happieft fermentation of the blood can produce nothing but chimerical ideas in a brain compofed of vicious or ill-difpofed organs ; which are confequently incapable of reprefenting nature to a poet, fuch as it appears to other men. The copies he draws of nature have no refemblance, becaufe his glafs (to ufe this expreffion) is untrue. Now creeping along the ground, and now foaring above the clouds, if he happens fometimes to touch the truth, 'tis merely by accident. Such were amongft us the

---

[a] *Pacuvium putatis in fcribendo leni animo ac remiffo fuiffe? fieri nullo modo potuit ; fæpe enim audivi poetam bonum neminem, fine inflammatione animorum exiftere poffe, & fine quodam afflatu quafi furoris.* Cic. de orat. l. 3.

author

authors of the poems on St Mary Magdalen and St Lewis, both of them full of poetic rapture, tho'. never reprefenting nature, becaufe they copied her. intirely from the whimfical empty notions they had formed in their own extravagant imaginations : They both ftrayed equally wide, tho' by different roads, from the refemblance of truth.

On the other hand, if a brain furnifhed with a good difpofition of organs fhould want that fire, which proceeds from a warm blocd full of fpirits, its productions will indeed be regular, but flat withal and infipid.

Impetus ille jacet, vatum qui pectora nutrit.
OVID de Pont. l. 4. el. 2.

The fire is fpent, which warms the poet's breaft.

If the poetic fire warms him fometimes, it is foon extinguifhed, and throws out only a glimmering light. Hence 'tis faid, that a man of wit is able to write a ftanza, but he muft be born a poet to be capable of writing three. Thofe who are not born poets, are foon out of breath when they attempt to climb up Parnaffus. They have a glimpfe of what they ought to make their perfonages fay, but they cannot form any diftinct notion thereof, and much lefs exprefs it. They remain frigid, while they endeavour to engage us. *Nervi deficiunt animique.*

When the right quality of blood unites with a happy difpofition of organs, this favourable concurrence conftitutes, methinks, a picturefque or poetic genius ; for I diftruft all phyfical explications, confidering the imperfection of this fcience, in which we are continually obliged to have recourfe to conjecture. But the

the facts I have here explained, are certain, and these facts, tho' not so easily accounted for, are sufficient to support my system. I fancy therefore that this happy assemblage is, physically speaking, that divinity which the poets say dwells within their breasts.

Est Deus in nobis, agitante calescimus illo,
Impetus hic sacræ semina mentis habet.
OVID. fast. l. 1.

Within us dwells a God, who gives us fire ;
And seeds of life divine our souls inspire.

'Tis in this that divine fury consists, so often mentioned by the ancients ; on which a modern writer composed a learned treatise about fifty-five years ago [a]. This is what Montagne meant by the following words [b]: *Why should not those poetic sallies, which transport their author beyond himself, be ascribed to his happy fate, since he acknowledges, that they surpass his strength, and that they come not from himself, nor are they in any manner subject to his power ? The same may be said of painting, where some strokes happen to drop from the painter's hand, which are so superior to his own conception and knowledge, as to throw him into admiration and surprize.*

This happy fate consists in being born with a genius. Genius is the fire which elevates painters above themselves, and enables them to infuse a soul into their figures, and motion into their compositions. 'Tis the enthusiasm which seizes poets, when they behold the graces skipping along the meadows, where others see nothing but flocks of sheep. Hence their vein happens not to be always at their own disposal.

[a] *Petitus de furore poetico.* [b] Essays, book 1. chap. 23

I

Hence

Hence likewife their fpirit feems to abandon them fometimes ; and at other times *to pull them by the ear*, as Horace expreffes it, to oblige them to write or paint. Our genius, as we fhall explain more at large in the courfe of thefe reflections, ought to feel the effect of all thofe alterations, to which our machine is rendered fo fubject by feveral unknown caufes. Happy thofe painters and poets, who have a particulat command over their genius, who break loofe from the enthufiafm when they leave off work, and who never bring with them into company the drunkennefs of Parnaffus.

'Tis fufficiently evinced by experience, that all men are not born with talents proper for rendering them poets or painters : We have feveral inftances of thofe, whom a labor, continued for the fpace of many years rather with obftinacy than perfeverance, could never taife above the degree of fimple verfifiers. We have feen likewife men of very good parts, who after having copied feveral times the moft fublime productions in painting, have waxed old with their pencil and pallet in hand, without ever rifing higher than the rank of indifferent colorifts and fervile imitators.

Men born with the genius which forms the great general, or the magiftrate worthy of enacting laws, frequently die before their abilities are difcovered. A perfon poffeffed of fuch a genius cannot difplay it, unlefs he be called to thofe employments for which he is qualified ; and he frequently dies before he is intrufted with them. Suppofing even that he happens to be born within fuch a diftance of thefe employments, as to be able to reach them in the courfe of human

human life, he oftentimes wants the art neceſſary for acquiring them. Tho' he is capable of exer-
ciſing them with dignity, yet he is incapable of following the road which in his days leads to their
attainment. Genius is almoſt conſtantly attended with a kind of loftineſs and grandeur. I do
not mean that which conſiſts in tone and air ; for
this is no more than a ſurly look which indicates a
narrow mind, and renders a man as contemptible
in the eye of a philoſopher, as a footman dreſſed in
a diſcarded miniſter's livery is in the eyes of courtiers. I mean that loftineſs which conſiſts in the
nobleneſs of the ſentiments, and in an elevation of
mind which fixes a juſt price on the preferments to
which we aſpire, as alſo on the trouble which a perſon muſt be at to obtain them ; eſpecially if he is
obliged to apply to perſons whom he does not conſider as competent judges of merit. In fine, men
are qualified by virtues to fill the moſt eminent places,
but it frequently happens in all ages, that the way
to obtain them is by meanneſs and vice. There are
conſequently a great many geniuſes, born with a capacity for the higheſt employments, who die without
having ever had an opportunity of ſhewing their talents. Thus a perſon born with military or political
talents has not been intruſted with the command of armies, or with the government of provinces : and a
man born with a genius for architecture, has been re-
fuſed the direction of a ſtructure in which he might
have diſplayed his abilities.

Men who have a talent for poetry or painting are
not of the number of thoſe who depend, as it were,
on the ſmiles and good-will of fortune, to make their

appearance

appearance in public. Fortune cannot deprive them of the helps that are requisite for making their abilities known : This we shall explain here more at large.

The mechanic part of painting is very laborious, but it is not unsurmountable to those who are born with a genius for that art. They are supported against the disagreableness thereof by the allurement of a profession for which they find themselves qualified, and by the sensible advancement they make in their studies. Novices in the art find every where masters, whose direction contributes to shorten their journey. Be they eminent or indifferent masters in their professions, it does not signify ; a disciple that has a genius will always benefit by their instructions. 'Tis enough for him that they are capable of teaching him the practical part of the art, which they cannot be ignorant of, after having professed it ten or a dozen years. An able scholar learns to perform well, by seeing his master perform ill. The force of genius changes the most ill-digested precepts into right nourishment : It enables a person to do that best, which he has learnt of no body but himself. *Lessons given by masters*, says Seneca [a], *are like grains of seeds. The quality of the fruit which the seeds produce, depends principally on that of the soil, in which they have been sown. The very poorest produces good fruit in an excellent soil. Thus when precepts have been sown in a well-disposed mind, they shoot up most beautifully, and the mind brings*

[a] *Eadem praeceptorum ratio, quae seminum ; multum efficiunt, etsi angusta sint ; tantum, ut dixi, idonea mens accipiat illa, & in se trahat, multa invicem generabit, & plus praestet quàm acceperit.* SEN. ep. 38.

forth

forth, as it were, a better sort of grain than that which was sown. How many eminent men, in all kinds of professions, have learnt the first elements of the arts which raised them to immortality, from masters whose sole reputation is that of having had such illustrious disciples?

Thus Raphael, instructed by a painter of a midling rank, but supported by his own genius, raised himself much above his master after a few years practice. He had only occasion for Pietro Perugino's lessons to initiate him. The same may be said of Annibal Caraccio, of Rubens, Poussin, Le Brun, and other painters, whose genius we so much admire.

With respect to poets, the principles of their art are so very easy to be understood, and carried into execution, that they do not even so much as want a master to point out the method of studying them. A man of genius may learn of himself in two months time all the rules of French poetry. He is even capable of tracing these rules in a short time to their very source, and of judging of the importance of each by those principles which first established them. Wherefore the public never fixed any idea of glory to the chance of teaching the elements of poetry to scholars, who have afterwards filled succeeding ages with the fame of their reputation. There has never been any mention made of the masters, who first taught Virgil or Horace the art of poetry. We do not even so much as know who shewed Moliere and Corneille, tho' so near our own days, the cæsura and measure of our verse. Those masters are not supposed to have had a sufficient fhare in the glory of their difciples, to merit our giving ourfelves the trouble of inquiring and retaining their names.

C H A P. III.

That the impulfe of genius determines men to be painters or poets.

THERE is no great merit in being the firft to induce a young poet to take pen in hand, his very genius would have made him take it. A genius does not depend merely on the folicitation of friends, to fhew himfelf to the public. He is not difcouraged, becaufe his firft effays have not fucceeded ; he pufhes on with perfeverance, and makes his way at length acrofs the heedlefnefs and wanderings of youth.

'Tis not employments of too elevated, or too low a nature ; nor an education which feems to remove a man of genius from an application to things for which he has a talent; nor any thing elfe in fine, that can hinder him from fhewing at leaft the fphere of his genius, tho' he happens not to fill it. Whatever is propofed to him as the objeft of his application, can never fix him, unlefs it be that which nature has allotted him. He never lets himfelf be diverted from hence for any length of time, and is always fure to return to it, in fpite of all oppofition, nay fometimes in fpite of himfelf. Of all impulfes, that of nature, from whom he has recei ved his inclinations, is much the ftrongeft.

Cuftode

Cuftode & curâ natura potentior omni.

JUV. fat. 10.

For nature is a better guardian far,
Than fawcy pedants, or dull tutors are.

DRYDEN.

Every thing is converted into pallets and pencils in the hands of a boy endowed with a genius for painting. He makes himfelf known to others for what he is, when he does not yet know it himfelf.

The Annalifts of painting relate a vaft number of facts in confirmation of what I have here afferted. The moft eminent painters were not born in the fhops or work-houfes of their profeffion. There are very few painters fons, who, purfuant to the common cuftom of other arts, have been bred up in their fathers profeffion. Among the illuftrious artifts who reflect fo great an honor on the two laft centuries, Raphael was the only one, as far as I can remember, that was fon to a painter. Giorgione's, and Titian's parents, as well as thofe of Leonardo da Vinci, and Paolo Veronefe, never handled either pencil or chifel. Michael Angelo's father, according to common fame, was of a very good extraction, and lived without practifing any lucrative profeffion. Andrea del Sarto was a taylor's fon, and Le Teintoret fon of a dyer. The father of the Caraccio's did not profefs handling a pencil. Michael Angelo di Caravaggio was a mafon's fon, and Correggio's father a plowman. Guido was the fon of a mufician, Dominichino of a fhoemaker, and Albano of a mercer. Lanfranco was a foundling, who learned to paint of his own genius, almoft in the fame manner as Paf-

C 2

chal

chal learnt the mathematics. Rubens's father had neither fhop nor workhoufe, but was one of the magiftrates of Antwerp. The father of Vandyke was neither painter nor fculptor. Frefnoy, who has favoured us with a poem on the art of painting, which has merited a tranflation and notes from Monfieur de Pile, and has left us alfo feveral good pictures, was bred a phyfician. The parents of the four beft French painters of the laft century, Valentine, le Sueur, Pouffin, and le Brun, were not painters. The genius of thofe great men went, as it were, in fearch of them to their parents houfe, to conduct them thence to Parnaffus : For painters afcend Parnaffus as well as poets.

Poets who have attained to any degree of fame, are ftill a ftronger inftance of what I have advanced concerning the impulfe of genius. There never would have been a poet, had not the force of genius determined particular men to the profeffion ; for never was a parent known, that defigned his fon for this employment. Befides, thofe who are charged with the education of a boy of fixteen, endeavour always, for a very obvious reafon, to divert him from poetry, as foon as he fhews an extraordinary paffion for this art. Ovid's father was not fatisfied with bare remonftrances, in order to extinguifh the poetic fire of his fon ; but fuch was the force of genius, that our little Ovid is faid to have promifed in verfe to leave off making verfes, when he was whipt for this paffion. Horace's firft profeffion was that of bearing arms : Virgil was a fort of a jockey ; at leaft we read in his life, that he made himfelf known to Auguftus by his fecrets

crets for the curing of horfes, for which this great poet was introduced into this emperor's ftables. But to wave any further inftances drawn from ancient hiftory, let us reflect on the vocation of the poets of our own times. Examples drawn from facts whofe circumftances are diftinctly known, will be much more effectual than thofe that are borrowed from paft ages ; and we fhall be eafily induced to believe, that what has happened to the poets of our days, happened in like manner to thofe of all ages.

The moft eminent French poets, who honoured the reign of Lewis XIV. were by birth and education remote from the profeffion of poetry. None of them had been engaged in the employment of inftructing youth, nor in any of thofe occupations, which lead a man of genius infenfibly to Parnaffus. On the contrary, they feemed to have been kept at a great diftance from thence, either by profeffions they had already engaged in, or by employments, for which their birth and education defigned them. Moliere's father brought his fon up an upholfterer ; and Peter Corneille wore a counfellor's gown, when he wrote his firft pieces. Quinault was clerk to a lawyer, when he gave himfelf up to his inclination for poetry ; for his firft comic effays were wrote on papers half dawbed over with lawyers fcrollings. Racine wore an ecclefiaftic habit, when he compofed his three firft tragedies. The reader will find no difficulty in believing, that the retired gentlemen, who bred Racine up from his infancy, and were intrufted with the care of his education, never encouraged him to write for the ftage. On the contrary, they left

no

no ftone unturned to extinguifh the violent ardor he had for rhiming. Monfieur le Maitre, who had him particularly under his care, was as diligent in concealing from him all forts of books of French poetry, as foon as he difcovered his inclination that way ; as Pafchal's father was careful in keeping his fon from the knowledge of any thing that might lead him to think of geometry. La Fontaine's employment among the waters and forefts ought to have deftined him for the planting and cutting of trees, and not for making them fpeak. If Monfieur L'Huillier, Chapelle's father, could have directed the occupations of his fon, he would have applied him to any thing rather than poetry. In fine, every body knows by heart the verfes, in which Boileau, who was fon, brother, uncle, and coufin to a recorder, gives an account of his vocation from the duft of the rolls to the fmiling verdure of Parnaffus. All thefe great men are a convincing proof, that 'tis nature, not education, as Cicero obferves, which forms the poet [a]. Without afcending higher than our own times, let us caft an eye on the hiftory of other profeffions that require a particular genius. We fhall find that the greateft part of thofe who have diftinguifhed themfelves in thefe profeffions, were not engaged therein by the counfels or impulfe of their parents, but by their own natural inclination. Nanteuil's parents ufed the fame endeavors to hinder him from being an ingraver, as the generality of parents employ to ingage their children to

[a] *Poetam natura ipfa valere & mentis viribus excitari, et quafi divino quodam fpiritu afflari.* Cic. pro Arch poet.

a particular profeſſion. He was obliged ſometimes to climb up into a tree, and conceal himſelf there in order to exerciſe himſelf in drawing.

Le Fevre, born an algebraiſt and great aſtronomer, began to exerciſe his genius, when he followed a weaver's trade at Liſieux. The very threads of his loom contributed to improve him in the knowledge of numbers. Roberval, while tending his ſheep, could not eſcape the influence of his ſtar, which had deſtined him to be a great geometrician. He was learning geometry before he knew there was any ſuch ſcience. He was occupied in drawing lines and figures on the ground with his crook, when a perſon chanced to paſs by, who taking notice of the child's amuſement, undertook to procure him an education more ſuitable to his talents, than that which he received from the peaſant he lived with. The adventure which happened to Monſieur Paſchal has been publiſhed by ſo many different hands, that it is known all over Europe. His father, far from exciting him to the ſtudy of geometry, very induſtriouſly concealed from him whatever might give him an idea of this ſcience; from an apprehenſion of his growing too fond of that ſtudy. But he found that the child had attained by mere dint of genius to underſtand ſeveral propoſitions of Euclid. Deprived of guide or maſter, he had already made a moſt ſurprizing progreſs in geometry, without having any notion of ſtudying that ſcience.

The parents of Monſieur Tournefort tried every method imaginable to divert him from purſuing the ſtudy of botany. He was obliged, when

he

he had a mind to go a fimpling, to conceal himfelf, as other children hide themfelves to lofe their time at play. Monfieur Bernoulli, a gentleman of a very great reputation even from his youth, and who died thirty-five years ago profeffor of mathematics in the univerfity of Bafil, gave himfelf up to the ftudy of this fcience, notwithftanding the long and continual efforts his father ufed to divert him from it. He ufed to hide himfelf to ftudy the mathematics, which made him afterwards take for his device, a Phaeton with thefe words : *Invito patre fidera verfo.* *Thro' ftars I roll againft my father's will.* This infcription is at the bottom of his portrait in the library of the city of Bafil. Let the reader pleafe to recollect here likewife all that he has read and heard from ocular witneffes, concerning this very fubject. I fhould tire his patience, were I to relate all the facts that can be alledged to prove, that there is no obftacle unfurmountable to the impulfe of genius. Was it not againft his parent's inclination, that the modern writer of the life of Philip Auguftus and Charles VII. [a] applied himfelf to the compofing of hiftory ; a tafk for which he was bleft with fuch eminent talents ? Would Hercules, Soliman, and feveral other theatrical pieces have been ever compofed, had not the genius of their authors ufed violence to oblige them to fall into the occupation they fancied moft, in fpite of the education they received, and the profeffion they embraced ? What if we were to quit awhile the republic of letters, in order to run thro' the hiftory of other profeffions, and efpecially of great generals ? Is it not

[a] *Monfieur Baudot de Julli receiver of the land tax at Sarlat.*

commonly

commonly in oppofition to the advice of their parents, that thofe who are not born in a military family, venture to embrace the profeffion of arms?

Mens birth may be confidered two different ways.
Firft with regard to their phyfical conformation, and
the natural inclinations which refult from thence.
Secondly with refpect to the fortune and condition
in which they are born as members of a particular
fociety. Now the phyfical birth always prevails over
the moral one. This requires a little explication.
Education, which is incapable of giving a particular
genius or inclination to children that have it not from
nature, is unable likewife to deprive them of this
genius, or to ftrip them of this inclination, if they
have brought it with them into the world. Children
are conftrained only for a certain time, by the education they receive in confequence of their moral birth ;
but the inclinations that arife from their phyfical na-
tivity, laft with a greater or leffer degree of vivacity
as long as life itfelf. They are the effect of the conftruction and arrangement of our organs, and inceffantly impel us where our propenfity leads us.

Naturam expellas furca, tamen ufque recurret.

HORAT.

Strive to expel ftrong nature, 'tis in vain,
With double force fhe will return again,
And conquering rife above the proud difdain.

CREECH.

Befides, thefe inclinations are in their higheft vigor
and impetuofity exactly at that very period of life,
in which we are freed from the conftraint of education.

I   C H A P.

CHAP. IV.

Objection against the preceding propofition, and anfwer to the objection.

IT will be objected here, that I have not a juft idea of what paffes in fociety, if I imagine that all genius's anfwer their vocation. You know not (fome will fay) that the neceffities of life inflave, as it were, the greateft part of mankind to that condition of life in which they were educated from their infancy. Now the mifery of thefe conditions muft ftifle a great number of genius's, who would have diftinguifhed themfelves, had they been fo happy as to have been born in a more elevated fituation.

Ut fæpe fumma ingenia in occulto latent !
Hic qualis imperator, nunc privatus eft.

PLAUT. capt. act. 1. fcen. 2.

How oft are great abilities conceal'd
From public view ! how mean a garment hides
A genius fit for ftratagems of war ?

The greateft part of mankind being put out from their infancy to low mechanic trades, wax old in life before they have an opportunity of attaining to a proper degree of learning, in order to enable their genius to take wing. Some will tell me, perhaps in a pathetic ftrain, that yon poor coachman in tattered rags, who gets his wretched livelihood by lafhing to death a pair of meagre ftarved horfes, tied to a rotten coach juft ready to fall to pieces, would have

been

been perhaps a Raphael or a Virgil, had he been fo fortunate as to have been born of a genteel family, and
received an education proportioned to his natural
talents.

I have already granted, that thofe who are born
with a genius for the command of armies, or for
any other great employments, and even if you
will, for architecture, cannot difplay their abilities, unlefs they have a lift from fortune, and are
feconded by lucky conjunctures. Wherefore I
acknowledge, that the greateft part of thefe men
are ranked amongft the vulgar clafs of mankind, and
quit this life without leaving pofterity the leaft veftige
of their exiftence. Their talents lie buried becaufe
fortune does not help to difcover them. But the
cafe is quite different with refpect to fuch as are born
painters or poets, and 'tis thefe only who fall under
our prefent debate. With regard to thefe, I confider
the arrangement of the different conditions which
form fociety as a kind of fea : Your indifferent geniufes are overwhelmed by the waves ; but great
ones find means to reach the fhore.

Men are not, when born, what they are at thirty
years of age. Before they become mafons, plow-
men, or fhoemakers, they are a long while in a ftate
of childhood. During their youth they are a confiderable time fit for the apprenticefhip of a profeffion,
to which their genius has called them. The time
which nature has allowed to children, for their
prenticefhip in painting, lafts till their five and
twentieth year. Now the genius which forms a
poet or painter, prevents a perfon from his infancy, from falling into a fervile fubmiffion

to

to mechanic employments, and fets him upon feek-ing out ways and means of inftruction... Sup-pofing his parents to be in fo diftreffed a condition as to be incapable of giving him a fuitable education, upon his fhewing a much nobler inclination than his equals, fomebody elfe will take care of him ; the child himfelf will go in purfuit thereof with fo much ardor, that chance at laft will throw it in his way. When I fay chance, I mean every occafion particu-larly confidered ; for thefe occafions occur fo fre-quently, that the chance which makes the boy here mentioned embrace them, muft certainly come fooner or later. Children born with a fuperior genius, and men who make it their bufinefs to inftruct fuch chil-deren, muft certainly meet fome time or other.

'Tis no difficult matter to comprehend, how chil-dren of bright capacities, who are born in towns, fall into the hands of people capable of inftructing them. With regard to the country, in the beft part of Eu-rope, it is ftrewed with convents, whereof the teligi-ous never fail to take notice of a young peafant, who fhews a curiofity and aptnefs fuperior to his equals. He is foon taken in to ferve Mafs, where he has an opportunity of making his firft ftudies. Then he is fure of his point ; for the wit and capacity he has an opportunity of fhewing, engage other people to af-fift him ; nay he goes half way himfelf to meet the fuccours that are coming to him. Monfieur Baillet, to whom we are indebted for a great number of books, ftocked with very fingular erudition, was caught in this net.

Befides, the genius which determines a child to learning, or painting, infpires him with a great

averfion

averfion to thofe mechanic employments, to which he fees his equals applied. He conceives a hatred to low trades, by which his parents or friends would debafe the elevation of his mind. This forcible conftraint during his infancy, grows infupportable, in proportion as he advances in years, and becomes fenfible of his capacity and mifery His inftinct, and what little he hears of the world, furnifhes him with fome confufed ideas of his vocation, enough to convince him he is not in his right place. At length he fteals away from his father's houfe, as Sixtus Quintus and many others have done, and paffes to fome neighbouring town. If his genius inclines him to poetry, and confequently to a love for polite learning, his bright capacity will render him worthy of the attention of fome good-natured perfon or other. He will fall into the hands of fome body that will deftine him for the church; for all Chriftian focieties abound with charitable perfons who think it their duty to procure a proper education for poor fcholars who fhew any glimpfe of genius; and this in order to render them one day an ornament to their community, or church. Thefe children, when they grow up do not always think themfelves obliged to follow the pious views of their benefactors. If their genius leads them to poetry, they refign themfelves to it, and embrace a profeffion for which they were not defigned, but fitted by their education. How can we imagine, that good feeds will lye dead on the ground, when people are fo ready to pick up thofe, that give the leaft appearance of hopes?

Again.

Again. Were we even to grant that a malignity of conjunctures had inflaved a man of genius to an abject condition, before he had learnt to read, (which is to fuppofe the moft ill-natured treatment of fortune) yet his genius will fome way or another make its appearance. He will learn to read when he is twenty years old, to enjoy independent of any body that fenfible pleafure, which verfes afford to a'man who is born a poet. His next ftage will be to

poets rife from the fhops of none of the moft noble trades; the famous joiner of Nevers, and the fhoemaker, *repairer of Apollo's bufkins?* Has not Aubry, a mafter paver at Paris, exhibited within thefe fixty years tragedies of his own making? We have even feen a coachman, who knew not a letter, make verfes, which tho' very bad ones indeed, are fufficient neverthelefs to prove, that the leaft fpark of the very groffeft poetic fire cannot be fo fmothered, but it will throw out fome glimmering light. In fine,

a poet; 'tis his poetic genius that is the caufe of his learning, by forcing him to look out for means of attaining to a proper knowledge for perfecting his talent.

A child born with a picturefque genius, begins, when he is ten years old, to fketch with a coal the faints he fees painted in churches : Can twenty years elapfe before he finds an opportunity of cultivating his talent ? Will not his capacity make an impreffion on fomebody, who will carry him to a neighbouring town, where under the direction of a bungling mafter he will render himfelf deferving of the

attention

attention of an abler inftruftor, whom he will foon
go in fearch of from one country to another? But
let us fuppofe the boy ftays in his hamlet ; he will
cultivate there his natural genius, till his pictures
will furprize fome body travelling that way. This
was the fate of Correggio, who had raifed himfelf to
an eminent degree in painting, before the world knew,
that there was in the village of Correggio a very pro-
mifing young man, who was beginning to fhew a
new kind of talent in his art. If this be an accident
that feldom happens, 'tis becaufe 'tis rare to find
fuch great geniufes as Correggio, and ftill more rare
that they are not in their proper ftations when twenty
years old. Thofe who remain buried all their lives,
are, as I have already obferved, only weak capacities,
men who would never have thought of painting or
writing, had they not been defired to work ; men
who would never have gone themfelves in fearch of
the art ; but muft have had the way pointed out.
The lofs of thefe is not great, as they were never
defigned by nature for illuftrious artifts.

The hiftory therefore of painters and poets and of
other men of letters, abounds with facts which fufficiently evince, that children born with a genius will
furmount the greateft obftruftions their birth can
throw in their way to learning. In a fubjeft of
this nature facts are much ftronger than any reafonings whatfoever. Let thofe, who are unwilling to
give themfelves the trouble of reading this hiftory, re-
fleft a little on the vivacity and docility of youth,
and on the innumerable ways, whereof we have only pointed out a part, which can each in particular
conduft a child to fome fituation, in which he may
cultivate

cultivate his natural talents. They will be convinced of the impoſſibility there is, that out of a hundred geniuſes even one only ſhould remain for ever buried, unleſs he happens by a very odd caprice of fortune to be born among the Calmuc Tartars, or by ſome unaccountable accident to be tranſported in his infancy into Lapland.

C H A P. V.

Of the ſtudies and progreſs of painters and poets.

GENIUS is therefore a plant which ſhoots up, as it were, of itſelf ; but the quality and quantity of its fruit depend in a great meaſure on the culture it receives. The very brighteſt capacity cannot be perfected but by the aſſiſtance of a long courſe of ſtudy.

> *Natura fieret laudabile carmen an arte,*
> *Quæſitum eſt, ego nec ſtudium ſine divite vena,*
> *Nec rude quid profit video ingenium alterius ſic.*
> *Altera poſcit opem res & conjurat amicè.*
>
> HOR. de arte.

> *Now ſome diſpute to which the greateſt part,*
> *A poem owes, to nature, or to art ;*
> *But faith, to ſpeak my thoughts, I hardly know,*
> *What witleſs art, or artleſs wit can do :*
> *Each by itſelf is vain I'm ſure, but join'd*
> *Their force is ſtrong, each proves the other's friend.*
>
> CREECH.

Quintilian, another great judge of works of wit and learning, will not even allow us to diſpute, whether

'tis

'tis genius, or ftudy which forms the excellent orator. He determines, that there can be no fuch thing
as a great orator, without the concurrence of both.

But a man born with a genius, is foon capable of
ftudying by himfelf, and 'tis the ftudy which he
makes by his own choice, and determines by his
tafte, that contributes moft to accomplifh him. This
ftudy confifts in a continual attention to nature, and
a ferious reflection on the works of eminent mafters, attended with obfervations on what is proper to
be imitated, and what we fhould endeavour to furpafs. Thefe obfervations lead us to the knowledge
of many things, which our genius would never have
fuggefted to us of itfelf, or which it would not have
hit upon 'till very late. One becomes mafter in a
day's time of the manner and knack of execution,
which coft the inventer whole years of refearch and
labor. Even if our genius had vigor enough to
carry us fo far thro' an unbeaten road, we could not
however arrive there by the fole affiftance of our own
ftrength, unlefs we were determined to go thro' a
long and unwearied fatigue, fimilar to that of the firft
inventers.

Michael Angelo practifed in all probability a
long time, before he could draw the Eternal Father
with that character of Divine Majefty, in which he
has reprefented him. Perhaps Raphael, born with
a genius not quite fo bold as the Florentine, would
never have reached by the ftrength of his own wings

---

[a] *Scio quæri natura ne plus conferat ad eloquentiam quàm doctri-*
na. Quod ad propofitum noftri quidem operis non pertinet. Nec
enim confummatus artifex nifi ex utraque fieri poteft. Quint Inft.
lib. 11.

the fublimity of this idea. At leaft he would not have attained it, but after an infinite number of unfruitful attempts, and at the expence of feveral great and repeated efforts. But Raphael happens to have a glance of the Eternal Father drawn by Michael Angelo: ftruck with the noblenefs of the idea of this great genius, whom we may call a Corneille in painting, he lays hold thereof, and becomes capable in one day of throwing into the figures he draws in refemblance of the Eternal Father, the characters of grandeur, majefty, and divinity, which he had juft before admired in the performance of his competitor. Let us relate the ftory at length, as it is a better proof of what I advance, than a multiplicity of arguments.

Raphael was employed in painting the arched roof of the gallery which divides the apartments of the fecond floor of the Vatican ; which gallery is commonly called the lodges. The arched roof is not one continued vault, but is divided into as many fquare arches, as there are windows in the gallery, and thefe arches have each their particular center. Thus every arch has four facings, and Raphael was painting at that time, a ftory of the Old Teftament on each of the facings of the firft arch. He had already finifhed three days of the works of the creation, on three of thofe facings, when the adventure, I am going to mention, happened. The figure which reprefents God the Father in thofe three pictures is really noble and venerable ; but there is too great a foftnefs in it, without a fufficient mixture of majefty. 'Tis only a human head, Raphael having drawn it in the

tafte

tafte of thofe heads which painters make for Chrift; and if there be any difference, 'tis only that which, purfuant to the laws of art, ought to be between two heads, whereof one is deftined for reprefenting the Father, and the other the Son. Juft as Raphael commenced the frefcos of the vault of the lodges, Michael Angelo was employed in painting the vault of one of the Vatican chapels, built by Pope Sixtus IV. Tho' Michael Angelo, jealous of his ideas, had ordered no body to be fuffered to come into the

Struck with the Divine Majefty and the noble air of grandeur which Michael Angelo infufed into the figure of the head of the Eternal Father, which is

ing the great work of the creation, he condemned his own tafte in this point, and preferred that of his rival. Raphael has reprefented the Eternal Father in the laft picture of the firft lodge, with a more than human majefty. He does not infpire us mere-ly with veneration, he ftrikes us even with an aw-ful terror. 'Tis true, Bellori [a] difputes Michael An-

works the *tafte and manner* of Raphael. But the reafons alledged by this author do not appear to me folid enough to explode the common opinion founded on the tradition of Rome, and on other facts befides thofe which he denies.

Raphael was but an indifferent colorift, when he firft faw one of Giorgione's pieces. He inftantly per-ceived, that his art might draw from colors, far diffe-

[a] *Defcription of the pictures drawn by Raphael of Urbin in the chambers of the Vatican. p.* 86.

rent beauties from thofe, he had hitherto extracted. This convinced him that he had not a competent knowledge of the art of coloring. He attempted therefore to follow Giorgione's example, and guef-fing by mere force of genius, at that painter's manner of drawing, he fell very little fhort of his model. His effay was [a] a reprefentation of the miracle which happened at Bolfena, where the prieft who was celebrating mafs before the pope, and doubted of the truth of tranfubftantiation, faw the confecrated hoft become bloody in his hands. The picture here mentioned is commonly called the mafs of Pope Julius, and is painted in frefco on the top and fides of the window, in the fecond divifion of the fignature apartment in the Vatican. 'Tis fufficient to let the reader know, that this piece was drawn by Raphael in the prime of his practice, to convince him that the poetry muft be abfolutely marvelous. The prieft who had doubted of the real prefence, and had feen the con-fecrated hoft grow bloody in his hands during the elevation, feems penetrated with refpect and terror. The painter has exhibited each of the affiftants in his proper character ; but it affords a particular plea-fure to behold the aftonifhment of the pope's Swifs, who ftare at the miracle from the bottom of the pic-ture. Thus it is that this eminent artift has drawn a poetic beauty from the necefrity of obferving the *Coftume*, by giving the pope his ordinary retinue. By a poetic liberty, Raphael pitches upon the head of Ju-lius II. to reprefent the pope, in whofe prefence this miracle happened. Julius looks attentively at the mi-

[a] BELLORI, ibid.

racle,

racle, but does not feem to be greatly moved. The
painter fuppofes that the pope was too well convinced
of the real prefence, to be furprized with the moft
miraculous events that might happen to a confecrated hoft. 'Tis impoffible to characterife the vifible
head of the church, introduced into fuch an event, by
a nobler and more fuitable expreffion.   This expreffion fhews us alfo the ftrokes of Julius II's particular character.   We may eafily diftinguifh by his portrait the obftinate befieger of Mirandola.   But the
coloring of this piece, which was the firft caufe of my
mentioning it, is much fuperior to that of any of the
other pictures of Raphael.   There is no carnation
drawn by Titian, that reprefents more naturally the
foftnefs, which a body ought to have, that is compofed
of fluids and folids. The drapery feems to be made of
the fineft filk and woollen ftuffs juft come from the
hands of the taylor. Had Raphael drawn his other pieces with as true and rich a coloring as this, he would
have been ranked among the moft eminent colorifts.

The fame thing happens to young people that are
born poets ; the beauties which lye open in works
compofed before their time, make a lively impreffion upon them. They eafily catch the manner of turning verfes and the mechanic part of preceding authors.
I fhould be glad to be informed by fome authentic relation, how much Virgil's imagination was heated and
inriched upon his firft reading of Homer's Iliad.

The works of great mafters have another manner
of engaging young people of genius ; which is by
flattering their felf-love.   A young man of abilities difcovers in thofe works feveral beauties and
graces, of which he had already a confufed idea,

fet

fet off with all the perfection they can poffibly admit.
He fancies he traces his own ideas in the beauties
of a mafter-piece confecrated by the admiration of
the public. The fame adventure happens to him, as
that which befel Corregio, while he was yet a plain
burgher of the little town of Corregio, when he firft
faw one of Raphael's pictures. I faid a plain burgher, tho' a vulgar error debafes Corregio to the
condition of a peafant. Monfieur Crozat has extracted from the public regifters of the town of Corregio feveral proofs, which fufficiently demonftrate
that Vafari was miftaken in the idea he gives us of
Corregio's fortune, and efpecially in the recital he
makes of the circumftances of his death.

Corregio, who had not as yet raifed himfelf by
his profeffion, tho' already a great painter, was
fo full of what he had heard concerning Raphael,
whom princes contended to heap with prefents and
honors, that he fancied, an artift who made fo great
a figure in the world, muft have had a much fuperior degree of merit to his, which had not as
yet drawn him out of his mediocrity of fortune.
Like a man unpractifed in the world, he judged of the
fuperiority of Raphael's merit by the difference of his
circumftances. But as foon as he got fight of a
piece done by that eminent mafter, and after examining it with attention, he had confidered how he
fhould have treated the fame fubject himfelf, he
cried out, *I am a painter as well as he.* The fame
thing perhaps happened to Racine, the firft time he
read the Cid.

Nothing, on the contrary, is a greater indication
of a man's want of genius than to fee him examine
coldly

coldly the performances of thofe, who have excelled
in the art he pretends to profefs. A man of genius
cannot fo much as mention the faults committed by
great mafters, without previoufly commending the
beauties of their productions. He fpeaks of them
only as a father would mention the defects of his
fon. Cæfar, born with a military genius, was moved, even to fhed tears, at the fight of the ftatue of
Alexander. The firft idea which occurred to him
when he beheld the effigy of that Greek hero,
whofe glory had been carried by the wings of fame
to the moft diftant corners of the earth, was not of
the faults which Alexander had committed in his expeditions. Cæfar did not compare them with his great
exploits; no, he was ftruck with admiration.

I do not mean by this, that we muft conceive immediately a bad opinion of a young artift for criticifing
fome defects in the works of great mafters : for defects
they really had, as they were men. A genius, inftead
of hindering them from feeing thofe faults, will lay them
open. What I look upon as a bad prefage, is to fee a
young man very little moved with the excellency of the
productions of great mafters : that he is not tranfported into a kind of enthufiafm when he fees them :
that he wants to calculate the beauties and defects he
finds, in order to know whether he is to fet a value
upon them, and does not chufe to form a judgment on their merit, 'till after he has balanced his
account. Had he that vivacity and delicacy of fentiment, which are the infeparable companions of genius, he would be fo ftruck with the beauties of celebrated pieces, that he would fling away his fcales
and compaffes to judge of them, as other people

have

have always done, that is, by the impreffion made by thofe works. A balance is very unfit for deciding the value of pearls and diamonds. A rough pearl of a bad water, let it be ever fo heavy, can never be of an equal value with the famous *peregrine*, that pearl for which a merchant ventured to give a hundred thoufand crowns, reflecting, fays he to Philip IV. that there was a king of Spain in the world. An infinity of ordinary beauties thrown together, have not (to make ufe of this expreffion) fo much weight, as one of thofe ftrokes, which the moderns, even thofe who deal in eclogues, muft commend in Virgil's Bucolics.

Genius is foon diftinguifhed in the works of young people ; they give a proof of their being endowed with it, even before they are acquainted with the practice of their art. We find in their pieces fome ideas and expreffions, which have not occurred before, but are what we may call new thoughts. We obferve amidft a great number of defects, a fpirit that aims at very eminent beauties, and in order to attain his end, performs things which his mafter is incapable of teaching him. If thefe young fellows are really poets, they invent new characters, they fay fomething that one has not read before, and their verfes are full of turns and expreffions, which do not occur elfewhere. For inftance, your verfifiers of no genius that undertake to write operas, can give us nothing but thofe thread-bare expreffions, *which Lulli* (to make ufe of Boileau's words) *ufed to beat again with the founds of his mufic.* As Quinault was the author and inventer of the proper ftyle of operas, this ftyle is an argument that Quinault had a particular genius, which thofe

who

who can only trouble us with a repetition of what he faid before them, muft certainly want. On the contrary a poet, whofe genius renders him capable to give a being to new ideas, is able at the fame time to produce new figures, and to create new turns to exprefs them. We are very feldom obliged to borrow words to exprefs our thoughts. 'Tis even rare that we are at any great trouble to find them; fince thought and expreffion rife generally at the fame time.

A young painter of genius begins to differ foon from his mafter, in things wherein his mafter difagrees with nature. This he fees with his eyes almoft half fhut, and frequently better than he that pretends to inftruct him. Raphael was only twenty years old, and yet an eleve of Pietro Perugino, when he was employed at Sienna. Yet he diftinguifhed himfelf fo well, that he was intrufted with the compofition of feveral pictures. One fees here that Raphael had already ftrove to vary the airs of the head; that he endeavoured to give life to his figures; that he defigned the naked part under his draperies; in fine, that he did feveral things, which probably he never learnt of his mafter. Nay, his mafter himfelf became his difciple, for 'tis vifible by the pieces drawn by Perugino in Sixtus's chapel in the Vatican, that he learnt of Raphael.

Another mark of genius in young people, is to make a very flow progrefs in thofe arts and practices, which form the general occupation of the common run of mankind during their youth, at the very time that they advance with gigantic ftrides in the profeffion for which nature has intirely defigned them. Formed only for this
profeffion,

profeſſion, their capacity ſeems very mean, when they attempt to apply themſelves to other ſtudies. If they learn
them, 'tis with difficulty, and they execute them with a
very bad grace.   Wherefore a young painter, whoſe
mind is intirely taken up with ideas relating to his
profeſſion ; who is not ſo expeditiouſly fitted, as other
young fellows his equals, for the converſation and
practice of the world ; who appears whimſical in his
vivacity ; and whom an abſence of mind proceeding
from a continual attention to his ideas renders auk-
ward in his manners and carriage ; ſuch a young
painter, I ſay, generally turns out an excellent artiſt.
His very failings are a proof of the activity of his
genius.   The world to him is only an aſſemblage
of objects proper to be imitated with colors.   To
him the moſt heroic action in the life of Charles V.
is this great emperor's ſtooping to pick up Titian's
pencil.   Do not ſtrive to undeceive a young artiſt
thus prejudiced with the notion of the regard due to
his art ; let him fancy at leaſt, during the firſt years
of his practice, that men illuſtrious in the arts and
ſciences hold the ſame rank now in the world, as
they formerly held in Greece.   Do not, I ſay, endeavour to undeceive him, experience will too ſoon
perhaps ſet him right.

CHAP. VI.
Of artiſts without genius.

WE have already obſerved, that there is no
man, generally ſpeaking, but what brings
ſome talent with him into the world, proper for the
neceſſities

neceffities or conveniences of fociety ; but thefe talents are all very different. Some are born with a talent fuited for a particular profeffion ; and others for various pro- feffions. The latter are capable of fucceeding in many, but their fuccefs cannot be very confiderable. Na- ture places them in the world to fupply the fcarcity of men of genius, who are deftined to perform wonders in one fphere, out of which they have no activity.

In fact, a man fit to fucceed in feveral profeffions, is very feldom likely to be eminent in any one of them.   'Tis thus a foil proper for producing feveral forts of plants, cannot give fuch a perfection to any particular plant, as it would have attained to in a foil peculiarly fit for it, tho' improper for any other fpecies. A land equally fit for bearing grapes as well as corn, will produce neither of them in any eminent degree of perfection.   The fame qualities which render a ground particularly adapted for one fort of plant, difqualify it for another.

When one of thofe indeterminate fpirits, who are fit for every thing, only becaufe they are proper for nothing, happens by fome conjuncture to find the way to Parnaffus, he learns the rules of poetry well enough to avoid committing grofs miftakes.   He is generally attached to fome author, whom he chufes for his model.   He feeds his mind with the thoughts of his original, and loads his me- mory with his expreffions.   As the perfons here mentioned, who are deftined to be the nurfery of middling artifts, have not a genius themfelves, our copier, by confining himfelf to fuch models, is deprived of courfe of a proper fubject of imitation in nature.   Thefe fubjects he can

discern

discern only in such copies of nature as are made by men of genius. If this imitating artist happens to be a man of sense, tho' of a poor genius, he gets nevertheless a comfortable subsistence from the plunder he makes of another man's property. His versification is so correct, and his rhime especially is so rich, that he acquires by his new performances a kind of credit in the world. If he does not pass for a man of genius, he is esteemed at least as a person of some parts. 'Tis impossible (people will say) to write such verses without being a poet. Let him only take care not to expose himself to the public assembled , that is, let him avoid writing for the stage. The most elegant verses, that are barren of invention, or decked only with borrowed imbellishments, ought never to be produced in public, but with the greatest circumspection. There are only some peculiar receptacles, where they should be nursed in the beginning ; they ought not to see light at first but before particular friends ; and strangers should not hear them, till they have been first informed, that such and such gentlemen have commended them. The prevention caused by these applauses, imposes upon people for some time.

If our imitating artist be not a man of sense, he makes an unseasonable application of the strokes and expressions of his model, whereof we are injudiciously reminded by his verses : He behaves in the publication of his works, as in the composing of them : He affronts the public with greater intrepidity than Racine and Quinault were masters of on the like occasions. Hissed at upon one stage ; he

gets

gets himſelf houted at and damned on another : Expoſed to more contempt in proportion as he is more known, his name is adopted by the public as a common appellation for a wretched poet ; happy even in this reſpect, if his ſhame and infamy do not ſurvive him.

Men of a midling capacity for a great variety of things, meet with the ſame fate when they apply themſelves to painting. A perſon of this ſtamp, who by ſome accident is become a painter, ſhews rather a ſervile than an exact imitation of his maſter's taſte in the contours and coloring. He grows a correct, if not an elegant deſigner, and if we cannot commend the excellence of his coloring, we do not however obſerve any very groſs miſtakes contrary to truth, becauſe there are rules to direct him : But as none but men of genius can learn by rules to ſucceed in the ordonnance and poetic compoſition, his pictures are extremely defective in theſe articles. His works are agreable only by detached pieces, becauſe having never formed one general idea of his plan, but having licked it out by piece-meal, the parts are unconnected.

Infelix operis ſumma quia ponere totum
Neſciet.   Hor. de arte.

But he's a ſot, unhappy in his art,
Becauſe he cannot faſhion every part,
And make the whole complete.   Creech.

In vain a perſon of this ſtamp ſerves his apprenticeſhip under the beſt of maſters ; he can never make in ſuch a ſchool, the ſame progreſs as a man of genius can with the aſſiſtance of an indifferent

different inftructer. A mafter, as Quintilian obferves [a], *is incapable of communicating to his difciple
the talent and art of inventing, which are the chief
accomplifhments of orators and painters.* A painter
may therefore impart the fecrets of his practice, tho'
he cannot his talents for compofition and expreffion.
A difciple void of genius, is frequently incapable of
attaining even to that perfection which his mafter is
arrived to in the mechanic part of his art. A fervile
imitator will naturally fall fhort of his model,
becaufe he adds his own faults to thofe of the
perfon he imitates. Befides, if the mafter be a man
of genius, he will foon be tired of inftructing fuch
a difciple. He finds he is upon the rack, as Tully [b]
expreffes it, when he fees his pupil fo extreamly dull
in what he himfelf comprehended fo quickly when
he was a fcholar.

We meet with nothing new in the compofitions
of painters of no genius, nothing fingular in their
expreffions. They are fo very barren, that when
they have copied after others for a confiderable
time, they fall at length to copying themfelves ;
and as foon as we know what picture they have
promifed, we find it eafy to guefs at the greateft
part of their figures. The habit of imitating
others, leads us to imitate ourfelves. The idea
of what we have painted, occurs always eafier
to our minds than what has been done by
others. 'Tis the firft thing that prefents itfelf to

[a] *Ea quæ in oratore maxima funt, imitabilia non funt. Ingenium,
inventio, vis, facilitas & quidquid arte non traditur.* QUINT.
[b] *Quod enim ipfe celeriter arripuit, id cum tarde percipi videt,
difcruciatur.* CIC. pro Rofcio.

thofe

thofe who feek for their compofition and figures in their memory rather than in their imagination. Some, like Baffano, have no fcruple in making a downright repetition of their own works. Others, endeavouring to conceal the thefts they have made from their own productions, introduce their per-fonages again upon the ftage, under a difguife indeed, but fuch a difguife as may be eafily dif-covered ; by which means their theft becomes ftill more odious. The public confiders a work in its poffeffion as its real property, and thinks itfelf extremely ill ufed to be obliged to purchafe a fecond time, what it already had bought at the price of its commendations.

As it is eafier to follow a beaten track, than to open a new road, an artift without a genius attains quickly to that degree of perfection to which he is capable of rifing : He foon arrives to his proper height, and then grows no taller. His firft effays are frequently as perfect as the works he produces in his full maturity. We have feen painters without a genius, but grown famous for fome time by the dexterity of putting themfelves forward, who per-form much worfe when they come to the ftate of man-hood, than during their youth. Their mafter-pieces are in thofe countries where they made their ftudies ; and they feem to have loft one half of their merit by repaffing the Alps. In effect thefe artifts, when they come back to Paris, do not find fo eafy an opportunity there, as at Rome, of ftealing pieces, and fometimes intire figures to inrich their compofi-tions. Their pictures grow extremely poor, when they have no longer an opportunity to pick up from the per-

formances

formances of eminent mafters, the head, the foot, the attitude, and fometimes the ordonnance they wanted.

We may compare the magnificent parade of the ancient and modern mafter-pieces, which render Rome the moft fuperb city in the world, to thofe fhops where a great quantity of jewels are expofed to fale. Let thofe jewels be fet forth in ever fo great a profufion, the number you bring home, will be only in proportion to the money you took with you for the purchafe. Thus there is no folid benefit reaped from the great mafter-pieces of Rome, but in proportion to the genius with which they are confidered. Le Sueur, who never was at Rome, and had feen only from afar, that is, in copies, the riches of this great capital of the polite arts, reaped more benefit from thence than feveral painters who are apt to boaft of having dwelt many years at the foot of the capitol. In like manner a young poet improves by reading Virgil and Horace in proportion only to his genius, by the light of which he ftudies the ancients.

Let thofe who are born with an indeterminate genius, fuch as have an aptnefs and capacity for every thing, apply themfelves therefore to thofe arts and fciences, in which the moft knowing are the moft eminent. There are fome profeffions, in which the imagination or art of inventing is as prejudicial, as it is neceffary in poetry and painting.

C H A P.

CHAP. VII.

That Genius's are limited.

MEN born with a genius for a particular art or profeſſion, are the only people capable of any eminent degree of ſucceſs ; but then 'tis obſervable, that theſe are the only profeſſions and arts, in which they can poſſibly excel. They fall into a very low character, when they quit their own ſphere ; and loſe their vigor and penetration of mind, as ſoon as they enter upon things for which nature has not formed them.

The men here mentioned are not only debarred from excelling in more than one profeſſion, but are likewiſe generally confined to one of thoſe branches into which the profeſſion is divided. *'Tis almoſt impoſſible,* ſays Plato, *that the ſame man ſhould excel in works of a different nature. Tragedy and comedy are, of all poetic imitations, thoſe which have the greateſt reſemblance ; and yet the ſame poet has not an equal ſucceſs in both. Actors who play in tragedies, are not the ſame as thoſe who act in comedies* [a]. Thoſe painters who have excelled in drawing the ſouls of men, and in a juſt expreſſion of the paſſions, were but indifferent coloriſts. Others have

---

[a] Οὐκοῦν κỳ περὶ μιμήσεως; ὁ αὐτὸς λόγος, ὅτι πολλὰ ὁ αὐτὸς μιμεῖσθαι εὖ, ὥσπερ ἕν, ἐ δυναΤός. Οὐ γὰρ ἔν. Σχολῇ ἄρα ἐπιΤηδεύσει γί τι ἅμα τῶν ἀξίων λόγα ἐπιΤηδευμάτων, κỳ πολλὰ μιμήσεΤαι, κỳ ἔΤαι μιμηΤικός· ἐπεί Τε ἐδὲ τὰ δοκᾶνΤα ἐγΓὺς ἀλλήλων εἶναι δύο μιμήμαΤα δύνανΤαι οἱ αὐτοὶ ἅμα εὖ μιμεῖσθαι, οἷον κωμῳδίαν κỳ τραγῳδίαν ποιᾶνΤες. PLATO *de Repub.* 1 3.

made the blood circulate in the flesh of their figures; but they have not been so well acquainted with the expression, as the midling artists of the Roman school. We have known several Dutch painters endowed with a genius for the mechanic part of their art, and especially for 'the marvelous talent of

row space, a talent for which they have been indebted to a particular patience of mind, which enabled them to hang for a long time over the same work, without being seized with that vexation and fretting, which is apt to rise in men of a livelier disposition, when they see their efforts prove several times abortive. These flegmatic painters have investigated with a kind of obstinacy, and by an infinite number of attempts, the teints, the mezzo-tintos, and in short every thing necessary for the degradation of the colors of objects; and by their perseverance they have learnt to paint even light itself. We are inchanted with the magic of their chiaro-scuro; for the various shadows are not better laid out in nature, than in their pieces. But those very painters have been unsuccessful in other parts of their art, of no less consequence. Bare of all invention in their expressions, and incapable of raising themselves above such objects as were present to them, they have drawn nothing but low passions, and a mean ignoble nature. The scene of their pieces is a shop, a guard-house, or a country kitchen; and their heroes are a parcel of sneaking fellows. The Dutch painters here mentioned, who have attempted historical pieces, have drawn works that are admirable for their chiaro-scuro, but in every other

other refpect ridiculous. The dreffes of their perfonages are extravagant, and their expreffions low
and comic. They draw Ulyffes without art or cunning, Sufanna without modefty, and Scipio without
any ftroke of grandeur or courage. Thus the pencil of thefe frigid artifts deprives thofe illuftrious
heads of their known character. Our Dutchmen,
(among whom 'tis plain I do not rank the painters
of the fchool of Antwerp,) were perfectly fenfible of
the value of local colors, but they were incapable
of drawing the fame advantage from thence as the
painters of the fchool of Venice. The talent of coloring, as practifed by Titian, requires invention ;
and depends more on a fecundity of imagination in
contriving proper expedients for the mixture of colors, than upon an obftinate perfeverance in re-touch-
ing the fame thing a hundred times.

We may rank Teniers in the number of the painters here mentioned ; for tho' he was born in Bra-
bant, yet his genius determined him to imitate the
tafte of the Dutch painters, rather than that of Rubens and Vandyke, his countrymen and cotemporaries. Never was there a painter, that had greater
fuccefs than Teniers in low fubjects, fuch was the
excellency of his pencil. He underftood the chiaro-
fcuro perfectly well, and furpaffed all his competitors in the knowledge of local colors. But when he
attempted hiftory-painting, his fuccefs was even inferior to that of indifferent painters. His *pafticci*,
whereof he has drawn a vaft number, are immediately known by the mean and ftupid air of the
heads of the principal perfonages. We commonly
give the name of *paftrci* to pictures drawn by an

impoftor,

impoſtor, who imitates the hand and manner of com- poſing and coloring of another painter, under whoſe name he has a mind to expoſe his work to the public.

There are to be ſeen at Bruſſels in the gallery of the Prince de la Tour ſome large hiſtorical pieces, deſigned for Cartoons to a ſuit of hangings, and re- preſenting the hiſtory of the Turriani of Lombardy, from whence the houſe of la Tour Taxis is deſcend- ed. The firſt pictures are done by Teniers, who cauſed the reſt to be finiſhed by his ſon. Nothing can be more indifferent with reſpect to compoſition and expreſſion.

M. de la Fontaine had certainly a natural ge- nius for poetry ; but his talent was for tales and fables, which he has treated with an agreable erudi- tion, of which this kind of writing did not ſeem ſuſ- ceptible. When La Fontaine attempted to write comedies, they never miſſed being received with the hiſſes and cat-calls of the pit ; and the ſame fate, 'tis known, attended his operas. Each kind of poe- try requires a particular ability, and nature cannot beſtow an eminent talent upon a man, without refu- ſing to favor him with other qualifications. Where- fore 'tis ſo far from being aſtoniſhing that La Fon- taine compoſed bad comedies, that it would have been a ſubject of ſurprize, had he wrote good ones. If Pouſſin had colored as well as Baſſano, he would have made as great a figure among painters, as Julius Cæſar among heroes. Had Cæſar been juſt, his clemency would have rendered him the moſt illuſtrious of all the Romans.

'Tis

'Tis therefore a matter of great importance to the noble artifts here mentioned, to know wha tkind of poetry and painting their talents have defigned them for, and to confine themfelves to that for which nature has formed them. Art can only per-fect the *aptitude* or talent which we have brought with us into the world, but cannot give us a talent which nature has refufed us. It makes indeed a great addition to our abilities, but this is when we ftudy a profeffion for which we have been deftined by nature. *The principal part of art*, fays Quintilian [a], *confifts in attempting things that are becoming. But this is a point that can neither be learnt without art, nor be intirely acquired by precepts.* It often hap-pens that a painter remains concealed among the croud, who would have been ranked among the moft eminent of his profeffion, had he not been be-witched by a blind ambition, attempting to excel in fome kinds of painting for which he had no capacity; whereby he *neglected* the parts, for which he had a natural ability. The works he attempted, are, if you will, of a fuperior clafs : But would it not have been more honourable for him to have held the firft place among land-fkip painters, than the laft among the painters of hiftory ? Is it not a greater credit to be mentioned as one of the principal por-trait-painters of our time, than as a wretched ranger of lame and ignoble figures ?

The paffion of being efteemed an univerfal genius, debafes a great number of artifts. When the value of an artift is rated in general, we are apt to take as

<hr />

[a] *Caput eft artis decore quod focies Ita neque fine arte, neque totum arte tradi poteft.* QUINT. Inft. l. 11.

much

much notice of his indifferent, as of his valuable pieces: Wherefore he runs the rifk of having a character or definition given of him as author of the former. What a number of eminent authors fhould we have had, if their writings had been lefs voluminous! Had Martial left us only thofe hundred epigrams, which men of learning in all countries generally know by heart; had his book contained no larger a collection than that of Catullus; there would be no fuch great diftinction made between him and that ingenious Roman knight. At leaft there would never have been a great wit [a] fo incenfed at feeing thefe two writers compared, as to commit every year with great ceremony a copy of Martial to the flames, in order to appeafe by this whimfical facrifice the poetic manes of Catullus.

Let us return to the limits prefcribed by nature to the moft extenfive genius, and conclude, that the leaft limited genius is that, whofe bounds are not of fo narrow a compafs as thofe of others. *Optimus ille qui minimis urgetur.* Now there is nothing more proper for difcovering the limits of an artift's genius, than his performances in fome branch or kind, for which nature has not defigned him.

Emulation and ftudy can never enable a genius to leap beyond the bounds which nature hath prefcribed to his activity. Labor indeed may perfect him, but I queftion whether it can give him a greater extent than he has received from nature. The extent which labor feems to communicate to genius's, is only apparent; and art inftructs them to conceal their limits, but it never extends them. The fame thing happens to men in all profeffions, as in that of gaming. A man who has attained in a particular kind of play to the utmoft extent of his ability, advances no farther, and the leffons of the beft mafters, and even the continual practice of gaming for the fpace of feveral years, are incapable of giving him any greater improvement. Wherefore labor and experience will enable painters, as well as poets, to give a greater correctnefs, but not a greater fublimity, to their productions. They cannot make them bring forth works of a character fuperior to their natural capacity. A genius who has only received of nature the wings of a dove, will never learn to foar with the flight of an eagle. We feldom acquire, as Montagne obferves, by ftudying other men's works, the talent they had for invention. [a] *The imitation of fpeaking is foon acquired ; that of judging and inventing is not fo eafily attained. Women's manteaus and attire may be borrowed ; but ftrength and nerves cannot.*

The leffons of an eminent mufician unfold our organs, and learn us to fing methodically : And yet they make but a very fmall alteration in the found and extent of our natural voice, notwithftanding they feem to give it a foftnefs and fome kind of extent.

Now that which conftitutes the difference of our minds, as long as the foul continues united to the body, is a thing no lefs real than what difcriminates our voices and faces. Philofophers of all fects agree, that the character of our minds proceeds from the conformation of thofe organs of the brain, which affift the foul to difcharge its functions. Now it de-

[a] Effays, book 2. chap. 5.

E 4   pends

pends no more on us to change the conformation, or configuration of thefe organs than to alter that of the mufcles and cartilages of our face and throat. If ever there happens any phyfical alteration in thefe organs, 'tis not produced by the mere effort of our will, but by fome phyfical change fupervening in our conftitution ; and they are altered in the fame manner as the other parts of the body. Our minds do not therefore attain to a refemblance by looking at one another ; unlefs it be as our voice and faces are capable of acquiring a likenefs. Art does not augment the phyfical extent of our voice, or increafe our genius, only inafmuch as the exercife, wherein confifts the practice of the art, is capable of making a real change of fome part of the conftruction of our organs. Now the change which exercife is capable of making is a very fmall matter. Art does no more remove the defects of organization which it learns to conceal, than it augments the natural extent of fuch phyfical talents as are improved by its leffons.

C H A P. VIII.

Of plagiaries : What it is they differ in from thofe, who improve their ftudies to the beft advantage.

BUT cannot (fome will fay) an artift fupply the want of elevation and the fterility of his genius, by tranfplanting into his works thofe beauties which are fo much admired in the productions of eminent mafters ?

mafters ? Can't he foar by the counfels of his friends, to where the ftrength of his own genius would never have been able to carry him ?

.With refpect to the firft point, my anfwer is, that it was always allowable to receive the affiftance of other people's wit, provided it be done without pla-giarifm.

. That which conftitutes a plagiary, is the publifh-ing another man's work for one's own. 'Tis giving for our own compofition, intire verfes which we have had neither trouble nor merit in tranfplanting from another man's performance. I fay, when we have tranfplanted without trouble, for if we happen to adopt the verfes of a poet, who has wrote in a dif-ferent language from our own, we are not then guilty of plagiarifm. The verfe becomes in fome mea-fure ours, becaufe the new expreffion, with which we have clad another perfon's thought, is our proper-ty. There is fome merit in committing fuch a theft, as it cannot be executed well without trouble, and without being endowed at leaft with the talent of expreffion. There is as much induftry requifite to fucceed in this, as was neceffary in Sparta to fteal like a gentleman. To difcover in our own language pro-per terms, and equivalent expreffions to thofe which the ancient or modern author has made ufe of : To be able to give them a proper turn, in order to convey the energy of the thought, and prefent us with the fame image as the original, is not the tafk and bufinefs of a fcholar. Thefe thoughts tranf-planted thus from one language into another, can fucceed only in the hands of thofe, who have at leaft the talent of inventing terms. Wherefore

when they fucceed, one half of their beauty belongs to thofe who fet them in a new light.

The reputation therefore of Virgil cannot be di-
minifhed, by fhewing that he borrowed a vaft number
ber of things from Homer. Fulvius Urfinus put
himfelf to a great deal of trouble to very little purpofe, if he collected all the paffages which the Latin poet imitated in the Greek, merely to afperfe the
character of the Latin writer. Virgil has acquired,
as it were, a right to the property of all thofe ideas
which he borrowed of Homer. They belong to him
fairly in Latin, becaufe of the elegant turn and con-
cifenefs with which he has rendered them in his own
language, and the dexterity with which he fets thofe
fragments in a regular building whereof he is the
architect. Thofe who imagined they might leffen
Boileau's reputation, by printing by way of com-
ment, at the bottom of the text of his works, the
verfes of Horace and Juvenal which he inchafed in
his, were very much miftaken. The verfes of the
ancients, which this poet has fo artfully turned into
French, and fo completely rendered an homogeneous
part of the work in which he ingrafts them, that
the whole feems to be one connected thought of the
fame perfon, are as great an honour to Boileau, as
thofe that flow quite new from his vein. The original turn he gives his tranflations, the boldnefs of
his expreffions, as free as if they had rifen with his
conception, difplay almoft as much invention as the
production of a new thought. This is what made
La Bruyere fay [a] that Boileau feemed to create other
mens ideas.

[a] Harangue to the Academy.

It

It even adds a peculiar grace to one's works, to imbellifh them with antique fragments. The verfes of Horace and Virgil well tranflated, and feafonably applied in a French poem, have pretty near the fame effect as the antique ftatues in the gallery of Verfailles. The readers are pleafed to fee in a new drefs, the thought with which they were formerly delighted in Latin. They are glad to have an opportunity of reciting the verfes of an ancient poet, in order to compare them with thofe of a modern imitator, who ftrives to vie with his original. There is nothing fo inconfiderable but felf-love fets a value upon when it flatters our vanity. Wherefore authors moft celebrated for the fecundity of their genius, have not difdained to add this kind of grace or ornament to their works. Was it a fterility of imagination which obliged Corneille and La Fontaine to borrow fo many things from the ancients ? Moliere has frequently done the fame, and tho' he was rich enough with his own fund, he tranflated neverthelefs ten verfes fucceffively from Ovid, in the fecond act of the Mifanthrope.

We may admit of the affiftance of thofe poets, who have wrote in the modern tongues ; as we may benefit by the help of the works of the Greeks and Romans ; but when we make ufe of the productions of modern poets, we ought, methinks, to mention whom we are indebted to, efpecially if we borrow a confiderable part. I do not approve, for inftance, M. de la Foffe's borrowing the intrigue, characters, and principal incidents of the tragedy of Manlius [a], from Mr.

[a] *Manlius was acted in 1697.*

Otway's

Otway's Englifh play, intitled, *Venice Preferved*[b], without mentioning the work which had been of fuch fervice to him. All that can be alledged in defence of M. de la Foffe, is, that he has only ufed reprifals in quality of a Frenchman, becaufe Otway himfelf borrowed from the hiftory of the confpiracy of Venice, by the abbot of St Real[c], the fubject, the principal characters, and the moft beautiful paffages of his piece. If M. de la Foffe has taken from Otway fome things which the Englifh poet did not borrow of the abbot of St Real, as the epifode of the marriage of Servilius, and the Cataftrophe, 'tis by reafon that he who retakes a fhip which had been made a prize by the enemy, is fuppofed to have a right to the goods, which they have added to the freight of the veffel.

As all painters fpeak, as it were, the fame language, they cannot borrow the famous ftrokes of another painter, if his works be ftill exifting. Pouffin might have adopted the notion of the Greek painter, who reprefented Agamemnon with his head veiled at the facrifice of Iphigenia, in order to convey a ftronger idea of the excefs of grief which overwhelmed the father of the victim. He might have made ufe of this ftroke for the fame expreffion, by reprefenting Agrippina hiding her face with her hands in the picture of the death of Germanicus. The Greek painter's piece was no longer exifting, when the Frenchman drew his. But Pouffin would have been charged with having ftole this ftroke, were it to be feen in one of Raphael's or Caraccio's pictures.

a *Acted in* 1682.   b Printed in 1674.

I   As

As there is no merit in ftealing a head from Raphael, or a figure from Dominichino ; as the theft is not attended with any great labor, 'tis forbidden under pain of public contempt : But as both talent and labor are required to animate the marble of an antique figure, and to make of a ftatue a living figure, which fhall concur to the fame action with other perfonages, 'tis a commendable performance. A painter is therefore allowed to make ufe of an Apollo of Belveder, to reprefent Perfeus, or fome other hero of Perfeus's age, provided he animates this ftatue, and is not fatisfied with copying it correctly, in order to place it in the picture juft as it is in the niche. Let painters therefore give life to thofe ftatues before they make them act. This is what Raphael has done, who feems, Prometheus like, to have ftole fire from heaven to animate them. I refer thofe who defire further inftructions on this fubject, to a Latin writing of Rubens, concerning the imitation of antique ftatues. It were to be wifhed, that this great genius had always practifed his own leffons.

Painters who make the fame ufe of antiques as Raphael, Michael Angelo, and fome others have done, may be compared to Virgil, Racine, or Boileau. Thefe have made ufe of poems that were ancient with regard to the time in which they compofed, in the fame manner as the illuftrious painters above-mentioned made ufe of antique ftatues. As for painters who have no poetic rapture, whofe intire compofition confifts in laying, as it were, the pictures of great mafters under contribution, demanding two heads of one, an arm of another, and from the richeft of

all

all a group ; robbers, that frequent Parnaſſus only to plunder paſſengers ; I compare them to patchers of centons, the moſt contemptible of all verſifiers. Let them take care they don't fall into the hands of the officer whom Boccalini placed on the double mount ; for he will be ſure to ſtigmatize them.

There is a vaſt difference between carrying off from a gallery the painter's art, or between appropriating the manner of operating peculiar to the admired artiſt, and transferring into our Portofolio a part of his figures. A man of no genius is incapable of converting, like Raphael, the grand and ſingular things he remarks, into his own ſubſtance. Without laying hold of the general principles, he is ſatisfied with copying what he has before his eyes. He therefore takes a figure along with him, but he does not learn to treat in the ſame taſte a figure of his own invention. A man of genius gueſſes at the artiſt's manner of performing. He ſees him, as it were, at work, by looking at his performance ; and laying hold of his manner, 'tis in his imagination only he carries off the booty.

With regard to the counſels of people of underſtanding, 'tis true they may prevent painters and poets from committing errors ; but they cannot ſuggeſt the expreſſions and the poetic ſtile, nor ſupply the defect of genius. They may ſtraiten the tree, but they cannot render it fertile. Theſe counſels are fit only for correcting miſtakes, and principally for rectifying the plan of a work of ſome extent ; ſuppoſing the authors happen to ſhew a ſketch of their plan, and thoſe whom they conſult, conſider

and

and examine it well, and have it, purfuant to Quintilian's [a] advice, as prefent in their minds as if they
had made it themfelves. 'Tis thus Boileau gave
thofe counfels to Racine, which proved fo frequently
of ufe to him. What can a poet in reality expect
from reading a work to a friend, to which he has
already put the laft hand, than to be fet right concerning fome word, or at furtheft with refpect to
fome fentiment? Let us even fuppofe, that after a
fingle reading we may be able to give good advice
to the artift with refpect to the plan of his
work; is it to be imagined he would be patient and
docile enough to comply with us, and to mould
anew a work which he had already finifhed,
imagining he was to have no farther trouble about
it?

The moft fublime genius's are not born great artifts, but only capable of becoming fuch. 'Tis by
dint of labor they rife to their higheft point of perfection.

Doctrina fed vim promovet infitam,
Rectique cultus pectora roborant. Hor. od. 4. l. 4.

Yet the beft blood by learning is refin'd,
And virtue arms the folid mind.

But the impatience of appearing in public fpurs us
on; and we attempt to write a poem, when we are
fcarce yet able to turn a verfe. Inftead of beginning
to work for ourfelves, we muft labor, forfooth, for

[a] *Diligenter legendum eft, ac pæne ad fcribendi follicitudinem.*
Nec per partes modo fcrutanda funt omnia, fed perfectus liber utique
ex integro refumendus. Quint. de inft.

the public. Such is particularly the fate of young poets ; but as they do not know their own genius, and have not as yet formed a ftyle fuitable to their character, and proper for expreffing the ideas of their imagination, they are confequently miftaken in chufing fuch fubjects as are not agreable to their talents, and in imitating in their firft productions, the ftyle, turn, and manner of thinking of other writers. For example, Racine [a] wrote his firft tragedy in the tafte of Corneille, tho' he had not a talent of treating tragedy in the manner as Corneille has handled it. Racine would have never been able to fupport himfelf, had he, to make ufe of this expreffion, continued to walk in his predeceffor's bufkins. 'Tis therefore very natural for young poets, who inftead of imitating that fide of nature which their genius points out to them, ftrive to copy the part which others have imitated ; who ufe violence to their talent, and endeavour to force it to purfue the fame track which others have beaten with fuccefs ; 'tis very natural, I fay, for them to write very indifferent pieces in the beginning ; pieces that may be faid to be unworthy of primogeniture with refpect to their younger brothers.

'Tis in vain neverthelefs to attempt to perfuade young people, preffed by emulation, excited by the fire and activity of youth, and fpurred on by the impatience of their genius to the purfuit of fame, to defer making their appearance in public, till they have difcovered their kind of talent, and fufficiently improved it. It would be to no purpofe to tell them, that it would be gaining a great point to furprize

[a] *Les freres ennemis, or the brothers at variance.*

the

the public ; that they would be much more refpected, were they never to appear as apprentices in their profeffion ; that unexpected mafter-pieces, againft which envy has no time to form a party, make a much greater progrefs than works long expected, which find rival critics upon their guard, and the character of whofe author may be defined from fome indifferent poem or picture. Nothing is capable of reftraining the impetuofity of a young man, feduced by the flattering incentive of vanity, whereof the excefs only is to be cenfured in youth. Befides, as Cicero [a] obferves, *Prudence does not fall to young people's fhare.*

Thefe precipitate performances remain, but 'tis unjuft they fhould injure the memory of illuftrious artifts. Is not a prenticefhip neceffary in all pro-feffions ? Now a prenticefhip confifts in committing faults, in order to become capable of avoiding them. Do we even fo much as dream of reproaching a perfon that writes good Latin, with the barbarifms and fole-cifms with which his firft exercifes muft have been un-doubtedly ftuffed. If painters and poets have the mif-fortune of ferving their prenticefhip under the infpection of the public, we ought not however to lay thofe little miftakes to their charge, in giving a defcription of their character after they have attained to the rank of eminent artifts.

But artifts without a genius, who are as fit to be Pouffin's as Titian's eleves, jog on all their life in the road in which hazard has firft engaged them ; whereas men endowed with genius perceive, when they chance to be led aftray, that they have got into a wrong road : Upon

[a] *Prudentia non cadit in hanc ætatem* Cic. pro Cœlio.

which they abandon it to take up with another, and
quit that of their matter to go in pursuit of a new
one. By master I understand here performances as
well as persons. Raphael, tho' dead above two
hundred years ago, may still train up pupils. Our
young artist therefore, who is blest with a genius,
enters upon a practice of his own to imitate nature,
and this practice he forms from maxims resulting
from his own and other people's labor. Every day
adds some new improvements to his former knowledge. Each elegy and picture he makes, contributes to render him a better painter or poet ; and
he excels at length those who probably had the advantage of him in masters and models. There is
nothing but what affords him an opportunity for
some useful reflection ; and in the midst of an open
field he makes as useful a study, as if he were in his
cabinet. In fine, his merit, raised to its highest
pitch of perfection, supports itself with credit, till
his organs growing feeble thro' old age, his trem-
bling hand is no longer able to accompany his yet
vigorous imagination. Genius is the last thing that
grows old in man. The most decrepit and broken
with age become warm, and assume an air of youth,
when they enter into a discourse of things relating
to the profession, for which they received a genius
from nature. Let yon withered old officer speak of
war, he seems seized with inspiration, as if he were
sitting upon a tripod ; he talks like a man of forty,
and finds matter and expressions with the same readi-
ness and ease, as that which a blood fermenting
with spirits affords for conception and speech.

Several

Several ocular witneſſes have aſſured me, that Pouſſin was, to the very end of his life, a youthful painter with reſpect to his imagination. His merit ſurvived the dexterity of his hand, and he ſtill continued to invent, when he had no longer the talents requiſite for the execution. In this reſpect, there is ſome kind of difference between poets and painters. The plan of a long poem, the diſpoſition of which, to be good for any thing, ſhould be formed in the head of the inventer, cannot be executed without the aſſiſtance of memory ; inſomuch that the plan muſt feel the effect of the infeebling of this faculty ; a conſequence that too commonly attends old age. The memory of old men is treacherous with regard to new things. Hence aroſe the defects which occur in the plan of the latter tragedies of the great Corneille. The adventures are not properly brought on, and the perſonages are frequently thrown into ſituations, in which they can have nothing that is good or natural to ſay : Yet we may diſtinguiſh now and then the elevation, and even the fecundity of Corneille's genius, by means of the poetic ſtyle.

C H A P. IX.

Of the obſtacles which retard the progreſs of young artiſts.

ALL geniuſes ſhew themſelves ſome time or other, but they do not all attain to that degree of perfection which nature has rendered them

capable

capable of acquiring.   Some there are, whofe progrefs is ftopt in the very middle of their courfe.   A
young man cannot make all the advancement he is
capable of in the art of painting, unlefs his hand be
perfected at the fame time with his imagination.
'Tis not fufficient for painters to conceive noble
ideas, to imagine the moft elegant compofitions, and
to difcover the moft pathetic expreffions ; their hand
muft acquire likewife a docility of bending a hundred different ways, to become capable of drawing
with exactnefs the lines prefcribed by their imagination.   " We fhall be incapable of performing any
" thing worth notice, fays Frefnoi in his art of
" painting, unlefs our hand be taught to fpread on
" canvafs the beauties which our mind produces."

Sic nihil ars operâ manuum privata fupremum
Exequitur, fed languet iners uti vinêta lacertos,
Difpofitumque typum non linguâ pinxit Apelles.

FRESNOI de arte graphica.

Genius hath its arms tied, as it were, in an artift
whofe hand is not docile and pliant.   The fame
pretty near may be faid of the eye as of the hand.
The eye of a painter ought to be accuftomed early,
to judge by a fure and eafy operation, what effect
may arife from a certain mixture or oppofition of colors ; what effect a figure of a particular height may
have in a group ; and what may be the effect of a
particular group, after the picture is colored.   If the
imagination hath not a hand and eye at its difpofal
capable of forwarding its views, its compleateft ideas
will be able to produce only fome coarfe picture,
which the very artift that has drawn it will defpife ;

fo

fo inferior will he find the execution of his hand to the invention of his mind.

The ftudy neceffary, for perfecting the eye and hand, does not confift in giving fome hours to an interrupted labor. It demands an intire attention and conftant perfeverance for the fpace of feveral years. Every one knows the maxim which forbids painters to let a day pafs without drawing a ftroke ; a maxim fo very judicious, that it is commonly applied to all forts of profeffions. *Nulla dies fine linea.*

The proper time of life for acquiring this perfection of eye and hand, is that in which our internal and external organs are compleatly formed ; that is, from fifteen to thirty. The organs contract with eafe, during this period, all thofe habits, of which their firft conformation renders them fufceptible. But if thofe precious years are loft, if they flip away without being laid out to an advantage ; the docility of our organs leaves us, which all our repeated efforts will never be able to recal. Tho' our tongue is a much fuppler organ than our hand, yet we always mifpronounce a foreign language, which we have learnt after the age of thirty.

Unhappily for mankind, 'tis in thofe precious years we are moft apt to be called away from ferious applications. 'Tis then we begin to confide in our own knowledge, which can be no more than the very firft dawn of prudence. 'Tis then we lofe that docility for counfel, which ferves children inftead of a great many virtues ; and our refolution, as weak as our reafon, is not fufficient proof againft wearinefs and diflike. Horace defines a young man,

——— —— ——— *Monitoribus afper,*
Utilium tardus provifor, prodigus æris,
Sublimis, cupidufque, & amata relinquere pernix.

HOR. de arte.

Rough to reproof, and eafy bent to vice :
Inconftant, eager, haughty, fierce, and proud ;
A very flow provider for his good,
And prodigal of his coin and of his blood. }

CREECH.

Befides, every thing affords us, in this ftage of life, opportunities of indulging our pleafures. The various taftes of a young man are paffions, and his paffions are furies. The fire of their blood brings feveral of thefe upon them at a time ; and 'tis very extraordinary, if their infant reafon can be miftrefs only for a few moments.

I muft add here another reflection, which is, that the genius of poetry and painting cannot dwell in a man of a cold temperament, or of an indolent humor. That very conftitution which makes him a poet or a painter, inclines him to the livelieft of paffions. The hiftory of fuch eminent artifts as have not been fhipwrecked upon the rocks here mentioned, abounds at leaft with the dangers they have been expofed to, and their narrow efcapes : Some have been dafhed to pieces, but there are none of them but what have at leaft run a-ground.

I cannot conceive the caufe of the Bifhop of Alba's furpaffing himfelf in the defcription he gives us of the inquietudes and tranfports of a young poet tyrannized by a paffion, which ftruggles with his

genius,

genius, and drags him againſt his will from the occupations for which nature has formed him.

Sæpe etenim tectos immittis in oſſibus ignes
Verſat amor, molliſque eſt intus flamma medullas ;
Nec miſerum patitur vatum meminiſſe, nec undæ
Caſtaliæ, tantum ſuſpirat vulnere cæco,
Ante oculos ſimulacra volant nocteſque dieſque
Nuncia virginei vultus, quem perditus ardet.
Nec potis eſt alio fixam traducere mentem
Saucius.   VIDA art. poet. l. 1.

Oft hidden fires on all his vitals prey,
Devour the youth, and melt his ſoul away
By ſlow degrees ; —— blot out his golden dreams,
The tuneful poets, and Caſtalian ſtreams ;
Struck with a ſecret wound, he weeps and ſighs ;
In every thought the darling phantoms riſe ;
The fancied charmer ſwims before his ſight,
His theme all day, his viſion all the night :
The wandering object takes up all his care,
Nor can he quit th' imaginary fair.   PITT.

The nature of the waters of Hippocrene does not
render them proper, as yet, for extinguiſhing this
ſort of conflagration.

The paſſion of drinking is ſtill more dangerous
than the foregoing : It occaſions a great loſs of
time, and diſables a young artiſt from making a good
uſe of what little leiſure it leaves him.   Exceſs of
liquor is not one of thoſe vices, which age is apt to
correct in man : And yet it deprives the mind in a
few years of its vigor, and the body of great part
of its ſtrength.   A man too much addicted to liquor,
is ſurly and heavy without his bottle, and what little

ſpirits

spirits he has, arise only from the digestion of a sto-
mach, which must necessarily be spoiled before its
time.

Horace, when he speaks seriously, says that a
young man who has a mind to excel in any profession, ought to be very temperate.

Abstinuit venere & vino. ——   HOR. de arte.

Nor taste the joys of wine, nor sweets of love.
CREECH.

Petronius, the least austere of all writers, requires a
young man, who intends to distinguish himself in
his studies, to be very sober. *Frugalitatis lege pal-
leat exacta.* Juvenal speaking of the poets of his
time, who wrote large works, says, that they abstain-
ed from wine even on those days, which were set aside
by custom for the pleasures of the table.

——— ——— *fuit utile multis*
Pallere & vinum toto nescire Decembri.
JUV. sat. 7.

Then, then, 'twas worth a writer's pains, to pine,
Look pale, and all December taste no wine.
Mr. CHARLES DRYDEN.

I shall not be reproached with having summoned
the young people whom I intend here to arraign,
before too severe a tribunal.

In fine, as the hurry and precipitation of a young
painter is not always attended with success, he may
now and then chance to take a dislike to a laborious employment, the success of which does not answer
his expectations. The natural impatience of young
people is the cause of their wanting to reap immediately

diately after they have fown. The allurement of an exercife to which our genius invites us, helps us very much to furmount our diflikes, and withftand our pleafures : but 'tis always better, when the defire of making our fortune comes in to affift the impulfe of our genius. It were therefore to be wifhed, that a young man, whom his inclination determines to be a painter, fhould find himfelf in fuch a fituation, as to confider his art as the means of his eftablifhment, and to expect his figure and appearance in the world, in proportion to the improvement he makes in his profeffion. If a young man's fortune, inftead of engaging him in a conftant labor, concurs with the levity of his age to call him off from application ; what can we expect, but that he will let the time proper for the forming of his organs flide away infenfibly without improving in his art? A work frequently interrupted, and generally accompanied only with a fuperficial attention, is infufficient to perfect an artift. In fact, the fuccefs of our labor depends almoft as much on the difpofition we are in when we apply ourfelves; on what we were about before we began; and on what we intended to do after we finifh ; as on the duration of the very labor itfelf. When the force of genius brings a young painter back to a more ferious ftudy of his art, after the drunkennefs of his youth is paft ; his eyes and hands are no longer capable of improvement. If he has a mind to make good pictures, let him meddle only with that part which depends on the imagination, and let another hand be concerned in the execution.

Poets,

Poets, whofe prenticefhip is not attended with fo much difficulty as that of painters, can always render themfelves capable of anfwering their vocation. The very firft ardor with which their genius infpires them, is fufficient to learn the rules of poetry ; for 'tis not thro' ignorance that fo many writers tranfgrefs them. The greateft part of thofe who violate thefe rules, know them very well ; but they find themfelves deftitute of abilities fufficient for reducing them to practice.

'Tis true a poet may take a diflike againft entertaining us with long performances, becaufe of the trouble attending the difpofition of the plan. Perfeverance is not a virtue that young people are fond of. If they apply themfelves with ardor to the moft laborious and moft difficult exercifes, 'tis upon condition of the fhortnefs of their continuance. 'Tis therefore a great happinefs for fociety, when young poets are obliged by their fortune to engage in a continual application.

By the neceffity of making one's fortune I do not mean that of fubfifting. The extremity of indigence, which obliges a perfon to write for bread, contributes only to lead a man of genius aftray, who confulting not his talents, but his wants, pitches upon that kind of poetry which he finds moft lucrative. Inftead of compofing ingenious allegories and excellent fatyres, he fpends his time in fcribling wretched pieces for the ftage : for the ftage in France is the Peru of poets.

A poetic enthufiafm is not a talent, which the fear of ftarving can infpire. If, as Perfius fays, who
calls

calls the belly the father of induftry, *ingenii largi-*
tor venter, an empty belly fharpens people's wit,
writers muft certainly be excepted. Boileau obferves after Juvenal, that

Horace a bû fon faoul quand il voit les Menades.

When Horace Bacchus faw, his guts were full.

In fact, as the faid Latin poet explains exceedingly
well, to fet foot on the mount Olympus, to pene-
trate into the projects of the Gods, to give feafts and
entertainments to the Goddeffes, is not the bufinefs
of a poor fhabby fellow, that does not know where
to get a dinner. If Virgil, continues Juvenal, had
not had the eafe and conveniences of life, thofe hy-
dras, which he reprefents as fuch hideous monfters,
would have been no more than ordinary fnakes.
The fury, which fills the bofom of Turnus and A-
mata with rage, would have been, to fpeak after
our way, like only to the tranquil Eumenis of the
opera of Ifis.

Magnæ mentis opus, nec de lodice parandâ
Attonitæ, currus & equos faciefque Deorum
Afpicere, & qualis Rutulum confundat Erynnis.
Nam fi Virgilio puer & tolerabile defit
Hofpitium, caderent omnes a crinibus hydri.

Juv. fat. 7.

A wit fhould have no care, or this alone,
To make his rifing numbers juftly run.
Phœbus and Bacchus, thofe two jolly Gods,
Bear no ftarv'd poets to their bleft abodes.
'Tis not for hungry wit, with wants controll'd,
The face of Jove in council to behold:

Or

Or fierce Alecto, when her brand she toss'd
Betwixt the Trojan and Rutilian host.
If Virgil's suit Mæcenas had not sped,
And sent Alexis to the poet's bed,
The crested snakes had dropt upon the ground,
And the loud trumpet languish'd in the sound.

Mr. CHARLES DRYDEN.

Excess of want debases the mind, and a genius reduced thro' misery to write, loses one half of his vigor.

On the other hand, pleasures are as great an obstruction as want, to a poet's improvement. True it is that Lucan composed his Pharsalia, notwithstanding all the amusements and avocations, which are the common consequence of opulency. He received the compliments of his friends on the success of his poem, in his gardens inriched with statues of marble ; but one single example proves nothing. Of all those poets who have ever attained to a high degree of reputation, Lucan is the only one, to the best of my remembrance, that always lived from his earliest years in plenty. I believe every one will join issue with me, when I assert, that Moliere would never have taken the pains necessary for rendering himself capable of composing *Les femmes scavantes,* nor have been at the trouble of writing it after he had qualified himself for it, had he been in possession of an estate of a hundred thousand livres a year, at the age of twenty. Methinks I discover the proper situation of a young poet, in a witty expression of our king Charles IX. Poets and horses, (said that young prince in Latin, a language with which the custom of that time allowed even polite people to sprinkle
their

their converfation) ought not to be fattened, but fed. *Equi & poetæ alendi funt non faginandi.* The exceffive paffion which the great folks of that time had for their horfes renders this comparifon excufable, as the fafhion of thofe days authorifed it. The defire of improving his fortune raifes the fpirit of a poet who is in this fituation, without any danger of want to debafe his mind, and oblige him to run after a fordid ftipend, as fo many mercenary fcribblers of dramatic poems, who feem to trouble their heads very little about the fuccefs of their pieces, but to fix their attention on the money they expect.

Geftit enim nummum in loculos dimittere, poft hoc
Securus, cadat an recto ftet fabula talo.

HOR. ep. 1. l. 2.

He writes for gold, and if his pocket's cramm'd,
He cares not, let the play be clapp'd or damn'd.

CREECH.

As the mechanic part of our poetry is very difficult to thofe who write none but excellent verfes, and eafy to fuch as are contented with fcribbling indifferent ones, hence we have a greater number of bad poets than painters. Every one that has the leaft glimmering of wit, or the fmalleft tincture of learning, attempts to write verfes ; and unhappily for poets, every body becomes thus a judge, fo as to pronounce fentence on all new poems, with the feverity of a rival. Poets have complained a long time of the great number of competitors, who ftart up daily thro' the facility of the mechanic part of their art. " He that is not a pilot, fays Horace, ought not to " ftand at the helm. Thofe who have not ftudied
" the

" the virtue of fimples, fhould not pretend to make
" up medicines. None but phyficians ought to
" prefcribe bleeding to patients. Even the very
" meaneft trades are not practifed 'till after an ap-
" prenticefhip; but every body, capable or incapa-
" ble, will dabble in verfes."

Navem agere ignarus navis timet ; *Abrotonum ægro*
Non audet, nifi qui didicit, dare quod medicorum eft,
Promittunt medici ; *tractant fabrilia fabri* ;
Scribimus indocti doctique poemata paffim.

HOR. ep. 1. l. 2.

He that's no pilot, is afraid to fail,
Urge him to guide a fhip, you fhan't prevail ;
And only doctors will pretend to heal.
By fmiths alone are locks and ftaples made,
And none pretend but artifts in the trade.
But now for poetry we are all fit,
And fkilful, or unfkilful, all muft write.

CREECH.

The moft ftupid verfifiers generally write with the
greateft fluency and eafe. Hence we are peftered
with fuch a prodigious number of wretched performances, as are a fcandal to Parnaffus, and frequently hinder men of fenfe from affuming the glorious
title of a poet.

This brings to my mind what Boileau faid to Racine, concerning the facility of writing verfes. Racine had juft publifhed his tragedy of Alexander,
when he got acquainted with the author of the Art
of Poetry. As he was making mention of his ftudies, he told him that he had a furprizing facility in
compofing verfes. I will teach you, replied Boileau,

leau, to take pains with your verſification, a thing I am ſenſible you will quickly learn. Racine has been heard to ſay, that Boileau was as good as his word.

But theſe troubles and contradictions are incapable of giving a young man a diſtaſte of poetry, if he has had his vocation from Apollo himſelf, and is beſides excited with the deſire of acquiring a name and fortune in the world. He will attain ſooner or later to his higheſt degree of poetic merit ; but the uſe he will make of his abilities, will depend in a great meaſure on the times in which he lives. If his unlucky ſtars throw him into the world, when there is neither an Auguſtus nor a Mæcenas to protect him, his productions are not likely to be ſo frequent or ſo voluminous, as if he were born in a happy age with reſpect to the arts and ſciences. Virgil was at an infinite deal of labor and pains to compoſe a poem of ſuch an extent as his Æneid, notwithſtanding the reliſh his genius gave him for this kind of ſtudy, and tho' he was encouraged by the attention which Auguſtus gave to his verſes, and excited by a noble ſpirit of emulation. Had he lived at a time when there was neither an Auguſtus, nor a Mæcenas, nor a rival, he would ſtill have been determined by the impulſe of his genius, and love of glory, to improve his talent. Very likely he would have made himſelf capable of compoſing an Æneid ; but it can hardly be ſuppoſed he would have had perſeverance ſufficient to terminate ſo large a work. Perhaps we ſhould have had only ſome few eclogues of his, written in an eaſy fluent ſtyle, and a ſketch of the Æneid containing only one or two books.

3

Your

Your great artifts are not thofe, whofe productions are attended with leaft difficulty.   Their .inaction frequently proceeds from a dread they have of the pains which eminent works muft coft them; when people imagine 'tis lazinefs that keeps them unemployed.   As failors, who fet foot on fhore after having, to make ufe of the expreffion of an ancient writer, beheld death in every wave that drew near them, grow out of conceit for a while of expofing themfelves to the perils of the fea ; fo a poet, who is fenfible of the pains a good tragedy has coft him, is not fo very ready to attempt another.   He muft reft for a while ; and after being tired of his labor, he muft grow weary of idlenefs, before he goes to work again.

A poet cannot, without a vaft deal of labor and application, lay out the plan of a work of any extent. The pains of correcting and polifhing one's own verfes is likewife a very troublefome employment. 'Tis impoffible but a perfon muft foon grow tired of the ferious attention to trifling niceties, which this kind of fatigue requires : And yet he muft have the refolution to go through with it, be it ever fo tedious.   I appeal to the teftimony of thofe poets, who have been deficient in this kind of labor.   True it is, that poets feel a moft fenfible pleafure in the enthufiafm of compofing. The foul wrapt up in the ideas, which rife in the heated imagination, is not fenfible of the efforts fhe makes in their production ; 'tis only the laffitude and exhaufting of fpirits, which are the confequence of compofing, that convinces them of their labor.

Neque

Neque idem unquam
Æque eſt beatus ac poema cum ſcribit,
Tam gaudet in ſe. CATULL. epigr. 20.

He's never half ſo bleſt,
As when he writes and when the muſe proves kind,
Such is the joy that fills his raviſh'd mind.

Thoſe who write verſes without a poetic genius, are pleaſed with their own performances, rather thro' a kind of delirium than any real enthuſiaſm. The greateſt part of them, like Pygmalion, fall in love with their own ſhapeleſs or ſoft productions, and never trouble their heads about reviſing them ; for to fall in love implies being blind to the imperfections of what one loves. There never was a Greek tyrant, whoſe ears have been filled with ſo much flattery, as a poet pays to himſelf, when he cenſes thoſe pretended deities created by his pen. 'Tis chiefly to bad poets we ought to apply the following paſſage of Cicero. *I don't know how it comes to paſs, that rather in this than in other kinds every man thinks his own performance the beſt. I was never yet acquainted with a poet, who did not imagine himſelf the greateſt man in his profeſſion* [a]. But a good poet is not ſo eaſily ſatisfied with what he has committed to writing. He is not even pleaſed with his verſes, tho' they merit the approbation of others ; and the trouble he is at in poliſhing them to his mind, is attended frequently with impatience and diſquiet.

[a] *In hoc enim genere neſcio quo pacto magis quàm in aliis ſuum cuique pulcherrimum eſt Adhuc neminem cognovi poetam qui ſibi non optimus videretur.* Cic. Tuſc. l. 5.

CHAP. X.

Of the time requisite for men of genius to attain to that degree of merit of which they are capable.

THERE is a great difference with respect to the space of time requisite for men of genius to arrive to their highest degree of merit. In the first place, genius's born for professions, which demand a great share of experience and maturity of spirit, are formed later than those, whom nature has designed for professions in which a person may succeed with little prudence and a strong imagination. A great minister, for instance, a great general, a great magistrate, does not arrive to the height of his perfection and knowledge, but in a more advanced stage of life than that in which painters and poets attain to their highest degree of excellency. The first cannot be formed without such a knowledge and skill of things, as is acquired only by experience; a knowledge which a great extent of mind, a subtle imagination, and even a constant application, are incapable of supplying. In fine, these professions require a ripe judgment, and especially a constancy unmixt with obstinacy. One may be born with a disposition to these qualities, but none are possessed of them at their birth; nor is it even possible to acquire them very early in life.

As our imagination gathers its full strength much sooner than our judgment; painters, poets, musicians, and those whose talent lies chiefly in invention, are not so long a forming as others. The age of thirty

is,

is, methinks, that in which painters and poets, generally speaking, reach the higheft ftep of Parnaffus.
They may afterwards grow more correct and more
prudent in their productions, but they do not become
more fertile, more pathetic, nor more fublime.

  As fome genius's are flower than others (which is
what I had to fay in the fecond place) as their progrefs
may be retarded by all the obftructions now mentioned, we have not pretended to determine the age of
thirty as a critical year, before or after which there is
nothing more to be expected. There may be five or
fix years difference in the age, in which two great painters or poets attain to their higheft degree of perfection.   One may arrive to it at eight and twenty, and
the other at three and thirty. Racine was quite formed
at eight and twenty: La Fontaine was much older when
he wrote the firft of his excellent pieces. Even the kind
of poetry to which an artift applies himfelf, feems
to retard this happy year. Moliere was forty years
old, when he compofed the firft of his beft comedies.
But Moliere's being a great poet was not fufficient to enable him to write thofe pieces: it was neceffary likewife to have acquired a knowledge of men and the
world, a knowledge which is not fo early attained,
and without which the very beft poets can write
but indifferent comedies. A tragic poet ought to
reach his higheft degree of perfection much earlier
than the comic writer ; a genius, and a general knowledge of the human heart, fuch as we generally acquire in our firft ftudies, being fufficient to write an
excellent tragedy. But to write a comedy of an
equal character, befides genius and ftudy, 'tis neceffary to have converfed a long time with the world.

In

In fact, to compose an excellent comedy, we muſt know in what conſiſts the difference, which age, education, and profeſſion produce betwixt people, whoſe natural character is the ſame.   We muſt know what form is communicated by a particular character of mind to thoſe ſentiments which are common to all men.   In ſhort, we ſhould have a thorough knowledge of mankind, and be acquainted with the language of all the paſſions, ages, and conditions.   Ten years time is not too much for learning ſo great a variety of things.

'Tis very natural for great genius's to reach their higheſt point of perfection ſomewhat later than men of leſs elevation and extent.   Great genius's have occaſion for many more things than others ; they are like thoſe trees which bear excellent fruit, and in ſpring have ſcarce bloſſomed, when the reſt are already covered with leaves.   Quintilian, who by profeſſion was obliged to ſtudy the character of children, gives a moſt admirable deſcription of what we commonly call, *ſlow and forward capacities*.   " If the " body, ſays he, be not pretty plump in one's child " hood, it will never be well ſhaped when one " comes to full manhood.   Thoſe whoſe limbs are " formed too ſoon become afterwards infirm and " meagre: wherefore of all children thoſe are the " leaſt promiſing, in my opinion, *continues Quin* " *tilian*, who by the generality of people are ſup " poſed to have more wit and capacity than others, " becauſe their judgment is ſooner ripened.   But " this premature underſtanding proceeds from the " imbecillity of their minds: they are in a good " ſtate of health, rather by reaſon they have no bad
humors,

" humors, than becaufe of their having a robuft
" body ᵃ." I have given here a few ftrokes only
of this paffage, which is fo extremely beautiful, that
it deferves to be read intire.

And yet this is the character which fills mafters
prefently with great expectations. I fpeak of the
common run, for if the mafter himfelf be a man of
genius, he will be able to difcern whether his pupil
has a genius or no at eighteen. He will perceive it
by the very manner of repeating his leffons, and
by the objections he forms. In fine, he will diftinguifh it, by feeing him do what he did himfelf when
he was a fcholar. 'Tis thus Scipio Æmilianus difcovered Marius's genius, when in anfwer to thofe
that inquired of him, what perfon he looked upon as
fit for commanding the armies of the republic, in cafe
they fhould lofe him ; he told them Marius : Marius
notwithftanding was at that time a fubaltern officer,
and had performed as yet no exploit ; nor difplayed
any quality, that could have rendered him worthy in
vulgar eyes of being Scipio's fucceffor.

As foon as young people are arrived to that time,
in which they muft think and extract matters from
their own fund, the difference between a man of genius and one who has none, becomes obvious to all
the world. The former invents very faft, tho' he
does not invent right ; the other does not invent

ᵃ *Erit illud plenius interim corpus quod mox adulta ætas aftrin-
gat. Hinc fpes roboris, maciem uamque & infirmitatem in pofterum
minari folet protinus omnibus membris expreffus infans .... Illa
mihi in pueris natura minimum fpei dabit, in qua ingenium judicio
præfumitur .... Macies illis pro fanitate & judicii loco infirmi-
tas eft.* QUINT. l. 2. c. 4.

at

at all. But *'tis eafy*, as Quintilian fays [b], *to find a remedy for luxuriancy; there's no labor can furmount fterility.* Art which cannot make water rife where there is no fource, can confine rivers which overflow, to their beds. The more the man of genius, and he that has none, advance towards the ftate of manhood, the more the difference between them grows fenfible. The very fame thing happens in this refpect in poetry and painting, as we obferve in all other conditions of life. The art of a governor and the leffons of a preceptor change a child into a youth; they infufe into him a greater fhare of knowledge, than he could be naturally fuppofed to have at his age. But this very child, when he arrives to that ftage of life in which he muft think, fpeak, and act of himfelf, is ftript all of a fudden of his premature merit. His fummer is far from anfwering the fine bloffoms of his fpring. The too follicitous education he has received becomes rather prejudicial to him, by reafon of its being the occafion of his falling into the dangerous habit of letting other people think for him. His mind has contracted an internal lazinefs, which makes him wait for external impulfes to refolve and to act. The mind contracts a habit of lazinefs with as much facility as the legs and feet. A man who never ftirs without the affiftance of fome vehicle, becomes foon incapable of the fame free ufe of his legs, as a perfon who has a conftant practice of walking. As we muft lend a hand to the former when he walks, fo we muft help the other to think, and even to will.

[a] *Facile eft remedium ubertatis; fterilia nullo labore vincuntur.* QUINT. l. 2. c. 4.

In

In a child bred up with less care, his inward part labours of itself, and his mind grows active. He learns to reason and determine of himself, in the same manner as other things are learnt. At length he attains to argue and resolve rightly, by dint of reasoning and reflecting on the cause of his deception, when the events convince him of the error of his judgment.

The more an artist endowed with genius takes time to perfect himself, and the more he waits for experience to become moderate in his sallies, reserved in his inventions, and cautious in his productions, the further generally he carries his improvement. The noon of summer days is further from the sun's rising than that of winter. Cherries attain to their full maturity with the very first warmth; but grapes do not ripen but by the assistance of the summer heats, and the temperature of autumn. "Nature, says Quintilian[a], "has not thought proper to let any thing, that is "compleat in its kind, come quickly to perfection. "The more excellent and sublime the work is, the "greater difficulties must be surmounted to finish "it." This is the opinion of the author here mentioned, who certainly understood his subject perfectly well, tho' he never read Descartes. Wherefore, the more springs are requisite for the fibres of the brain, and the more numerous these fibres are; the more time they require to attain to all those qualities of which they are capable.

---

[a] *Nihil enim rerum ipsa natura voluit magnum effici citò, praeposuitque pulcherrimo cuique operi difficultatem, quae nascendi quoque hanc fecerit legem, ut majora animalia diutius visceribus parentum continerentur.* QUINT. Inst. l. 10. c 2.

Great

Great masters therefore are generally longer in the course of their studies, than common artists. Their apprenticeship, if you will, lasts longer, by reason that they continue learning at an age, at which ordinary artists are already masters of what little they are capable of knowing. Let no body be frightened at the mention of apprenticeship, for there are several apprentices whose abilities surpass those of their masters, tho' their masters commit less faults. But the difference is, as Pliny expresses it [a], *that the latter, with all their correctness, have no strokes deserving of applause; the former, amidst their mistakes, shew something worthy of commendation.*

When Guido and Dominichino had finished each their picture in a small church built in the garden of the monastery of St Gregory on *Mount Cælius*, and dedicated to St Andrew, Annibal Caraccio their master was pressed to decide which of those two eleves deserved the prize. Guido's piece represents St Andrew kneeling before the cross ; and that of Dominichino exhibits the flagellation of this apostle [b]. These were grand subjects, on which our two antagonists had a very spacious field for displaying their talents ; and they executed their pieces with so much the more care, as being painted in fresco one opposite to the other, they were to continue eternal rivals, and to perpetuate, as it were, the competition of their masters. Guido, said Caraccio, has performed like a master, and Dominichino as an ap-

---

[a] *Sed & his non labentibus nulla laus, illis nonnulla laus etiamsi labantur,* PLIN. epist.

[b] *Dominichino has repeated this very subject at St Andrea della valle,*

prentice ;

prentice ; but, continued he, the apprentice is fuperior to his mafter.   We fee indeed fome faults in
Dominichino's piece, which do not occur in Guido's ;
but we meet there alfo with fome touches, which are
not to be feen in his rival's.   There we perceive a
fpirit which aimed at beauties, to which Guido's foft
and tranquil genius had no thoughts of afpiring.

   The more we are capable of rifing, the more fteps
we have to afcend before we can attain to the higheft
pitch of elevation.   Horace muft have been a full-ag-
ed man when he made himfelf known as a poet : and
Virgil was near thirty when he wrote his firft eclogue.
Racine was pretty near the fame age, according to
Boileau, when he publifhed his Andromache, which
may be confidered as the firft tragedy of this great
poet. · Corneille was upwards of thirty when he compofed his Cid.   Moliere had not at that age wrote
any of thofe comedies, to which he is indebted for
the reputation he left behind him. Boileau was turned
of thirty when he publifhed his fatyres, fuch as we
have them at prefent.   True it is, that the contrary
may be inferred from the dates of his pieces inferted
in a pofthumous edition of his works ; but thefe
dates, which are frequently contradicted, even by the
piece of poetry to which they are prefixed, do not
feem to me to be of any weight.   Raphael was
about thirty when he difplayed the noblenefs and
fublimity of his genius in the Vatican.   'Tis there
we may behold his chief performances, worthy of
the great name he tranfmitted to fucceeding ages.

C H A P.

CHAP. XI.

Of works suitable to men of genius, and of artists who counterfeit other people's manner.

MEN of genius, that are jealous of their reputation, ought to publish none but large performances, since it is impossible for them to conceal their apprenticeship from the public. By this precaution they might avoid exposing themselves to disagreeable comparisons. When painters and poets of ever so eminent a genius happen to publish, either poems consisting of a small number of verses, or pictures containing a single figure without expression, and placed in a common attitude, their productions are exposed to very odious parallels. As a person may scribble four or five good verses without a genius, or draw a good picture of the Virgin Mary with a child in her lap, without being a great painter, the difference between the plain workman and the divine artist is not so obvious in such limited pieces, as in works of greater composition and susceptible of a larger number of beauties. In the latter this difference shews itself in its full extent.

There are some pictures of the Virgin Mary done by Carlo Maratti, which the favorers of this painter maintain to be equal in beauty to those of Raphael, for which we cannot charge them with any excessive exaggeration. And yet what immense difference is there in the composition of those two painters, and who is it that ever presumed to draw a parallel between them! Tho' painters are as apt to be

self-

felf-conceited as poets, yet Carlo Maratti himfelf did
not think himfelf worthy to mix his pencil with that
of Raphael. A little after the jubilee year of 1700,
there was a refolution taken to repair the ceiling of
the gallery of that palace at Rome, which goes by
the name of the Little Farnefe. This houfe was
built by Auguftine Chigi, who lived under the pontificate of Leo X. The paintings which Chigi
had caufed to be drawn here by Raphael, have
rendered the name of Chigi as famous in Europe, as the pontificate of Alexander VII. [a]   Carlo
Maratti having been chofen as the principal painter
at Rome, to take the above-mentioned ceiling in
hand, on which Raphael had reprefented the hiftory
of Pfyche, this able painter would not confent to
make any addition to the old work, but only to
touch it over again with the paftel ; becaufe, faid
he, if there fhould happen to rife hereafter, a perfon
worthier than I, of joining his pencil with that of
Raphael, perhaps he will efface my work, in order
to fubftitute his own.

Vander Meulen knew how to paint a horfe as well
as Le Brun, and Baptift could draw a bafket of flowers better than Pouffin. To come to poetry, Boileau
has wrote fome epigrams much inferior to thofe of two
or three poets, who would not fo much as prefume
to compare themfelves to him. We cannot judge
fo well of the fuperiority of one race-horfe over another, when they run too fhort a diftance : The difference is eafier to be diftinguifhed, when they ftart
for any confiderable length. It would be unneceffary
to explain here in what fenfe I underftand a fmall

[a] *This pope was of the family of the Chigi.*

work ;

work ; for a picture only three feet long, may be sometimes a large work ; and a poem of only three hundred verses may be a large poem.

I shall add here one reflection concerning those works, which do not require much invention ; 'tis that your forgers in painting counterfeit them with much greater ease than they can counterfeit those in which the imagination of the artist has full room to display itself. Your makers of *pasticci*, that is, those pictures which are drawn in imitation of the manner of a great artist, and are exposed in public under his name, tho' he never saw them ; those makers of *pasticci*, I say, are never able to forge the ordonnance, coloring, or the expression of eminent masters. We may imitate another man's hand, but we cannot, to express myself thus, imitate so well his mind ; we cannot learn to think like another so well, as we can learn to mimic his speech.

Were an indifferent painter to counterfeit a large composition of Dominichino's, or Rubens, he would be no more able to impose upon us, than one that would attempt to make a *pasticcio* under the name of Giorgione or Titian. We must have a genius almost equal to that of the painter we attempt to counterfeit, to be able to make our work pass for his. We cannot therefore counterfeit the genius of great men, but we may sometimes succeed so far as to imitate their hand, that is, their manner of laying on the colors, and drawing their strokes, the airs they used to give their heads, and the vicious parts of their practice. 'Tis much easier to imitate mens faults than their perfections. For instance, Guido is charged with having made his heads too broad. They fre-

I

quently

quently want a roundnefs, by reafon their parts are not diftinct, and do not rife fufficiently one upon another. In order therefore to imitate him in this particular, 'tis fufficient to be negligent, and not to give one's felf the trouble of practifing what the rules prefcribe with relation to the roundnefs of heads.

Jordano the Neapolitan, whom his countrymen call the *il fa prefto*, or the *quick difpatcher*, was, next to Teniers, the greateft maker of *pafticci*, that ever laid fnares for the curious. Flufht with the vanity of having counterfeited with fuccefs fome of Guido's heads, he undertook fome large compofitions in the tafte of that amiable artift, and in that of fome other eleves of Caraccio. All thofe pictures, reprefenting divers events of the hiftory of Perfeus, are to be feen at Genoa, in the palace of the marquis Grillo, who paid this forger much handfomer, than the great mafters, whofe ape he acted, had been paid in their time. Upon feeing thofe pictures, one cannot help being furprized, that a painter, who did not want talents, fhould have employed his labor and time fo ill, and that a noble Genoefe could have made fo bad a ufe of his money.

The fame remark holds good in poetry. A man of no genius, but who has read a great number of verfes, may, by a proper arrangement of fuch things as he recollects, compofe an epigram which will bear fo great a refemblance to thofe of Martial, as to pafs for one of that poet's. But a poet, who after diverting himfelf with writing a thirteenth book of the Æneid, fhould be bold enough to attribute it to Virgil, would find no body to fwallow the cheat.

Muretus

Muretus was able to make fix verfes of his own compofing, pafs for thofe of Trabea, a Latin comic poet, who lived in the fixth hundredth year after the foundation of Rome.

Here, fi querelis, ejulatu, fletibus
Medicina fieret miferiis mortalium,
Auro parandæ lacrimæ contra forent.
Nunc hæc ad minuenda mala non magis valent,
Quam næniæ præficæ ad excitandos mortuos,
Res turbidæ confilium, non fletum expetunt.

Mafter, if human miferies could be remedied by com-
plaints and weeping, tears would foon be purchafed
with gold. But thefe contribute no more to the leffen-
ing of our misfortunes, than the funeral fongs of a
hired mourner can avail towards raifing the dead.
Troubles in life do not call for tears, but counfel.

Jofeph Scaliger had been fo far deceived by thofe verfes, as to quote them in his commentary on Varro[a], as a fragment of Trabea difcovered in an ancient manufcript. If Muretus had attempted to forge a whole comedy in the ftyle of Terence, he could not have impofed upon Scaliger. Men that have a regard for their reputation, ought therefore to endeavour to put it out of the power of future impoftors, to im-pute fuppofitious works to their memory. 'Tis enough for them to anfwer for their own faults to pofterity.

[a] *Page* 212. Edit. ann. 1573.

CHAP.

C H A P. XII.

*Of illuſtrious ages, and of the ſhare which mo-
ral cauſes have in the progreſs of arts.*

ALL ages are not equally fertile in great artiſts. 'Tis a common obſervation that there
are ſome ages in which the arts and ſciences are in a
drooping condition, as there are others in which they
produce flowers and fruit in abundance. What compariſon is there between the poetic writings of the
Auguſtan age, and the productions of that art in
the age of Gallienus ! Was painting the ſame art,
in a manner, under Leo X. as in the two preceding
centuries ? But the ſuperior excellency of ſome ages,
in compariſon to others, is a thing too well known,
to require any arguments to evince it. Our
buſineſs here is to trace, if poſſible, thoſe cauſes
which render one particular age ſo vaſtly ſuperior
to others.

Before I enter upon my ſubject, I muſt beg leave
of the reader to uſe the word *age* in a ſignification
ſomewhat different from that in which it is rigorouſly
underſtood. The word age, in the civil ſenſe thereof, implies a duration of one hundred years ; but
ſometimes I ſhall make it import a duration of ſixty
or ſeventy only. I fancied I might uſe the word age in
this ſignification with ſo much the more liberty, as
the duration of an age is eſſentially arbitrary, and
the agreement of people in giving a hundred years
to each age, was only in order to facilitate the calculations and citations of chronology. There is no

I   phyſical

phyſical revolution in nature at the end of a hundred years, as there is at the expiration of one year, which is what we call the annual revolution of the ſun. Beſides, people are accuſtomed to make uſe of the word age, when they ſpeak of thoſe happy times in which the arts and ſciences particularly flouriſhed. One is uſed to ſay and hear on this occaſion, the age of Auguſtus, of Alexander, and of Lewis XIV.

'Tis eaſy to perceive, that moral cauſes have a great ſhare in the ſenſible difference there is in ages. I call here moral cauſes, thoſe which operate in favor of arts, without imparting any real capacity or wit to the artiſts, and in ſhort, without making any phyſical alteration in nature, but are only an inducement to perfect their genius, by rendering their labor eaſier to them, and by exciting them by emulation and rewards, to ſtudy and application. I give therefore the appellation of moral cauſes of the perfection of arts, to the happy ſituation in which painters and poets find their country at their ſetting out in their reſpective profeſſions ; to the inclination of their ſovereign and their fellow citizens for the polite arts ; in fine, to thoſe excellent maſters who flouriſh in their time, whoſe inſtructions abridge their ſtudies, and ſecure their ſucceſs. Is there any doubt but Raphael would have been a compleat painter four years ſooner, had he been the eleve of another Raphael ? Who can pretend to ſay, that a French painter who had taken wing at the commencement of the thirty five years war which ravaged France till the treaty of Vervins[2], could have

[2] *In the year* 1598.

the fame opportunities of improvement, or meet with the fame encouragement, as if he had begun to fly in the year fixteen hundred and fixty.

Is it poffible for the countrymen of great artifts to give fuch an attention to the polite arts, as may promote their fuccefs, unlefs they happen to live at a time when they are allowed to be more attentive to their pleafures than wants? Now this general attention to pleafure, fuppofes a long train of years exempt from thofe inquietudes and fears which are the general confequence of war, at leaft fuch as may endanger the eftates and fortunes of particulars, by aiming at the fubverfion of the conftitution of which they are members. The delicate tafte the Romans had for the polite arts was unknown to them, whilft they were engaged in their own country in wars, the events of which might have been fatal to their republic, becaufe the enemy upon the gaining of a victory might come and incamp upon the banks of the Tiber. They did not begin to relifh poetry and painting, till after they had transferred the feat of war into Greece, Africa, Afia, and Spain, when the battles fought by their generals did not decide the fate of their republic, but only its glory and extent of dominions. The people of Rome, as Horace obferves,

Et poft Punica bella quietus quærere cæpit
Quid Sophocles, & Thefpis, & Æfchylus utile fer-
 rent.   Hor. ep. l. 2. ep. 1.

Till Carthage ruin'd, fhe grew foft in peace,
And then inquir'd what weighty Sophocles,

What Æschylus, what Thespis taught the age,
What good, what profit did commend the stage.

CREECH.

The recompences of a sovereign come next to the attention of our countrymen and cotemporaries. If he diftributes his favors impartially, they are an encouragement to artifts ; which they ceafe to be, as foon as they are mifplaced.   Nay, it would be much better, were a sovereign not to diftribute any favors at all, than to do it without judgment.   An able artift may find means to comfort himfelf under the contempt and neglect into which his art is fallen. A poet may even bear with the difrelifh people chance to have for poetry ; but he is ready to burft with envy and fpite, when he fees a prize given to works that are far inferior to his own performances. He grows defperate at the fight of an injuftice which is a perfonal affront to him, and he renounces, as much as in him lies, the Mufes for ever.

Men are not generally fo felf-conceited, as people imagine, but have at leaft a glimpfe or imperfect knowledge of their intrinfic value, as well as of their eftimation in the eyes of the world.   Thofe who are neither sovereigns, nor minifters, nor too nearly related to one another, have frequent oppor- tunities of knowing their real value, which they can- not doubt of for any confiderable time, unlefs they be perfect fools.   One cannot commend and hug one's felf alone for any length of time ; and Cotin could not have been long ignorant that his verfes were hiffed at by the public.   That vanity therefore and conceit which appears in middling poets, is frequently af- fected,

fected, infomuch that their inward opinion differs from their outward fpeeches in commendation of their works. There is no queftion but poets are frequently infincere in fpeaking of the merit of their verfes. Is it not contrary to their inward conviction, that they commend as their very beft performance that which the public efteems the worft? But this is becaufe they want to give a reputation to a poem whofe weaknefs ftands in need of a fupport, by fhewing an affected prejudice in favor of this piece; whilft they abandon thofe works to their own fate, which are able to fupport themfelves with their own wings. Corneille was often heard to fay, that Attila was his beft piece; and Racine would fain make people believe, that he preferred Berenice to any. of his profane tragedies.

Great mafters ought therefore not only to meet with a recompence, but they fhould even be rewarded in a particular manner. Without this diftinction, prefents ceafe to be a recompence, and become a mere falary common to good and bad artifts, by which no one thinks himfelf particularly honored. The Roman foldiers would have ceafed to fet a value upon the crown of oaken boughs, for which they ufed to expofe themfelves to the greateft dangers, had the favor of a general beftowed it a few times on thofe who never deferved it.

We find that moral caufes were a great encouragement to the polite arts, in thofe ages in which painting and poetry flourifhed. Hiftory makes mention of four ages, whofe productions have been admired by fucceeding times. Thofe happy ages in which the arts attained to a perfection which they fell fhort of at other times, are, that which commenced ten years before the reign of Philip father of Alexander the Great, that of Julius Cæfar and Auguftus, that of Julius II. and Leo X. and finally, that of our king Lewis the fourteenth.

Greece was no longer afraid of being ravaged by Barbarians in the time of Philip king of Macedon. The wars which the Greeks waged amongft themfelves, were not of fuch a deftructive nature to fociety, as to drive particulars from their own houfe and home, or lead them flaves into an enemy's country ; fuch as thofe, which the barbarous conquerors emerging from the northern fnows, waged formerly againft the Roman empire. The wars which were then carried on in Greece, refembled thofe which have been frequently waged on the frontiers of the Spanifh Netherlands, that is, a kind of war in which the people, 'tis true, run a rifk of being conquered, but not of being made flaves, or of lofing their property, or of being expofed to fuch misfortunes as commonly happen in the wars between the Chriftians and Turks. The wars therefore of the Greeks amongft themfelves, were what may be properly called regular wars, in which the laws of civility and humanity were frequently practifed. It was forbidden by the law of nations at that time, to pull or beat down a trophy raifed by the enemy to perpetuate his glory and the oppofite party's infamy. Now all thofe laws of nations which difcriminate the engagements of armies from the combats of wild beafts, were fo religioufly obferved at that time, that the Rhodians chofe rather to erect a building in order to inclofe and conceal the trophy

raifed

raifed there by Artemifia after the taking of their town, than to deftroy it upon any account. Greece abounded at the fame time with fanctuaries equally refpected by the feveral contending parties. A perfect neutrality prevailed always in thofe afylums, and the weaker fide was always fecure from the attacks of the moft inveterate enemy. One may eafily form an idea of the little effufion of blood in thofe battles which wete fought between the Greeks, by the furprize with which Livy fays they were feized at the fight of the butcherly arms of the Romans, and of the great carnage and flaughter they made in the heat of battle. This furprize was like that of the Italians, when they firft faw the manner in which the French waged war, during the expedition of our king Charles VIII. to the kingdom of Naples.

People of all ranks muft have been vaftly at their eafe during the happy days of Greece. Society was then divided into mafters and flaves, by which means the feveral exigencies of the community were much better anfwered, than by a low and ill-educated clafs of people, who work only thro' ne-ceffity, and find themfelves deftitute of feveral things requifite for carrying on their bufinefs to an advantage, when they are reduced to labor. The wafps and hornets were not fo numerous with regard to the bees, as they are in our days. The Greeks, for inftance, did not bring up a part of their inhabitants to be unfit for every thing except the art of war ; a kind of education which has been a long while one of the moft dreadful fcourges of Europe. The generality therefore of the nation made plea-fure their principal occupation, in the fame man-

ner

ner as is practifed by fuch of our own countrymen as are born to an eftate of a hundred thoufand livres a year; and their climate gave them a greater fenfibility of the pleafures of the mind, amongft which poetry and painting are the moft bewitching allurements. Wherefore the greateft part of the Greeks were connoiffeurs, at leaft by acquiring a comparative tafte. Hence a workman became a celebrated artift in Greece as foon as his merit was eminent; and nothing gave a man a greater dignity than the fame of being illuftrious in the arts and fciences. This kind of merit changed a common fellow into a great perfonage, infomuch as to be thought upon a level with thofe that were intrufted with the higheft and moft important offices of the ftate.

The Greeks were fo much prevented in favor of all thofe talents which conduce to the amufement of fociety, that their very kings did not think it a difhonor to chufe players for their minifters [a]. *To appear upon the ftage for the public amufement*, fays Cornelius Nepos, fpeaking of the Greeks, *was never reckoned difhonorable among thofe nations, tho' with us 'tis efteemed an infamous, or at leaft a mean and indecent employment* [b].

The opportunities of receiving the applaufes and favors of great affemblies, were alfo very frequent in Greece. As we have congreffes in our

[a] Livius hiftor. l. 24. QUINT. dial. de orat.

[b] *In fcenam vero prodire & populo effe fpectaculo nemini in eifdem gentibus fuit turpitudini, quæ omnia apud nos partim infamia, partim humilia, partim ab honeftate remota ponuntur.* COR. NEPOS in proœmio.

times,

times, where the deputies of princes and ftates meet in order to terminate wars, and regulate the fate of provinces and the limits of kingdoms ; in like manner there were affemblies formerly from time to time, where the moft illuftrious perfonages of Greece rendevouzed, in order to decide the merit of the moft eminent painter, the moft moving poet, and the beft wreftler. This was the real motive which induced fuch multitudes of people to flock to thofe public games that were celebrated in different cities. The public porticos where the poets went to recite their verfes, or painters to expofe their pictures, were places where the better fort of company ufed generally to meet. In fine, *the works of great mafters,* as Pliny obferves[a], *were not confidered at the time here mentioned, as common moveables deftined to imbellifh a private perfon's apartment* ; *no, they were looked upon as the jewels of the ftate and as a public treafure, the enjoyment whereof was due to all the inhabitants.* The ardor which painters and poets had in thofe times to improve their talents, was not inferior to the eagernefs which we obferve in the people of our days to heap up money, and to attain to great employments in the ftate. Wherefore the Mufes, as Horace obferves, prefented the Greeks particularly with wit and eloquence, to recompence them for their conftant fervice and attendance, and for their difinterreftednefs in every thing, except the article of praife.

---

[a] *Non enim parietes excolebant dominis tantûm, nec domos uno in loco manfuras, quæ ex incendio rapi non poffent. Omnis eorum ars urbibus excubabat, picторque res communis terrarum erat.* PLIN. hift. l. 35.

H 4 *Graiis*

Graiis ingenium, Graiis dedit ore rotundo
Musa loqui, præter laudem nullius avaris.

HOR. de arte.

The Muses lov'd the Greeks, and blest with sense,
They freely gave them wit and eloquence.

CREECH.

If we do but confider the fituation of Rome, when Virgil, Pollio, Varius, Horace, Tibullus, and their cotemporaries were fo great an honor to poetry, we fhall find, that in their days Rome was the flourifhing capital of the greateft and happieft empire that ever exifted. This city enjoyed, after a long fucceffion of troubles and civil wars, the fweets of a repofe fhe had been long a ftranger to, and this under the government of a prince who was a real lover of merit, being poffeffed of a great fhare of it himfelf. Befides, Auguftus was obliged to make a good ufe of his new authority, in order to be more able to eftablifh it ; and confequently he could not confide it but to fuch minifters as were lovers of juftice, and likely to make a moderate ufe of their power. Thus riches, honors, and diftinctions were the fure encouragement and reward of merit. As a court was a new and odious thing at Rome, Auguftus was determined, that his at leaft fhould be fubject to no other reproach than that of being a court.

If we defcend to the age of Leo X. in which the arts and fciences, that had been buried ten centuries, rofe out of their tombs ; we fhall find, that under his pontificate Italy was in the greateft ftate of profperity it had been in fince

I

the

the time of the Cæfars. Thofe petty tyrants, who had *neſtled* themfelves with their officers and attendants in an infinite number of fortreſſes, and whofe friendſhip and quarrels were both a terrible fcourge to fociety, had been juſt exterminated by the prudence and courage of Pope Alexander VI. Seditions were now removed from the cities, the greateſt part of which formed themfelves at the clofe of the preceding century, into regular and fettled governments. We may venture to aſſert, that the foreign wars which commenced about that time in Italy by the expedition of Charles VIII. to Naples, were not fo grievous to fociety, as the perpetual dread of being carried off, upon going into the country, by the banditti of a villain, who was fettled, and, purfuant to the phrafe of thofe times, fortified in a ſtrong hold ; or as the apprehenfion of feeing one's houfe fet on fire in a popular tumult. The wars of thofe days refembled a ſtorm of hail which came by puffs, and ravaged only a fmall part or corner of the country. The art of exhauſting provinces for the fubfiſting of armies on the frontiers, that pernicious art which perpetuates the quarrels of fovereigns, and continues the calamities of war a long time after the concluſion of treaties, infomuch as to render it impoſſible for peace to flouriſh till feveral years after the war is finiſhed ; that pernicious art, I fay, had not been as yet invented. Two Popes had reigned fucceſſively, who were extremely defirous of leaving illuſtrious monuments of their pontificate, and found themfelves obliged of courfe to excite and encourage all thofe artiſts and men of learning, who by immortalizing themfelves

were

were capable of giving them immortality. Francis I. Charles V. and Henry VIII. grew jealous of their reputation, and rivalled them in their turns in the encouragement of arts and sciences. By this means learning and arts made a moft furprizing progrefs; and painting particularly was carried, in a very fhort term of years to its utmoft pitch of perfeſtion ; no wonder, *when*, to exprefs myfelf in Pliny's words, *it was courted by kings and nations, ennobling thofe whom it deigned to hand down to pofterity* [a].

The reign of our late king Lewis XIV was a moft favourable time for the arts and fciences. As foon as that prince took the reins of government into his own hands, he made the moft advantageous fettlements for men of genius, that were ever eftablifhed by any fovereign. The minifter whom he employed for this particular purpofe, was extremely capable of difcharging his office. M. Colbert's protection was never purchafed at the price of a fervile and affiduous flattery, nor of a pretended or real fubjeſtion to his will and pleafure. He had no other inclination but that of having his prince ferved by men of the beft capacities. Sole author of his maiter's decifions, and difpofer of his favors, he went himfelf in fearch of thofe that were thus qualified, and offered them his proteſtion and friendfhip, when they did not prefume to demand it. Merit therefore at that time, thro' the magnificence of the prince, and the wife conduſt of the minifter, became a kind of eftate or patrimony.

[a] *Cum expeteretur a regibus populifque, illos nobilitante quos dignata effet pofteris tradere.* PLIN. l. 35.

CHAP.

C H A P. XIII.

That physical causes have probably had also a share in the surprizing progress of arts and sciences.

THERE is no room, in fine, to question but that moral causes have contributed to the surprizing progress of poetry and painting in particular ages. But may not physical causes have had also their influence in this same progress? May they not contribute to the amazing difference we observe between the state of arts and sciences in two succeeding ages? Is it not the physical causes that put the moral causes in motion? Is it the liberality of sovereigns, or the applause of one's countrymen, that forms illustrious painters and poets? Or is it not rather the great artists who attract this liberality, and by their wonderful productions force an attention and regard for those arts, which the world did not shew them, while they were yet rude and imperfect. Tacitus observes, that *those times which are fertile of eminent men, abound likewise in such as are capable of doing justice to their merit* [a]. Have we not reason to believe, that there are times, in which men of the same country are born with greater capacity and wit than at other times? Is it possible to imagine, for example, that Augustus, had he been served even by two Mæcenas's, would have been able if he had lived in the time of Constantine,

---

[a] *Virtutes iisdem temporibus optimè æstimantur quibus facillimè gignuntur.* TAC. vit. AGRIC.

to change by his largeffes the writers of the fourth century into Livys and Ciceros? If Julius II. and Leo X. had reigned in Sweden, is it to be fuppofed that their munificence would have produced in thofe

Machiavels? Are all countries proper for producing great poets and painters? And are there not fome barren ages in countries capable of fuch productions?

Whilft I have been meditating on this fubject, a great variety of ideas have frequently prefented themfelves to my mind, which I look upon rather as fimple glimmerings than real lights. I cannot therefore after all my reflections, be pofitive, whether men who are born during a certain fpace of years, are as much fuperior to their anceftors and pofterity in extent and vigor of mind, as thofe firft men, of whom facred and profane hiftory makes mention, and who lived to a very great age, were certainly fuperior to their defcendants in an equality of humors and goodnefs of complexion. However there is a fufficient air of probability in thefe ideas, to think them worthy of entertaining my reader.

Men frequently attribute phyfical effects to moral caufes. Sometimes we impute to an unlucky or crofs accident, thofe chagrins whofe origin is intirely in the intemperature of our humors, or in fome difpofition of air that oppreffes our machine. Had the air been a little more ferene, perhaps we fhould have beheld with indifference, a thing which feems to throw us into the moft violent fits of defpair. I fhall therefore expofe here my reflections fo much the more readily, as in point of probability and conjecture, we

we fee ourfelves refuted with pleafure, upon difcovering a greater folidity in an anfwer than we really
expected. *We that are directed by probability* (to
make ufe of Cicero's words) *and are incapable of
exceeding the limits of what bears at leaft a refemblance to truth, are ready to refute without obftinacy, and to be refuted ourfelves without anger or
paffion* [a].

My firft reflection is, that there are countries and
times in which arts and fciences do not flourifh,
notwithftanding the vigorous concurrence of moral
caufes in their favor. The Achilles's who appear
in thofe times, do not find a Homer to fing their
exploits. Their great actions only furnifh future
poets with proper fubjects to excite them.

My fecond reflection is, that arts and fciences do
not arrive to their full perfection, by a flow advance,
proportioned to the time employed in their culture,
but by a very fudden progrefs. They attain this
perfection, when moral caufes do nothing particular
to promote them, but what they had done before
for a long time, without having produced any very
fenfible fruit of their activity. Arts and fciences
decline likewife at a time, when moral caufes redouble their efforts to fupport them in that point
of elevation, to which they rofe, in a manner, of
themfelves.

My third and laft reflection is, that great painters
have always been cotemporaries with great poets, and

---

[a] *Nos qui fequimur probabilia, nec ultra id quod verifimile occur-
rerit progredi poffumus, & refellere fine pertinacia & refelli fine
iracundia parati fumus.* Cic. Tufc. quæft. l. 2.

they

they have both flourifhed at the fame time with fuch of their countrymen as have been moft eminent in other profeffions. It feems as if a kind of fpirit of perfection in their days had fhed itfelf upon the inhabitants of their country. Thofe profeffions which flourifhed together with poetry and painting, fell with them at the fame time to neglect and ruin.

Firft REFLECTION.

IT would be needlefs to ufe many arguments to prove, that there are countries, which have never produced any eminent painters or poets. Every body knows, for inftance, that we have never had from the extremities of the North but wild poets, coarfe verfifiers, and frigid colorifts. Painting and poetry have never approached the pole nearer than the latitude of Holland; and even in this province we have feen only a poor ftarved kind of painting. The Dutch poets have fhewn a greater vigor and fpirit, than their painters. It feems (if I be permitted to jeft) that poetry is not fo much afraid of the cold as painting.

It has been obferved in all ages, that the glory of wit and capacity has been confined in fuch a manner to particular countries, that even neighbouring provinces have been unable to fhare it with them. Paterculus fays [a], that one fhould be no more furprized at feeing fo many illuftrious orators at Athens, than at not finding at Thebes, Sparta, or Argos, a perfon celebrated for eloquence. Experience had rendered familiar this unequal diftribution of capacities between neighbouring countries. *Different ideas,*

[a] PATERCUL. hift. lib. I.

fays

fays a modern author [a], *are like plants and flowers which do not grow alike in all kinds of climates. Perhaps our French foil is no more fit for the reafoning ufed by the Ægyptians, than it is proper for their palms; and without travelling fo far, probably our orange-trees which do not grow with fuch eafe here as in Italy, are an indication that there is a certain turn of mind in Italy, which is not altogether like that of France.* 'Tis abfolutely certain, that by the concatenation and reciprocal dependance between all the parts of the material world, the difference of climates which fhews itfelf fenfibly in the plants, muft extend itfelf likewife to the brain, and be productive there of fome effect or other. It were to be wifhed that this author had taken the trouble to unfold this principle. He would have cleared, much better than I can, thofe truths which I fhall endeavour to lay open; he who is poffeffed in fo eminent a degree of the moft precious talent a man of learning can be master of, that is, the gift of placing the abftrufeft fubjects within reach of common capacities, and of rendering the moft complicated truths intelligible, with tolerable attention, even to thofe who never made any ftudy but in his works, of the fciences they explain.

It will not avail to fay, that the reafon why arts and fciences have not flourifhed beyond the fifty fecond degree of North latitude, nor nearer than five and twenty degrees to the line, is becaufe they have not been tranfplanted to the torrid or frigid Zone. The arts rife of themfelves in proper climates: They muft therefore have their birth, their

[a] M. de Fontenelle, digreffion upon the ancients.

cradle,

cradle, and their inventers, before they can be tranfplanted. Who is it that firft brought the arts into Ægypt? No body. But the Ægyptians, favored by the climate of their country, gave them birth themfelves. The arts would rife of their own accord in countries that have a proper foil for them, were they never to be tranfplanted thither. Perhaps they would appear fomewhat later; however they would certainly make their appearance. Thofe, in whofe country the arts have never flourifhed, are people who live abfolutely in an improper climate. Were it not for this, the arts would rife in thofe places of themfelves, or at leaft they would have been tranfplanted thither by means of commerce.

The Greeks, for example, did not travel more frequently into Ægypt, than the Poles, as well as other northern nations, and the Englifh, travel at prefent into Italy. Neverthelefs the Greeks foon tranfplanted the art of painting from Ægypt into Greece, while its fovereigns and republics, ftill rude and unpolifhed, did not think the acquifition of this art to be an affair of any importance. 'Tis thus a field which is left unmanured clofe to a foreft, is fown of itfelf, and becomes quickly a copfe, when the foil is fit for the bearing of trees.

The Englifh thefe two centuries paft have been as fond of painting as any other nation; except the Italians; infomuch that foreign painters, who have fettled in England during this period, have gained three times more by their art, than they could have done elfewhere. 'Tis well known, what a value Henry VIII. had for pictures, and with what magnificence he recompenced Holbein. The munificence

of

of Q. Elizabeth encouraged all forts of arts during a reign of near fifty years. Charles I, who lived in great fplendor the firft fifteen years of his reign, carried his love for painting to a very great height ; infomuch that 'tis owing to his excefs of paffion for this art, that the price of pictures is rifen fo high in our days. As he employed agents all over Europe to make a collection for him at any rate, whilft Philip IV King of Spain opened his treafures for the fame purpofe with the greateft prodigality, the competition of thofe two monarchs enhanced the price of eminent performances. Thus the treafures of the art became the fource of real treafures in commerce [a]. And yet England has not hitherto produced fo much as one painter, who deferves to be ranked among the artifts of the firft, or even of the fecond clafs. The Englifh climate has been warm enough to produce a number of eminent men in moft fciences and profeffions. It has even given us good muficians and excellent poets, but it has not favoured us with painters, who have made fo great a figure, as the philofophers, poets, and other illuftrious worthies of the Englifh nation. The Englifh painters of note may be all reduced to three portrait painters [b].

Thofe painters who flourifhed in England under Henry VIII and Charles I were foreigners, who carried into that ifland an art which the inhabitants of the country could not keep. Holbein

[a] Dryden, *catalogue of painters.*
[b] Cooper, Dobson, Riley.

and Lely were Germans; and Vandyke a Flemming. Those who even in our days have been esteemed as the chief painters of the country, were not Englishmen. Vario was a Neapolitan, and Kneller a German. The medals struck in England in Cromwell's time, and those made there under Charles II and James II were very good work, but done by a stranger: This was Roëttiers of Antwerp, Guibbons's countryman, who was for a considerable time the principal sculptor in London.

We even observe that the design is generally bad in works done in England : If ever they are worth admiring, 'tis for the hand and execution of the workman, and not for the design of the artist. There are certainly no workmen in the world that have a greater beauty in the execution, or that know how to manage their tools better than the English. But they have not been able as yet to attain to that taste in their designs, which some foreign artists carried over with them to London; where it has never stirred out of their shops.

'Tis not only in excessive cold or wet countries, that the arts cannot flourish; there are even temperate climates, where they are in a drooping condition. Tho' the Spaniards have had several magnificent sovereigns, who have been as much captivated with the charms of painting, as any pope whatsoever; yet this nation, so fertile of great personages, and even of great poets in verse and prose, has not produced a painter of the first class, and can hardly furnish us with two of the second. Charles V,

Philip

Philip II, Philip IV, and Charles II, were obliged to employ foreign painters to work at the Efcu-
rial and in other places.

The liberal arts have never travelled further than
Europe, unlefs it be to take an airing, (if the expreffion be allowed me) on the coafts of Afia and Afric.
'Tis obfervable, that the Europeans, and thofe who
are born on the coafts bordering upon Europe, have
always been fitter than other people for arts and fciences, as well as political government. Wherefoever the
Europeans have carried their arms, they have generally
fubdued the inhabitants. They have vanquifhed them
when they were only ten to thirty, and very frequently when they have fought ten againft a hundred.
Without afcending fo high as Alexander the Great
and the Romans, let us only recal to mind with what
eafe a handful of Spaniards and Portuguefe, by the
help of their induftry and the arms they carried
with them from Europe, fubdued the two Indies.
To alledge that the Indians would not have been fo
eafily conquered, if they had been mafters of the fame
military machines, the fame arms and difcipline as
their conquerors, proves the fuperiority of genius in
the Europeans, who had invented all thofe things,
when the Afiatics and Americans had made no
fuch difcovery, tho' they had been continually at
war with one another.   If it be true that chance
taught the Chinefe fooner than us the ufe of gun-
powder and printing, we have carried both thefe
arts, as foon as we difcovered them, to fuch a degree of perfection, that we are capable now of giving leffons to the Chinefe.   Our miffionaries at
prefent have the direction of the cafting of their

cannon,

cannon, and we have taught them the practice of printing with separate types. Every body knows, that the Chinese used to print at that time with copper-plates, which could be of service only in the printing of one thing; whereas the separate types, without mentioning several other conveniences which they afford to printers, have likewise that of being of use in the impression of different sheets. We print Virgil's Æneid with the same types, that were used in printing the new Testament. When the Europeans first entered China, the astronomers of that country, who had been exceedingly well paid for many ages, were incapable of foretelling an eclipse with any exactness. 'Tis now upwards of two thousand years since the European astronomers have been most accurate in this kind of prediction.

The arts seem even to suffer, when they are kept at too great a distance from Europe. Tho' the Ægyptians were the first inventors of painting and sculpture, they have not had so great a share as the Greeks and Italians, in the glory of these arts. The sculptures which are agreed to have been done by the Ægyptians, that is, those which are seen on the ancient buildings of Ægypt, as their obelisks and mummies, are nothing to compare to such as were executed in Greece and Italy. If we happen to meet with a sphinx of surprizing beauty, 'tis probably the work of some Greek sculptor, who diverted himself with making Ægyptian figures, as our painters take a pleasure sometimes in imitating the figures of the basso-relievos, and the pictures of the Indies and China. Have we not had artists ourselves, felves, who have diverted themfelves with making fphinxes? There are feveral fuch in the gardens of Verfailles, which are original pieces done by our modern fculptors. Pliny does not extol in his work any one mafter-piece in painting and fculpture done by an Ægyptian, tho' he gives us fuch a long lift of the performances of famous artifts. We even find [a] that Greek fculptors ufed to travel to Ægypt for work. To return to Pliny's filence, it is obfervable that this author lived at a time, when the Ægyptian works were ftill extant. Petronius writes, that there were none but bad painters trained up in Ægypt. He obferves likewife that the Ægyptians had done a vaft deal of prejudice to this art, by inventing rules proper for rendering its apprenticefhip lefs tedious, and the practice lefs laborious.

'Tis now thirty years ago fince Sir John Chardin has given us the defigns of the ruins of Perfepolis. We may fee by thefe that the kings of Perfia, notwithftanding their immenfe opulence fo much boafted of in ancient hiftory, had but very indifferent workmen. Probably, the Greek artifts were not fo ready to go and feek their fortunes in the Perfian fervice as the Greek foldiers. Be that as it will, one is not at all furprized, after having feen thofe defigns, that Alexander fet fire to a palace, whofe ornament and furniture appeared coarfe and indifferent to him, in comparifon to what he had feen in Greece. The Perfians under Darius were what thofe that inhabit the fame country are at prefent, that is, extreme patient and able workmen, with refpect to their manual labor, but void

[a] Diodorus Siculus, book 1.

of

of genius to invent, and of talents to imitate the moft ingaging beauties of nature.

Europe is over-ftocked with ftuffs, china-ware, and other curiofities of China, and the eaftern parts of Afia. Nothing can be lefs picturefque than the tafte of the defign and coloring, which prevails in thefe works. There have been feveral tranflations publifhed of the poetic compofitions of the eaftern nations. When we find a ftroke in its proper place, or a probable adventure, we admire it ; and this·is as much as we can fay of them. Wherefore all thefe tranflations, which feldom go thro' a fecond edition, have only a tranfient vogue, for which they are in-debted to the foreign air of the original, and to the inconfiderate fondnefs which numbers of people have for fingular things. The fame curiofity which fets people a running after the countrymen of the authors of thofe writings, when they appear in France dref-fed after their own country fafhion, makes us defi-rous at firft of reading thefe tranflations.

If there had been any poets of equal merit with Homer among the Brachmans and ancient Perfians, the Greeks who travelled to inrich their libraries, in the fame manner as people in our days crofs the feas in order to fill their magazines, would in all pro-bability have rendered them into their language. One of their princes would have ordered a Greek tranflation of them, as one of the Ptolemies is faid to have had the Bible done into that tongue, tho' this prince had no notion of the Divine infpiration of its penmen.

When the Spaniards difcovered the continent of America, they found two empires that had flourifhed

for

for feveral years, thofe of Peru and Mexico : and the art of painting had been cultivated for a long time in thofe empires. The people endowed with an incredible patience and flight of hand, had even created the art of making a kind of Mofaic with the feathers of birds. 'Tis aftonifhing that human hands could have fufficient dexterity to range and reduce into the form of colored figures, fo many different filaments. But as thefe people had no genius, they were, in fpite of all their dexterity, very coarfe artifts. They underftood neither the moft fimple rules of defign, nor the firft principles of compofition, perfpective, or chiaro-fcuro. They did not fo much as know how to paint with minerals and other natural colors which come to us from their country. They have feen fince that time fome of the beft pictures of Italy, a vaft number of which have been fent by the Spaniards into the Weft-Indies. Their new mafters have likewife fhewn them how to make ufe of their pencil and colors, but have not been able to render them fkilful painters. The Indians, who have been fo docile in other arts, which they have learnt of the Spaniards, as to become better mafons, for inftance, than their mafters, have found nothing in the European pictures within their reach, except the vivacity of the colors. This they have not only imitated with fuccefs, but have even furpaffed their originals, by what I have heard from thofe who have feen feveral cupolas painted in Mexico by Indian artifts.

The Chinefe, who are fo curious in their own country paintings, have little or no tafte for the European pictures, in which we fee (fay they) too many

black

black fpots; for 'tis thus they call our fhades. After reflecting on what has been hitherto alledged, and on feveral other things which are generally known, and are fufficient to prove my propofition, I cannot help being of Fontenelle's opinion, who fpeaking of the knowledge and turn of mind of the eaftern people, fays; [a] *I am really inclined every day more and more to believe, that there is a certain genius, which has yet travelled but a very little way out of Europe.*

As there are countries, in which moral caufes have never been productive of great painters or poets; fo there are times wherein moral caufes are unable to form eminent artifts, even in thofe countries, which at other times produce them with the greateft eafe, and, as it were, fpontaneoufly. One would imagine, that capricious nature brings forth thefe great artifts, only juft when her fancy pleafes.

Before Julius II there had been feveral popes in Italy, who diftinguifhed themfelves by their liberality towards painters and men of letters, but could never with all their magnificence give wings to artifts, fo as to make them reach to that pitch of perfection, to which fuch numbers of their profeffion attained under the pontificate of this pope. Laurence of Medicis diftributed for a long time thofe royal bounties at Florence, which induced people to give him the firname of Magnificent; and the greateft part of his liberalities were beftowed with difcretion on all forts of real merit. The Bentivoglios did the fame thing at Bologna, and the princes of

[a] *Plurality of Worlds. Sixth evening.*

I   the

the houfe of Efte at Ferrara. The Vifcontis and the Sforzas were encouragers of the polite arts at Milan. And yet no body appeared in thofe times, whofe works could be compared to fuch as were afterwards produced, upon the reftoration of polite arts and learning. It feems as if men eminent in all kind of merit, who, purfuant to one's common way of thinking, ought to have been diftributed into feveral ages, all waited for the pontificate of Julius II to make their appearance.

Let us now turn our eyes a while to what paffed in France, with regard to poetry and painting. Did the moral caufes wait, 'till Le Sueur, Le Brun, Corneille, La Fontaine, and Racine had fhewn themfelves; before they would encourage painting and poetry? Can it be faid, that the effects have been feen to proceed fo quickly in our country from the action of moral caufes, that we muft attribute thereto the furprizing fuccefs of eminent artifts. Before Francis I we have had princes who have been very liberal to men of merit, without having been able, notwithftanding all their largeffes, of having the honor of producing a French painter or poet, whofe works could have been put any ways in competition in future times, with thofe which appeared under Lewis XIII and Lewis XIV. There are fcarce any fragments remaining of thofe times either in verfe or profe, that we can read with any pleafure. The chancellor de l'Hopital fays in his harangue, which he pronounced before the ftates of the kingdom affembled at Orleans: [a] *That good King Lewis XII ufed to take a pleafure in hearing the farces and*

[a] In 1561.

comedies,

comedies, even those which were written with the greatest liberty, because he said he learnt several things that were done in his kingdom, which would have otherwise escaped his knowledge. Of all those farces composed under Lewis XII or before, that of Patelin is the only one that is preserved in our cabinets.

The great king Francis was one of the moft zealous protectors, that the arts and fciences could ever boaft of. Every body knows what favor, or to fpeak more exactly, what friendfhip he fhewed to Roux, to Andrea del Sarto, to Leonardo da Vinci, (who died in his arms) as likewife to every one that was illuftrious for talent or merit.

With what profufion did not he pay for the pictures he had ordered to be made by Raphael ? His liberality and kind reception drew numbers of painters into France ; but tho' his bounties were beftowed continually on the profeffors of this art during a reign of thirty three years, they could never form an eminent painter amongft his own fubjects. Thofe painters who fettled at that time in France, died without eleves, fuch at leaft as were worthy of them ; in the fame manner as animals tranfported into a very different climate, die without leaving any of the fame breed behind them.

This generous prince was no lefs fond of poetry than painting, and he ufed even to write verfes fometimes himfelf. His fifter Margarite of Valois, the firft of the two queens of Navarre that bore that name, ufed likewife to compofe verfes. We have an intire volume of her poems, under the name of *Marguerites Francoifes,* or the *French pearls.* This reign produced therefore a great quantity of poems ;

but

but thofe of Clement Marot and St Gelais, are the only ones almoft that are read in our days. The reft ferve for ornament to thofe libraries, in which fcarce books are as much intitled to have a place as good ones. As the changes which have happened in our language do not hinder us from taking a pleafure ftill in reading thofe fragments that Marot compofed within the fphere of his genius, which was not fuited for great works ; fo they would not make us difrelifh the works of his cotemporaries, were they interfperfed with the fame beauties as thofe we find in the writings of poets who flourifhed under Lewis XIV.

Henry II and Diana of Valentinois were very fond of the Mufes. Charles IX refpected them fo far as to facrifice, as it were, his perfon to them ; and the verfes which he compofed for Ronfard, are equal to the very beft that were written by that illuftrious poet.

Ta lyre qui ravit par de fi doux accords
Te donne les efprits dont je n'ai que le corps,
Le maitre elle t'en rend, & te fcait introduire,
Ou le plus fier tyran ne peut avoir d'empire.

Thy lyre, which charms us with its tuneful firings,
Subdues thofe fouls that fcorn to yield to kings,
Extends thy fway and captivating hand,
Where the fierce tyrant can have no command.

This prince made the famous James Amiot, fon to a butcher of Melun, great Almoner of France. Every body knows the exceffive profufion of Henry III towards the French Pleiades, or the fociety of the feven brigheft ftars of the French poetry under

I   his

his reign. He did not practise towards them the above-mentioned maxim of his brother Charles IX relating to the subsistence proper to be given to poets. All the great wits who lived under Henry III, and even those who frequently abused their talents to preach and write against him, had a share in his prodigality. At the time here mentioned, poets and men of letters were admitted to a kind of familiarity with our kings. They approached them with as much privacy, and were as well received as the greatest lords of the court. And yet all these favors and honors were insufficient to carry even so much as one poet, during that period, to the top of Parnaffus. 'Tis surprising that so much encouragement produced so little fruit in a country, where one kind look from the sovereign is able to send twenty persons of distinction to dare certain death at a breach with the greatest intrepidity.

'Tis natural for a court to be passionately fond of every thing that is agreable to the inclination and taste of its master; and the court of France has constantly excelled all others in this respect. Wherefore I leave the reader to judge, whether it was thro' the fault of moral causes, that there was not a Moliere or a Corneille at the court of the princes of the house of Valois. Were not Terence, Plautus, Horace, Virgil, and the other great authors of antiquity, who contributed so greatly to form the poets of the seventeenth century, in the hands of the great wits of the courts of Francis I and Henry III? Is it because Ronsard and his cotemporaries did not understand the learned tongues, they composed works, whose taste has so little a resemblance with that of

the

the better fort of the Greek and Roman writings? No, fo far from that, their greateft defect is to have imitated them in too fervile a manner, and to have attempted to fpeak Greek and Latin with French words.

Our late king made feveral as judicious and magnificent foundations, as could have been eftablifhed by the Romans, in favor of thofe arts which depend on the defign. In order to give young people, that were born with a genius for painting, all imaginable conveniency and eafe for improving their talents, he founded an academy for them at Rome. This was giving them a kind of fettlement in the country of the polite arts. Thofe eleves that fhew any glimmering of genius, are maintained there long enough to have an opportunity of learning their profeffion. Thus refpect and recompence wait for the able artift, and even fometimes, as we ourfelves have feen, precede their merit. And yet fifty years care and expence has fcarce produced three or four painters, whofe works have the true ftamp of immortality.

'Tis alfo obfervable, that thofe three French painters, who were fo great an honor to our nation under the reign of Lewis XIV, were no ways indebted to thefe foundations, having been quite formed in their art before thefe fettlements were made. In the year fixteen hundred and fixty one, that is, the year in which Lewis XIV took the reins of government into his own hands, and in which his *Age* began, Pouffin was feventy years old, and Le Sueur was dead. Le Brun was then forty, and if the magnificence

ficence of the fovereign excited him to work, it was not that however which rendered him capable of excelling. In fine, Nature, whom this great prince obliged fo often to bend under his will, refufed obftinately to obey him in this article. She would not produce under his reign fuch a number of able painters as fhe brought forth of her own accord under Leo X. As the phyfical caufes denied their concurrence here with the moral ones, the whole power of this prince could never raife fuch a fchool in France, as thofe that were formed of a fudden at other times, at Rome, Venice, and Bologna.

The immenfe expences of Lewis XIV had no other fuccefs, but that of forming a large number of excellent fculptors. As a perfon that knows how to make handfome ftatues is a good fculptor ; and as it is not neceffary in order to merit this title, to have publifhed fome of thofe great works which we have fpoken of in the firft part of our refleftions ; we may venture to fay, that fculpture does not demand fo much genius as painting. A fovereign that cannot raife a certain number of young people, who by means of fuch helps as he fupplies them with, are capable of becoming fo many Raphaels or Caraccios, may find a great many who by his encouragement are able to attain to a great perfeftion in fculpture. The fchool which has not been erefted at a time, wherein the phyfical caufes concur with the moral ones, produces therefore men eminent in fculpture and ingraving, inftead of giving birth to painters of the firft order. This is exaftly what has happened in France. Since the reftoration of

arts,

arts, there have been no where fo many excellent fculptors and good ingravers of all forts, as in this kingdom under the reign of the late king.

The Italians, of whom we firft learnt the art of fculpture, have been obliged thefe many years to employ our artifts. Puget, a fculptor from Marfeilles [*], was preferred to feveral Italian workmen, to carve two of the four ftatues defigned for adorning the niches of the pilafters, which fupport the dome of the magnificent church of St Mary of Carignano at Genoa. 'Twas he alfo that made the ftatues of St Sebaftian and St Alexander Sauli. I am not inclinable to injure the reputation of Domenico Guidi who made that of St John, nor the other attift who carved the figure of St Bartholomew ; but the Genoefe themfelves regret at prefent that Puget did not carve the four ftatues. When the Jefuits at Rome erected, about five and forty years ago, the altar of St Ignatius in the church called by the name of Jefus, they publifhed their intention of giving the execution of the two groups of five figures of white marble, which were to be placed on each fide of this fumptuous monument, to whofoever fhould produce the beft model. The moft able fculptors that were then in Italy prefented each his model, and thefe having been expofed to public view, it was decided by general confent, that the model of Theodon, who was then fculptor of the fabric of St Peter, and that of Le Gros, both Frenchmen, deferved the preference. They made therefore thofe two groups, which are ranked at prefent among the mafter-pieces of *modern Rome*. The brazen baluftrade inclofing this al-

[*] Deceafed at Marfeilles 1695, aged 72.

tar, and compofed of angels fporting among rows of vines interwoven with ears of corn, is likewife the work of a French fculptor. The five beft ingravers in brafs we have ever feen, were Frenchmen either by birth or education ; and the fame may be faid of ingravers in other metals. The goldfmith's trade, whether in large or fmall work, as well as all thofe arts whofe value is raifed by the defign, are more perfect in France than in any other country. But as painting does not depend fo much on moral caufes, as the above-mentioned arts, the progrefs thereof has not been in proportion to the affiftances it has received within thefe fourfcore years.

Second REFLECTION.

That the arts attain to their higheft degree of elevation by a fudden progrefs, and that the effects of moral caufes cannot carry them to that point of perfection, to which they feem to have fpontaneoufly rifen.

THUS I have given my firft reafon for affirming, that men are not born with fo much genius in one country as in another, and that even in the fame country there are certain periods, in which people have not fo much genius as at other times. My fecond reafon feems to me as ftrong as the firft. This is, that there are particular times, in which men attain in very few years to a furprizing pitch of perfection in thofe very arts and profeffions, which they cultivated almoft ineffectually before for a long fucceffion of ages. This prodigy comes to pafs without any new intervention of the

moral

moral caufes, to which fo miraculous a progrefs can be attributed. On the contrary, arts and fciences decline, when moral caufes redouble their efforts to fupport them in that point of elevation, to which they feem to have been raifed by a fecret influence.

The reader is already aware of what kind of proofs I am going to alledge, in order to fbew that the progrefs of the polite arts was extremely rapid, and that thefe arts breaking thro' the bounds of a long fpace of time, leaped of a fudden from their dawn to their noon of perfection. Painting was revived in Italy as early as the thirteenth century, by *Cimabue*'s [a] pencil. There were feveral painters who acquired fome reputation in the two following centuries, but none of them attained to any eminent degree of perfection. The works of thofe painters, fo much cried up in their own times, have had the fame fate in Italy, as Ronfard's poems in France, that is, of not being any longer inquired for.

In 1480 painting was yet a rude and imperfect art, notwithftanding it had been conftantly cultivated during the fpace of two hundred years. They ufed to draw nature at that time with a very fcrupulous exactnefs, but without giving her a grand or. noble air. The heads were finifhed with fo much care, that one might tell the very hairs of their heads and beards ; the draperies were of the moft glittering colors and heightened with gold : In fine, the artift's hand had acquired fome eafe and dexterity, but without the leaft fire, or fpark of genius. No body had as yet hit upon the beauties that are

[a] boin in 1210.

drawn

drawn from the *naked* of bodies reprefented in action. There had been no difcovery yet made in the chiaro-fcuro, nor in the aerial perfpective, no more than in the elegance of the contours, or in the fine air of the draperies. Thofe painters knew how to range the figures of a picture, but without being able to difpofe them purfuant to the prefent rules of picturefque compofition. Before Raphael and his cotemporaries, the martyrdom of a faint feemed not to move any of the fpectators. The affiftants, whom the painter introduced into this tragic action, were only to fill up that fpace in the canvafs which the faint and the executioners left empty.

Towards the clofe of the fifteenth century, painting, which had hitherto walked with fo flow a pace towards its perfection, that its progrefs was almoft imperceptible, advanced all of a fudden with gigantic ftrides. A kind of Gothic painting commenced the ornaments of feveral edifices, whofe laft imbellifhments are the maſter-pieces of Raphael and his cotemporaries. Cardinal John Medicis[a] who did not grow old in his purple, having been chofen pope at thirty feven years of age, renewed the decoration of the church of St Peter of Montorio, and fet people to work at it a little after he had received his cardinal's hat. The chapels which are on the left hand coming in, and were done the firft, are imbellifhed with paintings and fculptures of a very indifferent tafte, and fomewhat bordering upon the Gothic ; but the oppofite chapels were adorned by artifts of the very firft clafs. The firft

[a] LEO X.

as you come into the church, is done by *Frà Seba-
ftiano del Piombo :* Another is inriched with ftatues
by Daniel of Voltera : In fine, we fee on the high
altar the transfiguration by Raphael, a picture as
well known in Europe as Virgil's Æneid.

The fate of fculpture has been the very fame as
that of painting. One would have imagined, that
the eyes of artifts, which had been hitherto fhut,
had been opened all of a fudden by a kind of miracle. A poet would fay, that every new performance of Raphael produced a painter. And yet the
moral caufes exerted themfelves no more at that
time in favor of the arts, than they had done before,
tho' to no purpofe, during the fpace of two centuries. The antique ftatues, and baffo-relievo's, which
Raphael and his cotemporaries knew how to make
fuch a good ufe of, were vifible to their predeceffors, without being of any fervice to them. If
fome antiques were difcovered, which their predeceffors had not feen, what a vaft number muft they
have beheld, which perifhed before Raphael could
have fight of them ? How comes it, that thefe
predeceffors did not rake and rummage into the
ruins of ancient Rome, like Raphael and his cotemporaries ? 'Tis becaufe they had no genius : 'Tis
becaufe their tafte differed from that which we
obferve in the Marcus Aurelius, and all the other
works of fculpture and architecture, which had
been difcovered and dug up a long while before
Raphael.

That fame prodigy which happened at Rome,
came to pafs at the fame time at Venice, Florence,
and all the other cities of Italy. Men fprung up

there,

there, as it were, from under ground, who immortalized their memories by their skill in their profesfions, and were all far superior to the masters they had learnt of ; men without predeceffors to imitate, and eleves of their own genius.   Venice faw itfelf inriched all of a fudden with excellent painters, notwithftanding the republic had not founded lately any new academies, nor propofed new prizes.   Thofe happy influences which were then fhed on the art of painting, went in fearch of Corregio to his village, to raife there a painter of a particular character.   He was the firft that attempted to hang figures really in the air, and which form a *cieling*, as painters exprefs it.   Raphael, in painting the nuptials of Pfyche on the vault of the faloon of the little Farnefe, has treated his fubject, as if it were done on a tapeftry faftened to the ceiling. Corregio hung figures in the air in the affumption of the virgin Mary, which he drew in the cupola of the cathedral church of Parma, and in the afcenfion of Chrift painted in the cupola of the abbey of St John of the fame city.   This very thing only would be fufficient to fhew the action of phyfical caufes in the reftoration of arts.   All thofe fchools that were formed at that time, led by different roads to the perfection of their art.   Their manner did not refemble one another, *tho' they were all fo extremely good*, as Cicero fays [a] upon a like occafion, *that we fhould have been vexed, had not each fchool purfued its own.*

[a] *Omnes inter fe diffimiles, ita tamen ut neminem velis effe fui diffimilem.* Cic. de orat. l. 3.

The

The North received likewife fome beams of this influence. Albert Durer, Holbein, and Luke of Leyden, were much better painters than any that had hitherto appeared in their country. There are feveral pictures of Holbein preferved in the cabinet of the library of Bafil, two of which demonftrate the furprifing progrefs which painting ma'e at that time. The firft of thefe pictures, which by an infcription at the bottom appears to have been made in 1516, reprefents a fchool mafter teaching children to read. It has all the faults with which we have reproached thofe paintings that were done before Raphael's time. The fecond, which exhibits the manner our Saviour was taken down from the crofs, and whofe infcription fhews it to have been done in 1521, is in the right tafte. Holbein had feen fome new pictures, and had benefited thereby, in the fame manner as Raphael improved by feeing the works of Michael Angelo. The Altar-piece which reprefents in eight feparate pictures the principal events of the paffion, and is preferved in the town-houfe of Bafil, muft have been drawn by Holbein before the Roman Catholic worfhip was fuppreffed in that city, or the proteftant Religion eftablifhed, and pictures expelled the churches in 1527. Thefe eight pieces may be compared with the beft performances of Raphael's eleves for the poetry, and preferred to them with refpect to the coloring. There appears even a greater knowledge of the chiaro-fcuro, than other painters were mafters of in thofe times. We perceive here fome marvelous incidents of light, efpecially in the picture re-

K 3 prefenting

prefenting Chrift made prifoner in the garden of Olives.

The fame event happened in France under the reign of Lewis XIII as that which fell out in Italy under Julius II. A bright fun was feen to fhine forth of a fudden, which had been ufhered in by a very weak dawn. Our poetry rofe up, as it were, in an inftant, and foreign nations, which had hitherto de-fpifed it, fell fuddenly in love with it. Peter Corneille, to the beft of my remembrance, is the firft French profane poet, of whom a piece of any extent has been rendered into a foreign language.

We find fome admirable ftanzas in the works of feveral French poets, who wrote before the time above pointed out as the epoch, from which we are to date the fplendor of the French poetry. Malherbe is inimitable in the number and cadence of his verfes : but as he had a better ear than genius, the greateft part of his verfes are commendable only for the mechanifm and harmonious arrangement of his words, for which he had a furprizing capacity. They did not even require at that time, that poems fhould confift, as it were, of *contiguous beauties* ; fome fhining paffages were fufficient to recommend a whole piece. The poverty of the other verfes was excufed, being confidered as made only for connecting the former, wherefore they were called, as we learn from abbot de Marolles's memoirs, *paffage-verfes*.

There are fome ftanzas in the works of Defportes and De Bettaut, that are able to vie with the very beft that have been wrote fince Corneille ; and yet thofe that would attempt the intire perufal of the works

of

of thofe two poets, on the credit of fome fragments they might have heard recited, would foon be tired of their undertaking.   The books now mentioned refemble thofe chains of mountains, where we muft traverfe a vaft deal of wild and defert land, before we can meet with a pleafant cultivated valley.

There had been a theatre for about two hundred years in France, when Corneille firft wrote his Cid. And yet what progrefs did our dramatic poetry make during that time? None at all.   Corneille found our ftage almoft as rude and barbarous, as it was under Lewis II.   Our drama made a greater progrefs from 1635 to 1665, and received far greater improvements during thofe thirty years, than all the three preceding centuries.   Rotrou appeared at the fame time as Corneille : Racine, Moliere, and Quinault ftarted up foon after.   Could one obferve a fufficient degree of perfection in the dramatic poetry of Garnier and Mairet, to have room to hope, that fuch eminent poets as Corneille and Moliere would fo foon appear in our poetic hemifphere ?   Who are the poetic anceftors, as it were, of La Fontaine ?   And to mention a word with regard to our painters, were Freminet and Vouet, who worked under Lewis XIII, deferving of the honor of being the immediate predeceffors of Pouffin, Sueur, and Le Brun ?

Thofe great men, who compofe what we call the Auguftan age, were not formed during the happy days of the reign of that emperor.   Every body knows, that the commencement of the age of Auguftus was a time of fire and fword.   Thefe days, fo happy for the whole univerfe, do not commence their date till the battle of Actium, when the tute-

lary

Iary genius of Rome overthrew with one blow, Antony, Difcord, and Cleopatra. Virgil was forty years old, when this event happened. Let us take notice of the following picture he draws of thofe very times, in which he was formed in his art, and which he fo elegantly defcribes to have been the reign of Mars and Fury.

Quippe ubi fas verfum atque nefas, tot bella per orbem,
Tam multæ fcelerum facies, non ullus aratro
Dignus honor, fquallent abductis arva colonis,
Et curvæ rigidum falces conflantur in enfem.
Hinc movet Euphrates, illinc Germania bellum ;
Vicinæ nuptis inter fe legibus urbes
Arma ferunt, fævi! toto Mars impius orbe.

VIRG. Georg. I. I.

Where fraud and rapine, right and wrong confound,
Where impious arms from ev'ry part refound,
And monftrous crimes in ev'ry fhape are crown'd.
The peaceful peafant to the wars is preft ;
The fields lye fallow in inglorious reft :
The plain no pafture to the flock affords,
The crooked fcythes are ftreigthened into fwords :
And there Euphrates her foft off-fpring arms,
And here the Rhine rebellows with alarms ;
The neighb'ring cities range on fev'ral fides,
Perfidious Mars long plighted leagues divides,
And o'er the wafted world in triumph rides.

DRYDEN.

Thofe who had raifed themfelves to any particular degree of credit or fame, were more expofed than others in the profcriptions, and during all the horrors of the fuft years of the reign of Auguftus.

Cicero,

Cicero, who was facrificed in thofe unhappy times abovementioned by Virgil, died the victim of his abilities.

Largus & exundans letho dedit ingenii fons
Ingenio manus eft & cervix cæfa.

Juv. fat. 10.

But both thofe orators fo much renown'd,
In their own depths of eloquence were drown'd:
The hand and head were never loft, of thofe
Who dealt in doggrel, or who punn'd in profe.

DRYDEN.

Horace was five and thirty years old, when the battle of Actium was fought. The liberality of Auguftus excited feveral great poets to write, but they were become eminent already in their profeffion before this encouragement.

But that which is fufficient alone to convince us that the moral caufes do but concur with another fecond caufe ftronger than themfelves, to the furprizing progrefs which arts and learning make in certain ages, is, that thofe arts and fciences fall into a ftate of decay at the very time when the moral caufes are ufing their utmoft effotts to fupport them in that point of elevation to which they fpontaneoufly rofe. Thofe great men, who formed themfelves, as it were, with their own hands, were never able to train up either by their leffons, or their examples, eleves of equal fame and ability with themfelves. Their fucceffors, who had received inftructions in their art from the moft eminent mafters; fucceffors, who for this and feveral other reafons, ought to have furpaffed their mafters, had

they

they been born with an equal genius, have occupied but not filled the place of their predeceffors. The firft fucceffors of thofe great mafters have been replaced by difciples of a ftill inferior merit. At length the genius of arts and fciences difappears intirely, till the revolution of ages comes to raife it out of its tomb, where it feems to bury itfelf for a long feries of time, after having fhewn itfelf only for a few years.

In that very fame country, where nature had produced fo liberally, and without any extraordinary affiftance, the famous painters of the age of Leo X ; the recompences and cares of the academy of St Luke, eftablifhed by Gregory XII and by Sixtus Quintus, the attention of fovereigns, and in fine, all the efforts of moral caufes have never been able to give a pofterity to thofe great artifts, who fprung, as it were, from their own loins. The fchools of Venice and Florence degenerated in fixty years. 'Tis true, painting fupported itfelf with fplendor at Rome during a greater number of years ; for even towards the middle of the laft century there were fome eminent mafters in that city. But thofe painters were all ftrangers, fuch as Pouffin, the eleves of the Caracci who came to Rome to difplay the abilities of the fchool of Bologna, and fome others. As this fchool had flourifhed later than that of Rome, it has alfo furvived the Roman fchool. But, if the expreffion be allowed me, there were no young trees that grew up near thofe great oaks. Pouffin, during thirty years conftant labor in a fchool in the very heart of Rome, formed only one eleve of any fame in painting, tho' this great man was as capable

of

of teaching his art, as any mafter that ever profeffed it. In the fame city, but not at fame fame time, Raphael, who died as young as his fcholars, had formed in the courfe of ten or a dozen years a fchool of five or fix painters, whofe works are at prefent a part of the glory of their mafter. In fine all the Italian fchools, fuch as thofe of Venice, Rome, Parma, Bologna, where great genius's appeared in fuch numbers during the flourifhing ftate of the art of painting, are grown at prefent intirely barren.

This decay happened juft at a time when Italy enjoyed the happieft days it had feen fince the deftruction of the Roman empire. All thofe conjunctures which could decide the fate of the polite arts (were it true that their fate depended intirely on moral caufes) concurred to make them flourifh at the very time they began to decline. The wars of Italy lafted from the expedition of our king Charles VIII to Naples, 'till the peace concluded at Cambray 1529 between the Emperor Charles the Vth and Francis I, which was foon followed with the laft revolution of the ftate of Florence. During the fpace of thirty four years, Italy, to exprefs myfelf in the words of her own hiftorians, had been trampled under foot by barbarous nations. The kingdom of Naples was conquered four or five times by different princes, and the ftate of Milan underwent more frequent revolutions. The Venetians faw feveral times their enemies armies from their turrets, and Florence was almoft conftantly in war, either with the family of Medicis, who wanted to inflave her, or with the inhabitants of Pifa, whom they were defirous of fubduing. Rome more than once beheld

hoftile

hostile or suspected troops within its walls, and this capital of polite arts was plundered by the arms of Charles V with as much barbarity as if it had been stormed by the Turks. And yet it was exactly during those thirty four years that the arts and sciences made that progress in Italy, which is considered in our days as a kind of prodigy.

Since the last revolution of the state of Florence to the close of the sixteenth century, the tranquillity of Italy was not interrupted but by wars on their frontiers, or of a very short continuance. During this space of time none of its cities were ransack'd, nor was there any violent revolution in the five principal governments, into which it is divided. The Germans and French made no more invasions, except the expedition of the duke of Guise to Naples under Paul the IVth, which was rather an inroad than a war. The seventeenth century was a time of rest and plenty for Italy 'till its very last year. It was during the time now mentioned, that the Venetians amassed immense sums of money, and made their famous gold chain, to which they added some new rings every year. Then it was that Sixtus Quintus put five millions of gold crowns into the apostolic treasure; that the bank of Genoa was replenished; that the Grand Dukes of Tuscany heaped up such immense sums; that the dukes of Ferrara filled their coffers; in short, that all those who governed in Italy, except the viceroys of Naples, and the governors of Milan, found, after the usual and cautionary expences, a superfluity which might be saved from the revenue of each year; which is undoubtedly the surest symptom

symptom of the flourishing state of a government. Nevertheless it was during those years of prosperity that the schools of Rome, Florence, Venice, and successively that of Bologna, grew poor and barren of good artists.   As their noon of perfection, if I may express myself so, was very near their first rising, so their setting succeeded quickly their noon. I am not willing to predict the decadency of our age, notwithstanding what a person of very great capacity has wrote upwards of forty years ago, speaking of the excellent works which his age had produced.   [a] *We must candidly confess, that 'tis now ten years since that happy time is elapsed.*   Before M. Boileau died he saw a lyric poet take wing, born with the talents of those ancient poets, to whom Virgil allots an honorable place in the Elysian fields, for having given the first lessons of morality to fierce and savage man.   The works of those ancient poets, which formed one of the first links of society, and gave birth to the fable of Amphion, did not contain maxims more sage than the odes of the author here mentioned, whom nature seemed to have favored with a genius, only to adorn morality, and give an amiable dress to virtue.   Others, who are still living, deserve I should make an honorable mention of their works, but as Velleius Paterculus says in an almost similar case, *Vivorum censura difficilis :* 'Tis too delicate a point to attempt to give a judgment of the living poets.

If we ascend to the age of Augustus, we shall find that learning and arts, especially poetry, began to decline, when every thing conspired to make

---

[a] *M. de Fontenelle, digression on the ancients and moderns.*

them

them flourifh : They degenerated in the moft glorious times of the Roman empire. Numbers of people think that the arts and fciences perifhed under the ruins of that monarchy fubverted and laid wafte by the northern nations. They fuppofed therefore that the inundations of Barbarians, attended with the intire confufion of fociety in moft of thofe places where they fettled, deprived the conquered people of the proper conveniences, and even of the very defire to cultivate the polite arts. The arts, they fay, could never fubfift in a country whofe cities were changed into fields, and their fields into deferts.

Pierides donec Romam & Tyberina fluenta
Deferuere, Italis expulfæ protinus oris.
Tanti caufa mali Latio gens afpera aperto
Sæpius irrumpens: funt juffi vertere morem
Aufonidæ vitti, victoris vocibus ufi.
Ceffit amor mufarum ; artes fubiere repentè
Indignæ ; atque opibus cuncti incubuere parandis.

VIDA Poetic. l. 1.

'Till from the Hefperian plains and Tyber chas'd
From Rome the banifh'd fifters fled at laft ;
Driv'n by the barbarous nations, who from far
Burft into Latium with a tide of war.
Hence a vaft change of their old manners fprung,
The flaves were forc'd to fpeak their mafter's tongue.
No honors now were paid the facred mufe,
But all were bent on mercenary views.

PITT.

This opinion is not the lefs falfe, for its being fo generally received. Falfe opinions are eftablifhed
with

with as much facility in hiftory, as in philofophy. The arts and fciences were already degenerated and fallen into a ftate of decay, notwithftanding they had been cultivated with care, when thofe nations, the fcourges of mankind, quitted the northern fnows. We may look upon the buft of Caracalla as the laft gafp of the Roman fculpture. The two triumphal arches erected in honor of his father Severus, the chapiters of the columns in the Septizon, which were afterwards removed into different churches, when that building was pulled down, and the remaining ftatues which are known to have been made at that time, fufficiently demonftrate that fculpture and architecture began to decline under that prince and his children. Every body knows that the Low-relieves of the largeft of thofe two triumphal arches were done by an indifferent hand. 'Tis natural however to fuppofe that the moft able fculptors were employed about it, were it only out of a regard due to the place where it was erected. This was in the moft confiderable part of the town at the further end of the *Forum Romanum*, and, as we have reafon to believe, at the foot of one of thofe ftairs deftined for afcending to the Capitol, which was called *the hundred fteps*. Now Severus's reign preceded the firft taking of Rome by Alaricus, upwards of two hundred years; and from that emperor's time the arts were continually in a ftate of decline.

The monuments that are extant, of the fucceffors of Severus, are ftill a lefs honor to fculpture, than the Low-relieves of the largeft of the two triumphal arches erected to the memory of that prince.

The

The Roman medals, ſtruck after the reign of Cara-calla, and that of Macrinus his ſucceſſor, who ſur-vived him but two years, are much inferior to thoſe that were ſtruck under the preceding emperors. Af-ter Gordianus Pius they degenerated in a mote ſen-ſible manner, and under Gallienus, who reigned fifty years after Caracalla, they became a moſt wretched coin. There is neither taſte nor deſign in their in-graving, nor judgment in their coining. As thoſe medals were a kind of coin deſtined to inſtruct poſte-rity with reſpect to the virtues and great exploits of the prince under whoſe reign they were ſtruck, as well as to ſerve the uſes of traffick, 'tis highly proba-ble, that the Romans, who were as jealous as any other nation of their honor, employed for this kind of work the moſt able artiſts they could find. 'Tis therefore reaſonable to judge by the beauty of the medals, of the ſtate of ingraving under each emperor ; for ingraving is an art which always goes hand in hand with ſculpture. The obſervations made by means of medals, are confirmed by what we remark in thoſe pieces of ſculpture, whoſe time is known, and which are ſtill exiſting. For inſtance, the medals of Conſtantine the Great, who reigned fifty years after Gallienus, are very ill ingraved, and of a poor taſte ; and we find likewiſe, by the triumphal arch erected to the memory of this prince, which is ſtill to be ſeen at Rome, that under his reign, and a hundred years before the Barbarians took poſſeſſion of that city, ſculpture was become as coarſe and imperfect an art, as it was in the commencement of the firſt Punic war.

I

When

When the senate and people of Rome determined to erect this triumphal arch in honor of Conftantine, there was not in all probability in the capital of the empire, a sculptor able to undertake the work. Notwithstanding the respect they had at Rome for the memory of Trajan, they stripped the arch, erected to that prince, of its ornaments; and without any regard to conformity or fitnefs, they employed them in the fabric of that which they erected to Conftantine. The triumphal arches of the Romans were not monuments invented merely by fancy, like ours; neither were their ornaments mere arbitrary imbellishments, directed only by the ideas of the architect. As we have no real triumphs, and after our victories we do not conduct the victor in a chariot preceded by the captives, the modern sculptors are confequently allowed, to make ufe of fuch trophies and arms as their fancy directs, in order to imbellifh their allegorical arches: for which reafon the ornaments of our triumphal arches are moft of them fuitable to any other building of that kind. But as the triumphal arches of the Romans were erected merely to perpetuate the memory of a real triumph, the ornaments taken from the fpoils which had appeared already in a triumph, and were proper for decorating the arch erected on that occafion, were not fit for imbellifhing that which they were to erect in memory of another, efpecially if the victory had been gained over a different people from thofe, whofe overthrow was the occafion of the firft triumph and arch. Every body could diftinguifh there the Dacian, the

L. Parthian,

Parthian, and the German, in the same manner as the French were known from the Spaniards, about a hundred years ago, when those nations wore each of them their peculiar dress. The triumphal arches of the Romans were therefore historical monuments, that required an historical verity, from whence they could not deviate without acting contrary to the rules of decorum.

Nevertheless, Constantine's arch was imbellished with captive Parthians, and trophies composed of their arms and spoils; ornaments all borrowed from Trajan's arch. Trajan had taken these spoils from the Parthians; but Constantine had not as yet been engaged in any quarrel with that nation. In fine, the arch was adorned with Low-relieves, in which all the world might then, and does at present, discover the head of Trajan. Nor can it be said, that it was for the sake of expedition that Trajan's monument was thus sacrificed to Constantine's arch; for as this could not be composed intirely of collected pieces, a sculptor of that time was obliged to make some Low-relieves, in order to fill up the vacant spaces. Such are the Low-relieves which are seen under the principal arch; as also the deities that appear on the outside, placed on the mouldings of the center of the two little arches; and likewise the broken Low-relieves, that are on the key-stones of these arches. All this sculpture, whose parts are distinguished from one another upon approaching the arch, is much inferior to the better kind of Gothic; tho' in all probability the most eminent sculptor of the empire was employed in the execution of it. In fine, when

when Conftantine wanted to imbellifh his new capital, Conftantinople, he knew of no better fcheme than to tranfport thither fome of the fineft monuments of Rome.   And yet as fculpture does not depend fo much on moral caufes as poetry and painting ; and as the phyfical caufes have not the fame empire over it as over the other two arts, it ought confequently to have a flower decline than thofe arts ; nay, even a flower decline than eloquence.   Befides, we find by what Petronius fays of painting, that this art began to degenerate even fo early as the emperor Nero's reign.

To come now to poetry, Lucan was fucceffor to Virgil ; and what a number of fteps do we find already, defcending from the Æneid to the Pharfalia ? Next to Lucan appeared Statius, whofe poetry is reckoned much inferior to that of Lucan.   Statius, who lived under Domitian, left no fucceffor behind him : neither was Horace fucceeded in the lyric kind of writing. Juvenal fupported fatyre under the empire of Adrian, but his poems may be confidered as the laft gafp of the Roman Mufes.   Aufonius and Claudian, who attempted to revive the Latin poetry, produced only a phantom that refembled it ; their verfes having neither the numbers, nor the force of thofe that were written under the reign of Auguftus.   Tacitus, who wrote under Trajan, is the laft Roman hiftorian, having no other fucceffor but the abridger of Trogus Pompeius. Tho' the learned feem to be divided with regard to the time when Quintus Curtius wrote his hiftory of Alexander, and tho' he is fuppofed by fome to be a later writer than Tacitus,

it

it seems to me notwithstanding, to be absolutely decided by a passage of his book, that he wrote about fourscore years before Tacitus. He says [a], in relation to the misfortunes which ensued after the death of Alexander, when the Macedonians chose several chiefs instead of one : That Rome had like to have been lately ruined by a project of restoring the republic. We distinguish in the magnificent recital he makes of this event, all the principal circumstances of the tumult which happened in Rome, when the senate attempted, after the decease of Caligula, to re-establish the republican government, and when their partisans made head against the prætorian cohorts, who insisted upon having an emperor. Quintus Curtius draws so particular a description of all the circumstances of the accession of Claudius to the empire, which calmed the tumult ; he gives such broad hints of Claudius's family, that it is impossible to hesitate with regard to the application of this passage, especially as the narrative cannot be applied to the accession of any of the thirty immediate successors of Claudius. This passage of Quintus Curtius can be understood only with respect to the accession of Claudius or that of Gordianus Pius.

Sixty years after the decease of Augustus, Quintilian wrote on the causes of the decay of the Roman eloquence. Longinus, who wrote under Gallienus, has given us a chapter *on the causes of the degeneracy of spirits,* at the end of his treatise on the Sublime. There was only the art of oratory left at that time ; but the orators themselves had disap-

[a] QUINTUS CURTIUS, l. 10. sect. 9.

peared.

peared. The decadency of arts and sciences was become already a sensible object ; and had made a sufficient impression on those who were capable of reflecting, to oblige them to enquire into the causes of this decay. This observation had been made a long time before the Barbarians had ravaged Italy.

'Tis observable also, that the arts and sciences began to decline under magnificent emperors, who cultivated the arts themselves. Nero, Adrian, Marcus Aurelius, and Alexander Severus knew how to paint : Can it therefore be supposed that the arts were disregarded during their reigns ? In fine, in the four centuries which elapsed from Julius Cæsar's time to the inundation of the Barbarians, there were successively several peaceable reigns, which may be considered as a real and historical golden age. Nerva, Trajan, Adrian, Antoninus Pius, and Marcus Aurelius, who succeeded one another immediately, and whose accession to the empire was as tranquil as that of a son who succeeds his father, were all great and good princes ; and their contiguous reigns compose almost an intire century.

True it is, that several emperors were tyrants ; and that the civil wars, by which a great number of those princes obtained or lost the empire, were very frequent. But the tyrannical humor of Caligula, Nero, Domitian, Commodus, Caracalla, and Maximinus, never discharged itself upon men of letters, and much less upon artists. Lucan, the only man of letters of any note, that was put to death in those times, was condemned for a conspiracy, and not as a poet. Did the death of Lucan discourage those, who were men of genius, from writing verses ?

L 3   Statius,

Statius, Juvenal, Martial, and many others who might have seen him die, were not deterred by his death from writing. The tyrannical spirit of those emperors was levelled principally against the great men of the state. The ambition, which even the cruelleft amongst them had of being upon good terms with the people, and which induced them to ingratiate themselves with the populace, by entertaining them with all forts of feasts and spectacles, engaged them to encourage the advancement of arts and learning.

As for the civil wars, which are fo much talked of in hiftory, the fcenes of the greateft part of them were out of Italy, and finished in two campaigns. They did not difturb forty years out of three hundred, which are computed from the time of Auguftus to that of Gallienus. The civil war of Otho and Vitellius, and that between Vitellius and Vefpafian, which did not laft both together fo long as nine months, could furely be never fo great a prejudice to learning and arts, as the civil war between Pompey and Cæfar, as that alfo of Modena, and the other civil wars which Auguftus waged againft the murderers of Cæfar, and againft Mark Antony. Neverthelefs the civil commotions, in which Julius Cæfar and Auguftus had a fhare, were no obftruction to the progrefs of learning. The death of Domitian was the effect of a plot of his own fervants, and the day after his death Nerva entered upon a peaceable reign. Things went pretty near in the fame manner at the death of Commodus, and at that of Pertinax, the two firft emperors that were killed and depofed after Domitian. Severus difpof-

3

feffed

feffed Didius Julianus without fighting, and the war he waged in the eaft againft Pefcennius Niger, as alfo that which afterwards broke out in Gaul between him and Clodius Albinus, did not interrupt the ftudies of the learned, nor the labors of the Roman artifts, no more than the fudden revolution that happened in Afia, and which difpoffeffed Caracalla to make room for Macrinus, and removed the latter to fubftitute Heliogabalus. 'Tis true, thofe tumultuous revolutions happened fometimes in Rome, but they generally ended in a day or two, without being attended with thofe accidents which are apt to retard the progrefs of arts and fciences.

Nero was depofed at Rome without fighting a blow. The murder of Galba, and Otho's acceffion to the throne, was a morning's work, and the infurrection coft only the lives of a hundred people. The Romans ftood and beheld the engagement between Vefpafian's and Vitellius's troops, with as much unconcernednefs as if they had been gazing at the combats of the gladiators. Maximinus was depofed, and the Gordians of Afric fubftituted in his place, with as much eafe and tranquillity as if fentence had been executed upon a private perfon. When the Gordians died in Afric, Puppianus and Balbinus fucceeded them without any difturbance, and it was but a two day's war which broke out between the people and the prætorian cohorts, when thefe two emperors were affaffinated, and Gordianus Pius fubftituted in their ftead. The other revolutions were very fudden, and we have already obferved that they happened out of Rome. In fine, the civil wars of the Romans, under their firft fifty empe-

L 4

tors, were only particular difputes between the armies contending which fhould have the honor of giving a matter to the empire. During thefe broils, the two parties took as much care of their refpective provinces, as our Chriftian princes take, in thofe wars in which they are but too often engaged, of fuch territories as they expect to conquer and preferve. There happen on thefe occafions a great many diforders, but not fuch as to bury the arts and fciences. 'Tis not every kind of war that obftructs the progrefs of the arts ; no, 'tis only fuch as endangers private people's fortunes, fuch as reduces them from a ftate of liberty to that of fervitude, or deprives them at leaft of their property.

Such were the wars between the Perfians and the Greeks, and fuch thofe between the Barbarians of the North and the Roman empire. Such alfo are the wars between the Turks and Chriftians, in which the whole body of the people run greater rifks, than the foldiers are expofed to in the common courfe of war. Wars of this fort generally fubvert the arts and fciences in thofe countries which they lay wafte ; but regular wars, in which the people are expofed to no other danger but that of changing mafter, and of belonging to one prince rather than to another, are not a neceffary caufe of the deftruction of the arts and fciences, unlefs it be in fome town fo unhappy as to be taken by ftorm. The terror fpread by fuch wars, can only retard their progrefs for a few years ; tho' it does not feem to produce even that effect. The arts and fciences (by what fatality I know not) never flourifh better than in the midft of thefe wars. Greece was expofed to a great

many

many such commotions in the learned age of Philip father of Alexander the Great. It was during the civil wars which tore the Roman empire under Cæsar and Auguftus, that the arts and sciences made such a furprizing progress at Rome. From the year 1494 to 1529, Italy was continually haraffed by armies confifting for the greatest part of foreign foldiers. The Spanifh Netherlands were attacked by France and Holland at the time the school of Antwerp flourifhed : and was it not in war time that the arts and sciences made their greatest progress in France ?

It does not therefore appear, upon mature inquiry, that during the three ages which followed the murder of Cæsar, the Roman empire was expofed to any of thofe frightful wars, which are capable of throwing the arts and sciences into a state of decay. The Barbarians did not commence to have any fixt settlements in the empire, nor the petty tyrants to rife up in particular provinces, till towards the reign of Gallienus. Thofe governors who made themfelves fovereigns, might have occafioned the devaftation of some countries, by the wars they waged with one another in such provinces, as had no fortreffes on their frontiers by reafon of their having been a long time fubject to the fame mafter : Yet thefe devaftations could never be the caufe of that great decay of the arts and sciences. The capital of a state is always the feat of arts in a connected government ; wherefore we may reafonably fuppofe, that the able artifts of the Roman empire were always to be met with at Rome. The devaftations therefore of this city only can be alledged as one of the caufes of the decline of the arts and sciences.

ences. Now Rome was the capital of a great empire, and continued to be imbellished with new edifices, till it was taken by Alaricus, an event which did not happen till four hundred and fifty years after the death of Cæsar. The tumults of the Prætorian Cohorts could be no obstruction to her having great painters, sculptors, orators, and poets, since they were no hindrance to an infinite multitude of indifferent artists. When the arts are cultivated enough to form a great number of indifferent artists, they might form excellent ones, were not the workmen destitute of genius.

Rome is to this very day full of tombs and statues, which by their inscriptions and the women's head-dress, are easily distinguished to have been made from the reign of Trajan to that of Constantine. As the Roman ladies used to change their head-drefs as often as the French ladies do theirs, the make of those head-dresses which are found in the Roman monuments, soon inform us under what emperor they were made; as we know by the medals of the wives and relations of the emperors, at what time a particular fashion prevailed. 'Tis thus one may judge of the time in which the figure of a French lady in a town drefs was made, by the help of a collection of the several modes which have obtained in France within these three hundred years, such as that published by Monfieur de Gaignieres.

Authors of the fourth century take notice, that there were more ftatues at Rome than inhabitants; and the finest ftatues, whose remains we prize so much to this day, were of this number. From Caracalla's la's time thefe ftatues were never able to form any good fculptors : Their efficacy and influence remained fufpended till the time of Pope Julius II.   And yet the people of Rome continued even in Conftantine's time to raife moft magnificent buildings, and confequently to employ great numbers of fculptors. Artifts of all kinds were never more numerous at Rome, than when they were leaft fkilful in their profeffion.   How many fumptuous buildings were erected by Severus, Caracalla, Alexander Severus, and Gordianus Pius ?   One cannot behold the ruins of Caracalla's hot baths, without being aftonifhed at the immenfe bulk of this edifice : even Auguftus himfelf never built one of fo great a fize.   There never was a more fumptuous fabric, more loaded with ornaments and incruftations, or which did a greater honor by its bulk to a fovereign, than the hot baths of Dioclefian, one of Gallienus's fucceffors.   The hall of this edifice is now the Carthufian church at Rome ; and one of the porters lodges makes another church, that of the begging friars of St Bernard at Termini.

Let us add one remark to thefe confiderations. The greateft part of the Roman fculptors made their apprenticefhip in the condition of flaves ; we may therefore fuppofe, that merchants who dealt in flaves, were very careful in examining, whether amongft the children they brought up for fale, there were not fome who had a particular talent for fculpture.   'Tis probable alfo, that when they found them capable of excelling in this art, they were very diligent in giving them a proper education for improving their abilities.   If a flave turned out a good

artift,

attiit, he proved a treasure to his master, whether he had a mind to sell his person or his works. Now the methods which may be employed to oblige a young slave to apply himself to business, are much more effectual than those which are used to engage free-born people. Besides, what a powerful incentive was it for slaves, to be flattered with the hopes of liberty! Those master pieces whose vestiges we so much admire, were still in all public places ; wherefore we can impute to moral causes the ignorance of those artists only, who did not appear till after Rome was taken and plundered by Alaricus.

Whence comes it, that the arts and sciences did not support themselves in Greece in that high degree of credit, to which they had been raised under the father of Alexander, and the successors of this conqueror? Whence comes it, that they continued always to decline, insomuch that the Greek artists were grown as rude and ignorant under Constantine, as they were two hundred years before Philip. Arts and learning fell into a sensible decay in Greece from the time of Perseus king of Macedon, who was defeated and made prisoner by Paulus Æmilius. Painting did not support itself so long, but began to degenerate, as Quintilian observes [a], as early as the first successors of Alexander. Lucian may pass for the only poet that appeared after that time, tho' he wrote in prose. Plutarch, and Dion Cassius, who is nearer to the latter's time than merit, are

[a] *Floruit autem circa Philippum & usque ad successores Alexandri praecipuè pictura.* QUINT. Inst. l. 11. c. 10.

esteemed

esteemed the best authors that wrote since Greece was become a province of the Roman empire. The writings of those two Greeks deserve our respect and veneration, being the works of judicious historians, who have transmitted to us in a very sensible manner, several curious and important facts, which we have only from their relations. Plutarch's books especially are the most precious remains we have of Greek and Roman antiquity, in respect to the details and facts, with which he acquaints us. The same pretty near may be said of Dion and Herodian, who wrote under Alexander Severus and Gordianus Pius; yet these historians are no way to be compared for strength and dignity, or for the art of painting great events, to Herodotus and Thucydides. We have already mentioned the use which may be made of medals, to know the condition the arts were in at the time they were struck. Now the medals which were struck in vast numbers with the emperors heads in those provinces of the Roman empire, in which the Greek language obtained, are very ill ingraved in comparison to such as were made at Rome at the same time by the authority of those senate, whose mark they bore. For example, those of Severus struck at Corfù, which are become now very common by means of the discovery of a treasure in that island about sixty years ago, are vastly inferior to the Latin medals of this same emperor, which were struck at Rome: Nevertheless the Corfù medals are ingraved the very best of any that were struck in Greece. Thus our general rule scarce admits of any exception.

Greece

Greece notwithstanding, from the death of Alexander till its subjection to the Romans, was exposed to none of those calamitous wars, which are capable of throwing the arts and sciences into oblivion. The tumult occasioned by the irruption of the Gauls into Greece about a hundred years after the death of Alexander, was of no long continuance. But were we even to grant, that the arts and sciences suffered by the wars which broke out between the successors of Alexander, and by those which the Romans carried on against two kings of Macedon and the Ætolians ; they ought nevertheless to have reverted again to their former state of perfection, as soon as the tranquillity of Greece was restored and settled by its submission to the Romans. The application and study of artists was no more interrupted after that period, but by the Mithridatic war and the civil wars of the Romans, which gave some little disturbance for four or five years to different provinces. At the very latest, the arts and sciences ought to have raised their heads under the reign of Augustus, who made them flourish at Rome. After the battle of Actium Greece enjoyed for the space of three hundred years, its sereneft days. Under the greatest part of the Roman emperors, the subjection of Greece to the empire was rather a kind of fee-dependance, which secured the public tranquillity, than a servitude burthensome to particulars, and prejudicial to society. The Romans had not a standing army in Greece, as in other provinces ; the most part of the cities were governed by their ancient laws, and generally speaking, of all foreign sovereignties never was there one which was less oppressive to conquered nations, than

that

that of the Romans. Their government had more of the nature of a rudder than of a yoke. Finally, the wars which the Athenians, Thebans, and Lacedemonians waged againſt one another ; thoſe likewiſe of Philip with the reſt of the Greeks, were much more dreadful for their duration and events, than the wars which Alexander, his ſucceſſors, and the Romans carried on in Greece. Yet the former wars did not debar the arts and ſciences from making that ſurprizing progreſs, which reflects to this very day ſo much honor on human underſtanding.

What has been hitherto alledged (ſome will ſay) does not prove that the Greeks had not under the Antoninus's and their ſucceſſors as much genius as Phidias and Praxiteles ; but their artiſts were degenerated, becauſe the Romans had tranſported the maſter-pieces of the moſt eminent artiſts to Rome, and conſequently had ſtript Greece of ſuch objects as were moſt proper to form the taſte and excite the emulation of young workmen. It was during the ſecond Punic war that Marcellus [a] removed to Rome the ſpoils of the porticos of Siracuſe, from whence the Roman citizens imbibed a reliſh for the arts, which ſoon became the general taſte of Rome, and was afterwards the cauſe of ſo many depredations. Even thoſe who were ignorant of the value and merit of ſtatues, vaſes, and other curioſities, ſeized notwithſtanding on every occaſion of carrying them to Rome, where they ſaw them ſo highly valued. 'Tis plain that Mummius, who intended to inrich Rome with the ſpoils of Corinth, underſtood nothing at all of their value, by the ridiculous

[a] Livius hiſt. l. 25

menace

menace he made to the masters of the veffels, who were charged with this magnificent freight [a]. Never could there have been a lofs more difficult to repair than that of this precious depofitum, confifting of fo many mafter-pieces of thofe illuftrious artifts, who contribute as much as the greateft generals to tranfmit the glory of their age to pofterity. Neverthelefs, Mummius recommending this treafure to their care, threatened them very ferioufly, that if they fhould chance to lofe the ftatues, pictures, and other things with which he intrufted them, he would be fure to have others of equal value made at their expence. But the Romans (to go on with the objection) foon emerged from this ignorance, and even the common foldier learnt to avoid breaking the precious vafes, when plundering the enemies towns. Sylla's army brought the Greek tafte for the polite arts from Afia to Rome, or to fpeak more correctly, they rendered it common in that city. *Then it was,* fays Salluft [b], *that the Roman foldiers firft learnt to wench, to drink, to admire ftatues, pictures, and emboffed veffels; then to get at them by ftealth or open violence, and to rob the temples of the Gods; polluting every thing they could lay holdfo either facred or profane.*

As early as the time of the republic there had been more Verres's than one, and more than one Roman who had exercifed a right of conqueft over

[a] VELL. PATERC. l. 2.

[b] *Ibi primùm infuevit exercitus populi Romani amare, potare, fignaque, tabulas pictas, vafa cælata mirari, ea privatim ac publicè rapere, delubra fpoliare, facra profanaque omnia polluere.* SALLUST. de Bell. CATILIN.

the

the subjected provinces. What a melancholy description of these excesses do we meet with in Cicero's fourth oration against this plunderer! This licentiousness, far from ending with the republican government, became a most lawless and unbridled rapaciousness under several emperors. The impudence with which Caligula plundered the provinces, is most notorious. Nero sent Carinas and Acratus, two *connoisseurs*, into Greece and Asia, to pick up all the fine pieces of sculpture that were remaining in those countries, in order to imbellish his new buildings. The poor Greeks, as Juvenal observes, were stript even of their houshold Gods : They did not so much as leave them the least diminutive God that was worth removing.

Ipsi deinde lares, si quod spectabile signum,
Si quis in edicula, Deus unicus. Juv. sat. 8.

Their·rapine is so abject and prophane,
They not from trifles, nor from Gods refrain ;
But the poor Lares *from the niches seize,*
If they be little images that please. STEPNEY.

All these facts are true, yet there was still such a great number of fine pieces of sculpture remaining in Greece and Asia, that it was impossible for the artists to be in want of models : There were objects enough left that were capable of exciting their emulation. The excellent statues which have been found in Greece within these two or three centuries, are a sufficient proof that the Roman emperors and their officers. had not stript the country. The Ganymedes which is to be seen in the library of St Mark at Venice, was found

in Greece about three hundred years ago.   The An-
dromeda belonging to the duke of Modena, was
discovered at Athens, when this town was plundered by the Venetians during the war, that was terminated by the peace of Carlowitz.   The relations of
travellers abound with descriptions of statues and
Low-relieves, which are still to be seen in Greece
and Asia Minor.   Did the Romans take away the
Low-relieves from the temple of Minerva at Athens?
But to come to letters, did they strip the Greeks of
all the copies of Homer, Sophocles, and other
writers of the best note? No; but these happy days
were past.   The industry of the Greeks was degenerated into a kind of artifice, and their penetration
and sagacity into a low spirit of cunning.   Thus they
were grown very coarse and ignorant, except in the
art of prejudicing one another.   During the last six
centuries of the empire of Constantinople, they were
less dextrous and knowing, especially in the arts,
than they had been in the time of Amyntas king of
Macedon.   'Tis true, that the happy age of Greece
lasted longer than the Augustan age, or that of
Leo X.   Learning maintained itself there after the
decay of the polite arts, because, generally speaking,
the Greeks in all ages have been superior in wit and
capacity to other nations.   One would imagine, that
nature has received a particular vigor and strength
in Greece, which she has not in other countries; so
as to communicate more substance to nourishments,
and more malignity to poison.   The Greeks, in fact,
have carried their vices and virtues to a much higher
point than any other nation.

The

The city of Antwerp was for a certain time the Athens of the countries on this fide the Alps. And yet when Rubens began to taife the credit of his fchool, the moral caufes did not feem then to exert themfelves in favor of his art. If the flourifh-ing ftate of cities and kingdoms were the fole caufe of the perfection of the polite arts, painting fhould have been fixty years fooner in its higheft fplendor. When Rubens firft appeared, Antwerp had loft one half of its grandeur, fince the new republic of Holland had ingroffed the greateft part of its commerce. The adjacent country was actually the feat of war, and a neighbouring enemy was every day making fome new attempts againft that city, by which the eftates of the merchants, clergy, and all the principal inhabitants, were continually expofed to the moft imminent dangers. Rubens left eleves fuch as Jordans and Vandyke, who were indeed a credit to their mafter, but left no difciples behind them to inherit their reputation. The fchool of Rubens has had the fame fate as other fchools, I mean that it dropt when every thing feemed to concur to fupport it. It feems as if Quellins, who may be looked upon as her laft painter, were likely to dye without leaving any eleves worthy of his name. We have heard of none as yet, and there is no likelihood he will acquire any pupils in his prefent retirement.

From what has been hitherto alledged, 'tis evident that the arts and fciences attain to the higheft point of their fplendor, by a fudden progrefs which cannot be attributed to moral caufes ; and 'tis alfo

plain

plain that they decline, when thefe fame moral caufes exert themfelves as much as poffible to fupport
them.

Third REFLECTION.

*That eminent painters have been always cotemporaries
with the great poets of their own country.*

IN fine the eminent artifts of every country have
been generally cotemporaries. The great painters of the feveral fchools have not only lived at
the fame time, but have been likewife cotemporaries with the moft famous poets of their own country. The ages in which the arts flourifhed, have been
alfo fertile of men eminent in all fciences, virtues,
and profeffions. There feems to be a peculiar time,
in which a certain fpirit of perfection fheds itfelf on
the inhabitants of a particular country. This fame
fpirit feems to withdraw itfelf after having rendered
two or three generations perfecter than the preceding
or following ones.

When Greece produced an Apelles, her fecundity
gave us at the fame time a Praxiteles and a Lyfippus.
Then it was, that her greateft poets, her moft eminent orators and philofophers flourifhed. Socrates,
Plato, Ariftotle, Demofthenes, Ifocrates, Thucydides, Xenophon, Æfchylus, Euripides, Sophocles,
Ariftophanes, Menander, and feveral others, lived
all in the fame age. What eminent men appeared
among the Greek generals of that time! What famous exploits did not they perform with fmall armies! What great princes were not Philip king of
Macedon

Macedon and his fon! Were we to collect all the illuftrious men that Greece has produced from the time of Perfeus king of Macedon down to the taking of Conftantinople by the Turks, we fhall not find in thofe feventeen centuries fuch a fwarm of men eminent in all profeffions, as appeared in the age of Plato. All other profeffions degenerated in Greece together with the polite arts. Livy calls Philopomenus, one of the prætors of the Achaians during the reign of Perfeus king of Macedon, the laft of the Greeks.

The Auguftan age had the fame fate as that of Plato. Among the monuments of Roman fculpture we meet with nothing more exquifite than thofe pieces which were made in the reign of Auguftus. Such as the buft of Agrippa his fon-in-law, which is to be feen in the gallery of the great duke of Tufcany; the Cicero of the Villa Matthei; as alfo the chapiters of the columns of Julius Cæfar's temple, which are yet ftanding in the middle of the *Campo Vaccino*, and which all the fculptors of Europe have agreed to take for models, when they treat of the Corinthian order. It was under Auguftus that the Roman medals began to grow fine; and ingraving is an art which generally follows the fate of fculpture. We diftinguifh the times in which a great many ingraved ftones were done, by the fubjects and heads which they reprefent. The fineft Roman ftones are fuch as we know were ingraved in Auguftus's time. Such is the Cicero on an agate which belonged to Charles II king of England, and the ftone in the king's cabinet reprefenting Auguftus and Livia. Such is the ftone which was given to the late king by M. Felch

M 3   of

of Bafil, where we fee an Apollo on a rock playing on his lyre. This is the attitude which characterifes the *Apollo Actiacus* in the medals of Auguftus, under whom this new divinity firft appeared, after he had gained the battle of Actium. We have likewife another reafon to believe that thefe medals were ingraved in Auguftus's reign : 'Tis the name of the ingravers which we read where the name of the artifts are fometimes ingraved in this kind of work. Now Pliny [a] and others inform us, that thofe excellent ingravers in ftone, lived under this emperor. We may alfo mention here the agate in *relievo*, which is to be feen in the emperor's cabinet at Vienna, and reprefents Auguftus and Livia; as likewife that whofe defign we have had from father Montfaucon in his travels thro' Italy [b], which reprefents Mark Antony and Cleopatra. In fine, the moft valuable of all the antique ftones, the agate of the holy chapel at Paris, whofe explication has employed the erudition of five of the moft illuftrious antiquarians, was ingraved under Auguftus or his two immediate fucceffors. This is a point that Peirefc, Triftan, Albert Rubens, M. le Roi, and father Hardouin are agreed upon.

We may affirm the fame of the Roman architecture, as has been now faid of fculpture. The theatre of Marcellus, the portico and inward decorations of the Rotonda, the temple of Julius Cæfar in the *Campo Vaccino*, that of Jupiter Anxur at Terracina, (which we know to be the work of the architect Pollio [c] by an infcription ingraved on one of

---

[a] PLIN. hift. l. 37.   [b] Pag. 242.

[c] Probably this was Vitruvius, whofe name was *Vitruvius Pollio*, and who lived under Auguftus.

the

the marble pieces of the great wall ;) and the temple of Caftor and Pollux, built at Naples at the expence of a freed-man of Auguftus, are efteemed the nobleft monuments of the Roman magnificence and the moft valuable for their architecture.

Every body knows, that the greateft Roman poets, or to fpeak more juftly, all the great Latin poets, except two or three, flourifhed in the age of Auguftus. This prince faw, or at leaft might have feen, Virgil, Horace, Propertius, Catullus, Tibullus, Ovid, Phæ-drus, Cornelius Gallus, and feveral others whofe works have perifhed, tho' they were admired as much in their days, as we admire thofe that are extant. He might have feen Lucretius, who died in the year of Rome 699, the very day that Virgil put on the *toga virilis*, or manly gown, as Donatus obferves in the life of Virgil. Mr. Creech, [a] the laft and beft commentator of Lucretius, is miftaken in the life he has given us of this author, by making him dye the fame day that Virgil was born. Hear what Horace fays of the merit of Fundanius, Pollio, and Varius, three other cotemporaries of Auguftus.

Arguta meretrice potes, Davoque Chremeta
Eludente fenem, comeis garrire libellos,
Unus vivorum, Fundani. Pollio regum
Fa&a canit, pede ter percuffo : forte epos acer,
Ut nemo, Varius ducit : molle atque facetum
Virgilio annuerunt gaudentes rure Camænæ.

Hor. ferm. l. 1. fat. 10.

[a] His book was printed at Oxford in 1695.

M 4

True comedy Fundanius only writes,
Pollio the acts of kings, and noble fights :
Strong epic poems Varius best can raise,
And Virgil's happy muse in eclogues plays,
Natural, and soft, and justly wins the bays. ⸱

$$\left.\begin{array}{c} \\ \\ \\ \\ \end{array}\right\}$$

C R E E C H.

'Tis a vast prejudice in favor of these poets, that
so judicious a writer as Horace, ranks them in the
same class with Virgil.

The greatest part of the above-mentioned poets
might have seen Cicero, Hortensius, and the rest of
the most celebrated Roman orators. They must
have seen Julius Cæsar as remarkable, when a citizen,
for his eloquence and several other civil virtues, as
famous, when a general, for his exploits and knowledge in the art of war. Livy the prince of the
Roman historians, Sallust an historian whom Paterculus and Quintilian [a] dare compare to Thucydides,
flourished under Augustus. They were likewise cotemporaries with Vitruvius the most illustrious of the
Roman architects. Augustus was born before the
death of Æsopus and Roscius the most eminent comedians mentioned in the Roman history. What
surprizing men were Cato Uticensis, Brutus, and
the most part of the murderers of Cæsar! What a
great man must Agrippa have been, who made so
prodigious a fortune under a prince so good a judge
of merit as Augustus? As Seneca the father observes, [b] *the most eminent orators that the Roman elo-*

[a] VELL PAT. l. 2. QUINT. Inst. l. 10 cap. 1.

[b] *Quidquid Romana facundia habet, quod insolenti Græciæ aut*
opponat aut præferat circa Ciceronem effloruit. Omnia ingenia
quæ lucem studiis nostris attulerunt tunc nata sunt. In deterius de-
inde quotidie data res est. M. ANN. SENEC. Controv. l. 1.

quence

quence had to compare or prefer to proud Greece, flou-
rifhed about Cicero's time. Then it was that thofe great
wits appeared, who illuftrated the feveral branches
of the Roman learning, which from that period has
been continually on the decline.

The pontificates of Julius II, Leo X, and Clement
VII, fo extremely fertile of great painters, produced
alfo the beft architects and the greateft fculptors that
Italy can boaft of. At the fame time there appeared
excellent ingravers in all thofe branches which this art
includes. The rifing art of prints was improved in
their hands, upon its firft appearance, as much as
painting was perfected in the pictures of Raphael.
Every one is acquainted with the fame and merit of
Ariofto and Taffo, who lived at leaft in the fame age.

Fracaftorius, Sannazarius, and Vida, compofed the
beft Latin verfes at that time, that had been wrote
fince the recovery of letters. What great men, each
of them in their kind, were Leo X, Paul III, the
cardinals Bembo and Sadoletus, Andrew Doria, the
marquifs of Pefcara, Philip Strozzi, Cofmus of Medicis ftiled the Great, Machiavel, and Guicciardin the
hiftorian? But in proportion as the arts have continued to decline, the places and profeffions of thofe
great men have ceafed to be filled with perfons of
their merit.

The moft eminent French fculptors, Sarazin, les
Anguiers, Hongre, les Marcy, Gyrardon, Dezjar-
dins, Coizevox, Le Gros, Theodon, Puget, and feveral others who are ftill living, flourifhed under the
reign of the late king, as alfo Pouffin, Le Sueur, Le
Brun, Coypel, Jouvenet, Les Bolognes, Foreft, Ri-
gault, and others who reflect fo great an honor on

our

our nation. Was it not under his reign that the Manfards diftinguifhed themfelves by their works? Then it was, that Vermeule, Mellan, Edelink, Simonneau, Nanteuil, les Poilly, Maffon, Piteau, Van-Schupen, Mademoifelle Stella, Gerard Audran, Le Clerc, Picard, and fo many other ingravers, fome of whom are ftill living, excelled in all forts of ingraving. We have had feveral goldfmiths and ingravers of medals at that time, fuch as Varin, who deferve that their reputation fhould be as durable as that of Diofcorides and Alcimedon. Sarrazin, the Corneilles, Moliere, Racine, La Fontaine, Boileau, Quinault, and Chapelle, were all fuccefflively the cotemporaries of thefe worthies. They lived at the fame time with *Le Notre*, a perfon famous for having perfected, and even created in fome meafure the art of gardening, which obtains at prefent in the greateft part of Europe. Lulli, who came into France fo very young, that he may be confidered as a Frenchman, tho' he was born in Italy, excelled to fuch a degree in mufic, that moft countries have been jealous of his reputation. In his days there were feveral very eminent in the art of playing on all kinds of inftruments.

All the various branches of eloquence and learning were cultivated under the reign of the late king by perfons, who may be cited as models to fuch as in future times will apply themfelves to the fame kinds of ftudy. Petau, Sirmond, Du Cange, Launoi, Monfieur de Valois, Du Chefne, Herbelot, Vaillant, Rapin, Commire, Mabillon, D'Acheri, Thomaffin, Arnaud, Pafcal, Nicole, Boffu, Monfieur Le Maitre, Rochefoucault,

Cardinal

Cardinal Retz, Bochard, Saumaife, Malbranche, Monfieur Claude, Defcartes, Gaffendi, Rohault, Abbot Regnier, Patru, Huetius, Monfieur de la Bruyere, Flechier, Fenelon, Boffuet, Bourdaloue, Mafcaron, Defmares, Vaugelas, Ablancourt, Abbot St Real, Peliffon, Monfieur Regis, Perrault, and fo many others, have lived in an age which produced fo many mafter-pieces in poetry, painting, and fculpture, as will perpetuate the glory of this age to pofterity.

In thofe two generations which furnifhed France with the illuftrious lift of the learned above-mentioned, we find a vaft number of men eminent in all kinds of profeffions. How many excellent magiftrates has this age, fo fertile in geniufes, produced? The name of the great Condè and that of marfhal Turennè, will be an appellation ufed for characterifing a great general, as long as the French nation fubfifts. What a great man would marfhal Guebriant have been, had not an untimely death fnatched him away in the vigor of his age? All the talents requifite in the military art have been difplayed by perfons of moft fingular merit. Marfhal Vauban is confidered not only by our French officers, but by all the military gentlemen of Europe, as the greateft of engineers. What reputation have not fome of the late king's minifters at this very time in Europe? Let us wifh for fucceffors to thofe worthies who are deceafed without having been yet replaced ; and that the Raphaels, who are yet living, in whatfoever kind of profeffion, may leave us their Julio Romano's to confole us for their lofs.

Velleius

Velleius Paterculus, who wrote his hiſtory towards the fifteenth year of the reign of Tiberius, examining into the fate of the illuſtrious ages that had preceded him, makes the ſame reflections as I have now made on thoſe very ages, and the other illuſtrious times which have ſucceeded that hiſtorian. Hear how he explains himſelf at the end of his laſt book [a]. *I cannot help committing to writing the ideas which riſe in my mind, without being capable to throw them into the form of a clear and continued ſyſtem. Is it not a ſurprizing thing to obſerve, when we reflect on the events of paſt ages, that the perſonages eminent in all kinds of profeſſions have been always cotemporaries, that they have flouriſhed always in the ſame period which has been of a very ſhort continuance. In a few years Æſchylus, Sophocles, and Euripides carried tragedy to its higheſt pitch of perfection? Ariſtophanes, Eupolis, and Cratinus, eſtabliſhed in a very ſhort ſpace of time, the ſpectacle which we call the ancient comedy. Menander, with Philemon and Diphilus his cotemporaries, if not his equals, perfected in a few years, what goes under the*

'   *name*

[a] *Cum hæc particula operis velut formam propoſiti exceſſit, quanquam intelligo, mihi in hac tam præcipiti feſtinatione, quæ me rotæ pronæve gurgitis ac verticis modo nuſquam patitur conſiſtere, pænè magis neceſſaria prætereunda, quam ſupervacua amplectenda : nequeo tamen temperare mihi, quin rem ſæpe agitatam animo meo, neque ad liquidum ratione perductam, ſignem ſtilo. Quis enim abundè mirari poteſt, eminentiſſima cujuſque profeſſionis ingenia, in eandem formam, & in idem artati temporis congruens ſpatium ; & quemadmodum clauſa capſa, alioque ſepto diverſi generis animalia, nihilo minus ſeporata alienis, in unum quæque corpus congregantur, ita cujuſque clari operis capacia ingenia in ſimilitudinem & temporum & profectuum*

name of the new comedy. They were inventers of a new kind of poetry, and left pieces behind them that were inimitable. The illustrious philosophers of the school of Socrates expired with his disciples Plato and Aristotle. 'Tis observable also that they lived at the same time as the great poets above-mentioned. Have there been any great orators since Isocrates? Have there been any heard of since his disciples, or at least since the eleves of his disciples? The age which produced those great men was so short, that they might all have been acquainted with one another.

The same thing which happened in Greece, is come to pass at Rome. If you ascend higher than Accius and his cotemporaries, you will meet with nothing but rusticity and coarseness in the Latin tragedy. The predecessors of this author can be commended only for one thing; which is, their having first broke the ice. The true wit and pleasantry of the comic stage appears only

in

tuum semetipsa ab aliis separaverunt? Una, neque multorum anno-rum spatio divisa, ætas, per divini spiritus viros, Æschylum, So-phoclem, Euripidem, illustravit tragædios: Una priscam illam & veterem sub Cratino, Aristophane, & Eupolide Comœdiam; ac no-vam comicam Menandro, æqualesque ejus ætatis magis quam operis, Philemon ac Diphilus, & invenere intra paucissimos annos, neque imitanda reliquere Philosophorum quoque ingenia, Socratico ore defluentia, omnium, quos paullo ante enumeravimus, quarto post Pla-tonis Aristotelisque mortem floruere spatio? Quid ante Isocratem, quid post ejus auditores, eorumque discipulos, clorum in oratoribus fuit? Adeo quidem artatum angustiis temporum, ut nemo memoria dignus, alter ab altero videri nequiverint. Neque hoc in Græcis quam in Romanis evenit magis. Nam nisi aspera ac rudia repetas, & inventi laudanda nomine, in Accio utcaque cum Romana tragædia est; dulcesque Latini leporis facetiæ per Cæcilium, Terentiumque, & Afranium sub pari ætate viruerunt. Historicos (ut & Livium

quoque

in the pieces of Afranius, Cæcilius, and Terence, three cotemporary writers. We find in the space of fourscore years, all the Roman historians of note, and even T. Livy. Among the historians of the preceding ages we meet only with such authors as Cato, that is, obscure and coarse annalists. The time so fertile of good poets has not lasted much longer than that which has abounded in good historians. The art of oratory and the Roman eloquence, and in short the perfection of the Latin prose, is visible in Cicero only and his cotemporaries. Amongst the orators that have succeeded him, we find very few that have left us any performances that are capable of pleasing ; and not one of them has wrote any thing that deserves our admiration. At the most we might make some exception in favor of Cato. But you will excuse me, you Publius Crassus, Publius Scipio, Lælius, Fannius, Sergius Galba, and both you Gracchi, if I cannot except you from the general law. Those

quoque priorum ætati adstruas) præter Catonem, & quosdam veteres & obscuros minus LXXX. annis circumdatum ævum tulit ; ut nec poetarum in antiquius citeriusque processit ubertas.   At oratio, ac vis forensis, perfectumque prosæ eloquentiæ decus, ut idem separetur Cato (pace P. Crassi Scipionisque & Lælii & Gracchorum, & Fannii & Ser. Galbæ dixerim) ita universa sub principe operis sui erupit Tullio, ut delectari ante eum paucissimis, mirari vero neminem possis, nisi aut ab illo visum, aut qui illum viderit.   Hoc idem evenisse grammaticis, plastis, pictoribus, sculptoribus, quisquis temporum institerit notis, reperiet ; & eminentia cujusque operis artissimis temporum claustris circumdata.   Hujus ergo præcedentisque seculi ingeniorum similitudines congregantis & in studium par, & in emolumentum, causas cum semper requiro, nunquam reperio, quas esse veras confidam, sed fortasse veri similes ; inter quas has maxime.   Alit æmulatio ingenia ; & nunc invidia, nunc admiratio incitationem accendit : naturaque, quod summo studio petitum est, adscendit in summum :
                                          diffici-

Those who will reflect seriously on the times, in which the famous grammarians, painters, statuaries, and sculptors have lived, will find that they were cotemporaries with the most eminent poets, historians, and orators of their country, and that the appellation of illustrious has been always confined to a small number of years. When I happen therefore to compare our age to the preceding ones, and to reflect how vainly we attempt to imitate our predecessors who were only men like ourselves, I cannot account for the sensible difference we observe between their productions and ours, by reasons that afford me any satisfaction.

Paterculus's sentiment carries so much the more weight with it here, as his cotemporaries had in their hands, when he wrote, a vast number of works which have since perished. As the greatest part of them therefore are no longer extant, we cannot decide this dispute at present so well as it

difficilisque in perfecto mora est ; naturaliterque, quod procedere non potest, recedit. Et, ut primo ad consequendos, quos priores ducimus, accendimur, ita ubi aut praeterire aut aequare eos posse desperavimus, studium cum spe senescit ; & quod adsequi non potest, sequi definit, & velut occupatam relinquens materiam, quaerit novam : praeteritoque eo, in quo eminere non possimus, aliquid in quo nitamur conquirimus : sequiturque, ut frequens ac nobilis transitus maximum perfecti operis impedimentum sit. Transit admiratio ad conditionem temporum, & urbium. Una urbs Attica pluribus annis eloquentia, quam universa Graecia, uberiusque floruit ; adeo ut corpora gentis illius separata sint in alias civitates, ingenia verò solis Athemensium muris clausa existimes. Neque Ego hoc magis miratus sim, quam neminem Argivuum, Thebanum, Lacedaemonium oratorem, aut dum vixit auctoritate, aut post mortem memoria dignum existimatum. Quae urbes, & multae aliae, talium studiorum fuere steriles, ni Thebas unum os Pindari illuminaret ; nam Alcmana Lacones falsò sibi vindicant. VELLEIUS PATERCULUS, lib. 1. hist. in fine.

I   could

could have been determined at that time. Besides, the experience of what has paſſed ſince Paterculus; adds a new ſtrength to his reflections : We have ſhewn, that the fate of the age of Leo X has been the ſame as that of the ages of Plato and Auguſtus.

CHAP. XIV.

How it is poſſible for phyſical cauſes to influence the fate of illuſtrious ages. Of the power of air over human bodies.

IN order to give an explication of the propoſitions above advanced, and proved by undoubted facts, may we not venture to affirm that there are countries, in which men are not born with the diſpoſitions requiſite for excelling in certain profeſſions, as there are ſoils where particular plants cannot grow ? May we not afterwards maintain, that as the grains which are ſown, and the trees that are come to their full growth, do not bear fruit every year of an equal perfection even in the moſt fertile and propereſt ſoil, ſo children educated in the happieſt climates, do not in all ages turn out men of like abilities ? Cannot ſome years prove more favorable than others to the phyſical education of children, as there are ſome more favorable than others to the vegetation of trees and plants ? In effect, the human machine is not much leſs dependent on the qualities of the air, on the changes to which theſe qualities are liable, and, in ſhort, on all the varia-

I   tions

tions which may obftruct or favor what we call the operations of nature, than the very fruits themfelves.

As two grains from the fame plant, produce a fruit of a different quality when they are fown in different foils, or even when they are fown in the fame foil but in different years; fo two children born with their brains formed exactly in the fame manner, will differ, when they grow up to the ftate of manhood, in fenfe and inclinations, if one of them be bred in Sweden, and the other in Andalufia. They will even differ in thefe refpects, though brought up in the fame country, if the feafons of their earlieft ftage of life differ confiderably in temperature.

During the life of man, and as long as the foul continues united to the body, the character of our minds and inclinations depends very much on the quality of our blood, which nourifhes our organs, and furnifhes them with matter of accretion during infancy and youth. Now the quality of our blood depends vaftly on the air we breathe; as alfo on the air in which we have been bred, by reafon of its having decided the quality of our blood during our infancy. The fame air contributes in our younger days to the conformation of our organs, which by a necef-fary concatenation, contributes afterwards in the ftate of manhood to the quality of our blood. Hence it comes, that people who dwell in different climates, differ fo much in fpirit and inclinations.

But the very quality of the air depends on that of the emanations of the earth; and according to the compofition of the earth, the air that inclofes it, is different. Now the emanations of the earth, which is a mixt body fubject to continual fermentations, can never be exactly of the fame nature in a particular country : And yet thefe emanations cannot vary without changing the tempe-rature of the air, and making fome alteration in its qua-lity. There muft be therefore, in confequence of this vicifiitude, fome changes now and then in the fpirit and humor of the people of a particular country, fince there muft be ages more favorable than others to the phyfical education of children. Wherefore fome generations will be more fenfible and livelier in France than others ; and this from a caufe of the fame nature as that which renders men more fenfible and acute in fome countries than others. This difference between two generations of the inhabitants of the fame country, will happen thro' the influence of that very caufe, from whence the different temperature of years, and the inequality of fruits of different harvefts, are known to pro-ceed.

Let us difcufs the reafons that may be alledged in fupport of this paradox, after defiring the reader to make a great difference between the facls above related, and the elucidations I fhall attempt to give of thofe facts. In cafe my phyfical explications happen not to prove folid, my error in this point will not hinder the facts from being true, or from proving that the moral caufes alone do not determine the fate of the arts and fciences. The effect will not be lefs certain, for my having given a wrong explication of the caufe.

The air we breathe, communicates to the blood in our lungs the qualities with which it is impregnated.

nated. It depofites alfo on the furface of the earth the matter which contributes moft to its fecundity, and the care generally taken to dig and manure it, proceeds from the experience people have, that the earth is much more fertile, when a great number of its particles have imbibed this aerial matter. Men eat one part of the fruits of the earth, and abandon the other to beafts, whofe flefh they afterwards convert into their own fub-ftance. The quality of the air is communicated alfo to the waters of fountains and rivers by means of fnows and rains, which are impregnated with a part of the corpufcles fufpended in the air.

Now the air, which certainly has a great power over our machine, is a mixt body compofed of ele-mentary air and of the emanations which efcape from the bodies it pervades, or which its continual action may chance to fet loofe. Naturalifts prove alfo that the air is likewife filled with an infinite number of fmail animals and their feeds. This is fufficient to make us eafily conceive, that it is fub-ject to an infinite number of alterations refulting from the mixture of corpufcles in its compofition, which corpufcles can neither be always the fame, nor always in the fame quantity. Hence 'tis alfo eafy to apprehend, that among the different alterati-ons to which the air is fucceffively expofed, fome muft laft longer than others, and fome muft favor more than others the productions of nature.

The air is alfo expofed to feveral viciffitudes pro-ceeding from external caufes, fuch as the action of the fun diverfified by its elevation, proximity, and expofition, and alfo by the nature of the foil, on

which

which its beams are reflected. The same may be said of the action of the wind, which blows from adjacent countries. These causes, which I call external, render the air subject to vicissitudes of cold and heat, drought and humidity. Sometimes the alterations of the air produce these vicissitudes, as it happens also that these vicissitudes are the cause of some alterations. But this discussion does not essentially belong to my subject, which we cannot disintangle too much from such things as are not absolutely necessary for clearing it up.

Nothing is more proper for conveying a just idea of the influence which the qualities peculiar to the air of a certain country by virtue of its composition, and which we may call permanent qualities, have over men and especially children, than to recall to mind the knowledge we have of the power which the simple vicissitudes, or transient alterations of the air have even over those, whose organs have acquired their full consistence. The quality of the air resulting from its composition, is much more durable than these vicissitudes.

Nevertheless the humor, and even the spirit and inclinations of adult people, depend very much on the vicissitudes of the air. According as this is dry or moist, according as it is hot, cold, or temperate, we are mechanically merry or sad, and pleased or vexed without any particular motive · In fine, we experience a facility or difficulty of turning and applying our minds to what objects we please. If these vicissitudes proceed so far, as to cause an alteration in the air, their effect must be still more sensible. The fermentation which prepares a storm, operates
rates

rates not only on our minds, infomuch as to render us heavy, and debar us from thinking with our wonted, liberty of imagination ; but moreover it corrupts even our provifions. It is fufficient to alter the ftate of a diftemper or a wound for the worfe ; and is frequently mortal to fuch as have been cut for the ftone.

The poet Vida had frequently experienced thofe critical moments, in which the work of the imagination grows difagreable ; and he attributes it to the action of the air on our machine. In fact, our minds may be faid to indicate the prefent ftate of the air with an exactnefs almoft equal to that of Barometers and Thermometers.

Nam variant fpecies animorum, & pectora noftra
Nunc hos, nunc illos, multo difcrimine, motus
Concipiunt : feu quòd cæli mutatur in horas
Tempeftas, hominumque fimul quoque pectora mutant.
VIDA poet. l. 2.

For ev'n the foul not always holds the fame,
But knows at diff'rent times a diff'rent frame.
Whether with rolling feafons fhe complies,
Turns with the fun, or changes with the fkies.
PITT.

We obferve even in animals the different effects of the action of the air. According as it is ferene or troubled, brifk or heavy, it infpires beafts with vivacity, or throws them into a heavinefs which a very fmall attention can render perceptible.

Vertuntur fpecies animorum, & pectora motus
Nunc alios, alios dum nubila ventus agebat,

N 3
Concipiunt :

Concipiunt : hinc ille avium concentus in agris,
Hinc lætæ pecudes, & ovantes gutture corvi.

VIRG. Georg. l. 1.

But with the changeful temper of the skies,
As rains condense, and sun-shine rarefies ;
So turn the species in their alter'd minds,
Compos'd by calms, and discompos'd by winds.
From hence proceeds the birds harmonious voice :
From hence the cows exult, and frisking lambs re-
joice.

DRYDEN.

The fame may be obferved of temperaments, which are inflamed by excefs of heat, almoft to a degree of madnefs. If there are twenty wicked actions committed at Rome in the fpace of a year, fifteen of them are perpetrated in the two months of the violent heats. There is a country in Europe where people that make away with themfelves, are not fo fcarce as in other parts. It has been obferved in the capital of that kingdom, where they keep bills of mortality, that out of fixty fuicides in one year, fifty of them happen towards the beginning or end of winter. There prevails in that country a north-eaft wind, which offufcates the fky, and makes a very fenfible impreffion even on the moft robuft. The magiftrates of the criminal courts in France make another remark pretty near to the fame purpofe. They obferve, that there are fome years which are more fertile of great crimes than others ; tho' the malignities of thofe years cannot be attributed to an extraordinary fcarcity of provifions, to a difbanding of troops, or to any other fenfible caufes.

Excefs

Excefs of cold congeals the imagination of fome ; and abfolutely changes the temper and humor of others. From fweet and good humored in other feafons, they become almoft favage and infupportable in violent frofts. I fhall produce here only one inftance of Henry III king of France. My author M. De Thou, a perfon of great dignity, whofe narrative I fhall tranflate, has given us the hiftory of a prince that died but a few years before he wrote, and with whom he had an intimate familiarity.

As foon as Henry III began to live regularly, he was very feldom out of order. He ufed only during the violent frofts to have a kind of melancholy fit, which was vifible to his domeftics, who then found him peevifh and difficult, whereas at other times he was an indulgent and good humored mafter. He was obferved therefore to have no relifh for his pleafures in very cold weather, but ufed to fleep little, and rifing earlier than ufual, he applied himfelf affiduoufly to bufinefs, determining affairs like a man governed by a rigid peevifh temper. It was in thefe fits, that this prince tired his chancellor and his four fecretaries of ftate with exceffive writing. The chancellor De Chiverni, who ferved him from his infancy, had been fenfible for a long time of the alteration caufed by cold weather in his temperament. I remember a particular piece of confidence which that magiftrate fhewed me concerning this fubjeɛ, when I happened to pafs by Efclimont, a feat of his in the country of Chartrain, in my way to Blois, where the court refided at that time. The chancellor foretold me in converfation, a few days before the Guifes were

N 4   *killed,*

killed, that if the duke continued to vex the king as he did in such weather, that prince would have him certainly dispatched between four walls without any form of trial. The king's spirit, continued he, is easily provoked, even to a degree of fury, during such a frost as we feel at present. In fact, the duke of Guise was killed at Blois the day before Christmas eve, a few days after the conversation between the chancellor de Chiverni and the president de Thou.

As the qualities of the air which we have distinguished by the name of permanent, have a greater power over us than its vicissitudes, the changes which happen in our machine, when these qualities are altered, must consequently be more sensible and durable, than those caused by the vicissitudes. Wherefore these alterations are sometimes productive of epidemic disorders which carry off in three months six thousand persons in a town, where hardly two thousand die in the common course of the year.

qualities of the air have over our minds, is what we experience when travelling. As we change air very often upon a journey, almost in the same manner as we should change it, were there an alteration in the air of the country we live in, the air of one tract of land diminishes our ordinary appetite, and that of another augments it. A French refugee in Holland complains at least three times a day, that his gaiety and vivacity of spirit has abandoned him. Our native air is oft-times a remedy to us : That distemper which is called the *Hemvé* in some countries,

and

and fills the fick perfon with a violent defire of returning to his native home, when, as Juvenal expreffes it,

———————— *notos triftis defiderat hædos,*

JUV. fat.

is an inftinct, which warns us, that the air we are in, is not fo fuitable to our conftitution, as that which a fecret inftinct induces us to long for. The *Hemvé* becomes uneafy to the mind, becaufe it is a real uneafinefs to the body. An air too different from that to which a perfon is accuftomed, is a fource of ailments and diftempers.

Nonne vides etiam cæli novitate & aquarum
Tentari procul a patria quicumque domoque
Adveniunt, ideò quia longè difcrepat aer.

LUCRET. de nat. rer. l. 6.

A traveller in ev'ry place he fees,
Or hazards, or endures, a new difeafe,
Becaufe the air, or water difagrees.

CREECH.

An air which is very wholefome perhaps to the inhabitants of the country, is a flow poifon to fome ftrangers. Who is it that has not heard of the *Tabardillo,* a kind of fever attended with the moft uneafy fymptoms, which attacks almoft all the Europeans a few weeks after their arrival in the Spanifh Weft-Indies? The mafs of blood formed by the air and nourifhments of Europe, being incapable to mix with the American air, or with the chyle produced by the food of that country, is confequently diffolved. The only way of curing

people

people feized with this diftemper, which proves' frequently mortal, is to bleed them plentifully, and to accuftom them by degrees to the food of the country. The fame diforder attacks the Spaniards born in America upon their coming to Europe; fo that the native air of the father proves a kind of poifon to the fon.

This difference between the air of two countries is imperceptible to our fenfes, and out of the reach of any of our inftruments; for we know it only by its effects. But there are fome animals, which feem to diftinguifh it by their fenfes. They do not pafs from the country they inhabit to adjacent provinces, where the air appears to us the fame as that which they are fo fond of. Thus we do not fee on the banks of the Seine a large kind of bird, with which the Loire is covered.

CHAP. XV.

The power of the air over our bodies proved by the different characters of nations.

WHENCE comes it that all nations are fo different from one another in fhape, ftature, inclination, and fpirit, tho' they defcend all from one and the fame progenitor? Whence comes it, that the new inhabitants of a country refemble in a few generations, fuch as inhabited the fame country before them, from whom they are not however defcended? Why are thofe people who dwell within the fame diftance from the line, fo different from one another?

another? A mountain only feparates a people of a robuft conftitution from one of a weak temperament; and a nation naturally couragious from another of a moft timorous difpofition. Livy [a] obferves, that in the war with the Latins, their troops might have been diftinguifhed from the Romans at the very firft fight : The Romans were fmall and feeble, whereas the Latins were tall and robuft. And yet *Latium* and the ancient territory of Rome were countries of a very inconfiderable extent, and bordering upon one another. Have the bodies of the Andalufian peafants the fame natural conformation, as thofe of the peafants of old Caftile ? Are the inhabitants of the adjacent provinces as fupple and nimble as the people of Bifcay ? Is it fo eafy to meet with fine voices in Auvergne, as in Languedoc? Quintilian fays, [b] *that one may difcover a man's country by his voice, as we may know the allay of brafs by its found.* The difference becomes ftill more fenfible when we examine the nature of very diftant countries : 'Tis furprizing between a Negro and a Ruffian. And yet this can proceed only from the difference of the air of the countries, where the anceftors of the prefent Negroes and Ruffians, who are all defcendants of Adam, went firft to fettle. The firft men who fettled near the Line, muft have left a pofterity, who differed very little from the pofterity of thofe who went in fearch of fettlements towards the Arctic pole. The grand-children born fome towards the Pole, and others near the Line, accord-

[a] Liv. hift. l. 6.

[b] *Non enim fine caufa dicitur barbarum Græcumve ; nam fonis homines ut æra tinnitu dignofcimus.* Quint. Inft. orat. l. 2. c. 5.

ing

ing to the progreffion of men's inhabiting the earth, muft have had a leffer refemblance. At length, this refemblance diminifhing every generation, and in proportion as colonies approached fome towards the Line, and others the Arctic Pole, the races of mankind arrived at laft to that difference, in which we behold them at prefent. Ten centuries might have been fufficient to render the defcendants of the fame parents, as different from one another. as the Negroes and Swedes.

'Tis only three hundred years fince the Portuguefe planted on the weftern coaft of Afric the colonies which they poffefs there at prefent ; neverthelefs the defcendants of the firft planters have no refemblance with the prefent natives of Portugal. The hair of the African Portuguefe is fhort and curled, their nofe flat, and their lips thick, like the Negroes whofe country they inhabit. They have imbibed long fince the complexion of thofe *Blacks* tho' they always claim the honorable appellation of *Whites*. On the other hand, the Negroes do not retain in cold climates the blacknefs they have in Afric : Here their fkin grows whitifh, infomuch that if a colony of Negroes were to fettle in England, they would probably lofe in a long feries of time their natural color, in the fame manner as the Portuguefe of Cape-Verd have loft theirs in the countries near the Line.

Now if the diverfity of climates is capable of producing fuch a variety and difference in the complexion, fize, fhape, and even in the very voice of men ; it ought confequently to caufe a greater difference in the genius, inclinations, and manners

of

of nations. The organs of the brain, or the parts of the human body, which, phyſically ſpeaking, decide the ſpirit and inclinations of men, are without compariſon more compounded and more delicate, than the bones and other parts which determine their ſtature and force: They are more compounded than thoſe which decide the ſound of the voice and the agility of the body. Wherefore two men who happen to have their blood of a quality different enough to occaſion an external diſſimilitude, will be much more unlike one another in mind; and will have a greater difference of inclinations than of ſhape and complexion.

Experience ſeems to confirm this way of reaſoning. All nations differ more in inclinations and mind than in make and color of body. As an ambaſſador of Rhodes ſaid before the Roman ſenate, [a] each people has its character, as well as every individual. Quintilian, [b] after having given the moral reaſons which were alledged for the difference between the eloquence of the Athenians, and that of the Aſiatic Greeks, ſays that we muſt look for it in the natural character of both nations. In effect, drunkenneſs and other vices are commoner in ſome countries than in others: and the ſame may be alſo ſaid of moral virtues. The conformation of the organs and the

[a] *Tam civitatum, quàm ſingulorum hominum mores ſunt. Gentes quoque aliæ iracundæ, aliæ audaces, quædam timidæ, in vinum, in venerem proniores alia ſunt* Liv hiſt. l. 45.

[b] *Mihi autem orationis differentiam feciſſe & dicentium naturæ videntur, quòd Attici limati quidam & emuncti, nihil inane aut redundans ferebant Aſiana gens tumidior alioqui & jactantior variore etiam dicendi gloria inflata eſt.* Quint. Inſt. l. 12. c. 10.

tem-

temperament of body give an inclination to particular virtues or vices, which influences the generality
of every nation. Wherefoever luxury is introduced,
it has always a fubferviency to the predominant inclination of the nation that falls into extravagance.
According to the different tafte of countries, people
are ruined either by fumptuous buildings, or magnificent equipages, or by keeping nice and delicate tables, or in fine by downright excefs of eating and
drinking. A Spanifh grandee fquanders his money
in intrigues and gallantry : but a Polifh palatine's profufion confifts in wine and brandy.

The Catholic religion is effentially the fame with
refpect to its ceremonial and dogmatic parts, wherefoever the Roman communion is embraced. Each
nation notwithftanding mixes fomething of its particular character in this worfhip. According to the
genius of every nation, it is exercifed with more or
lefs pomp, more or lefs dignity, and with more or lefs
fenfible demonftrations of gladnefs or repentance.

There are very few heads, whofe brains are fo ill
formed as not to make a man of wit, or at leaft a
man of imagination in a certain climate ; and quite the
contrary in another.

Tho' the Bœotians and Athenians were only fepa-
rated from one another by mount Cithæron, yet the
former were fo well known to be a coarfe heavy
people, that to exprefs a man's ftupidity, it was
ufual to fay, he feemed to have been born in Bœo-
tia ; whereas the Athenians paffed for the moft fenfible and ingenious people in the univerfe. I wave
citing here the encomiums, which the Greek writers

I   have

have given of the wit and taſte of the Athenians. The greateſt part of them (ſome will ſay) were either born or choſe to live at Athens. But Cicero, who knew the Athenians perfectly well, having lived a long time amongſt them, and who cannot be ſuſpected of a ſervile flattery to people that were ſubjects of his republic, gives the ſame teſtimony as the Greeks in their favor. *The judgment of the Athenians,* he ſays [a], *was always ſo ſound and prudent, that they could never liſten to any thing but what was pure and elegant.* What M. Racine ſays in the preface to his *Plaideurs,* that the Athenians never laughed at nonſenſe, is only a tranſlation in different words of the Latin paſſage of Cicero ; and thoſe who have cenſured the French author for writing it, have, to expreſs myſelf in Montagne's words, given him a box on Cicero's ear, a witneſs who cannot be excepted againſt in the fact here in queſtion.

The ſame reaſon which produced ſo great a difference between the Athenians and Bœotians, is the cauſe of ſo ſmall a reſemblance between the Florentines and ſome of their neighbours. Hence alſo it comes, that we ſee even in France ſo much ſenſe and ready wit in the peaſants of a province contiguous to another, where people of the ſame condition of life are almoſt ſtupid. Tho' the difference of air be not conſiderable enough in theſe people to make an external diverſity in their bodies, it is ſufficient notwithſtanding to create a diverſity in ſuch organs, as are immediately employed in the functions of the ſoul.

---

[a] *Athenienſes quorum ſemper fui [...] [...] truden'que iudicium, nihil ut p[...]ent niſi incorruptum audire et elegans.* **Cic. de orat.**

We

We even find minds which do not seem to be of the same species, when we reflect on the genius of people, whose difference is so considerable, as to be visible in their make and complection. Does a peasant of North Holland, and a peasant of Andalusia think in the same manner? Have they the same passions? Are they actuated alike by those passions they feel in common? Are they willing to be governed in the same manner? When this external difference grows still greater, the difference of minds is prodigious. *Behold,* says the author of the Plurality of worlds [a], *how much the face of nature is changed between this and China. Different faces, different shapes, different customs, and almost different principles of reasoning.*

I do not chuse to give here a particular description of the character of each nation, or of the peculiar genius of every age, but shall refer my reader to Barclay's Euphormio, who treats this subject in one of the books of that satire, which goes generally by the name of *Icon animorum.* But I shall add one reflection to what has been hitherto said, to shew how probable it is, that the understanding and inclinations of men depend on the air they breathe, and on the country where they are bred. 'Tis that strangers who have settled in any country whatsoever, resemble the ancient inhabitants after a certain number of generations. The principal nations of Europe have at present the same character as the ancient people of

[a] M. de Fontenelle, Plurality of worlds, 2d evening.

the

the countries they now inhabit, notwithſtanding they do not deſcend from thoſe ancient people. I ſhall illuſtrate this remark by a few examples.

The preſent Catalonians are deſcended, for the moſt part, from the Goths and other foreign nations, who upon their firſt ſettling in Catalonia, brought different languages and cuſtoms with them, from thoſe of the people who inhabited that country in the Scipio's time. 'Tis true, that thoſe ſtrange nations have aboliſhed the ancient language, which has made room for another compoſed of the different idioms which they ſpoke. This is a thing however that has been decided intirely by cuſtom : But nature has revived in the preſent inhabitants the manners and inclinations of the Catalonians in the Scipio's days. Livy ſays of the ancient Catalonians, *that it was as eaſy to deſtroy, as to diſarm them* [a] : Now all Europe knows whether the preſent Catalonians do not anſwer that character. Do not we diſcover the Caſtilians in the portrait Juſtin draws of the Iberians [b] ? *Their bodies are inured to hunger and fatigue ; and their minds are ſo prepared for death, as not to be afraid of it. They can live upon very little, and are as much afraid of loſing their gravity, as other people of loſing their life.* The Iberians had as different a character of mind from that of the Gauls, as the preſent cha-

---

[a] *Ferox gens nullam eſſe vitam ſine armis putat.* LIV.

[b] *Corpora hominum ad inediam laboremque, animi ad mortem parati Dura omnibus & adſtricta parcimonia. Illis fortior taciturnitatis cura quàm vitæ.* JUST

racter of the Castilians differs from that of the French.

Tho' the French descend, the greatest part of them, from the Germans, and the other Barbarians settled in Gaul ; they have notwithstanding the same inclinations and character of mind as the ancient Gauls. 'Tis easy to discover in the present French the greatest part of those strokes which Cæsar, Florus, and the ancient historians attributed to that people. A particular talent of the French, for which they are celebrated all over Europe, is a surprizing industry, in imitating with ease the inventions of strangers. Cæsar gives this talent to the Gauls, whom he calls, *a people of great quickness of mind, extremely fit for imitating and executing whatsoever they are taught* [a]. He was surprized to see how well the Gauls, whom he besieged, had imitated the most difficult military machines of the Romans, tho' they were quite new to them. Another very particular touch in the character of the French nation, is their insurmountable propensity to gaiety whether seasonable or not, which makes them conclude the most serious reflections with a song. Thus we find the Gauls characterised in the Roman history, and principally in a relation of Livy's. Hannibal at the head of a hundred thousand men, demanded a passage into Italy of the inhabitants of that country which is now called Languedoc, offering to pay ready money for what his men should consume, and menacing at the same time to lay their country waste with fire and sword, if they

[a] *Genus summæ solertiæ, atque ad omnia imitanda atque efficienda, quæ ab quoque traduntur aptissimum.* CÆS.

attempted

attempted to traverse his march.   Whilft they were
deliberating on Hannibal's propofition, the ambaffadors of the Roman republic, who had only a
very fmall retinue with them, demanded audience.
After having talked very big for a great while of the
fenate and people of Rome, whom our Gauls had
never heard mentioned but as enemies to fuch of
their countrymen as had fettled in Italy, the ambaffadors propofed to obftruct the paffage of the Car-
thaginians.   This was really defiring the Gauls to
make their country the theatre of war, in order to
hinder Hannibal from transferring it to the banks of
the Tiber.   The propofition was indeed of fuch a
nature, as not to be made but with great art and
precaution even to ancient allies.   *The audience*
therefore, fays Livy [a], *burfted out into a violent fit of*
laughter, infomuch that the magiftrates had much ado
to command filence, in order to give a ferious anfwer
to the ambaffadors.

Davila relates in the hiftory of our civil wars [b]
an adventure of this fort, which happened at the
conferences that were held for peace, during the
fiege of Paris by Henry IV [c].   Upon cardinal
Gondi's faying, that it was not hunger, but the
love for their king which induced the Parifians to
enter into a conference, the king's prefence could
not   prevent   the   young   lords   from   burfting
out into laughter at the cardinal's difcourfe, which

---

[a] *Tanto cum fremitu rifus dicitur ortus, ut vix a magiftratibus*
majoribufque natu juventus fedaretur.   LIV.

[b] Davila, l. 11.   [c] in 1590.

became really ridiculous by its boldnefs ; both parties being very well affured of the contrary. All Europe reproaches the French, to this very day, with their uneafinefs and levity, which makes them quit their own country, to ramble in fearch of employments, and to lift under every colors. Florus[a] has obferved of the Gauls, *that there were no armies to be found without Gallic foldiers.* If in Cæfar's time we meet with Gauls in the fervice of the kings of Judea, Mauritania, and Ægypt, do not we find Frenchmen in our days amongft all the troops in Europe, even among thofe of the king of Perfia and the Great Mogul ?

The prefent Englifh are not defcended, generally fpeaking, from the Britons who inhabited that ifland when the Romans fubdued it. Neverthelefs the ftrokes with which Cæfar and Tacitus characterife the Britons, are extremely well fuited to the Englifh : For the one were not more fubject to jealoufy than the other. Tacitus obferves[b], that Agricola found no better method of engaging the ancient Britons to make their children learn Latin, as well as Rhetoric and the other polite arts in ufe among the Romans, than to excite them by emulation, by making them afhamed to fee themfelves excelled by the Gauls. The fpirit of the Britons, faid Agricola, is of a better frame than that of the Gauls, and if they have a mind to take pains, it depends intirely on themfelves, to furpafs their neighbours. Agri-

[a] *Nullum bellum fine milite Gallo.* FLORUS.

[b] *Jam verò principum filios liberalibus artibus erudire & ingenia Britannorum ftudiis Gallorum anteferre, ut qui modò linguam Romaram abnuebant, eloquentiam concupifcerent.* TAC.

I

cola's

cola's artifice had its defired effect, and the Britons who before fcorned to fpeak Latin, grew even defirous of acquiring the beauties of the Roman eloquence. Let the Englifh themfelves judge, whether the artifice ufed by Agricola might not be employed amongft them at prefent with the like fuccefs ?

Tho' Germany is in a much different condition at prefent, from what it was when Tacitus defcribed it; tho' it is ftocked now with towns, whereas it had formerly nothing but villages; tho' the moraffes and the greateft part of the forefts have been converted into meadows and plowed lands; in fine, tho' the ancient manner of dreffing and living be confequently different in feveral things from that of the prefent inhabitants; we may diftinguifh neverthelefs the genius and character of the old Germans in thofe of our times. Their women, like thofe in former days, follow the cumps in much greater numbers than thofe of other countries. What Tacitus oblerves of the repafts of the old Germans, is true with regard to the generality of the moderns. Like their anceftors they reafon very well concerning affairs when they are warm at table, but they never come to a conclufion but in cool blood[a]. Thus we find in every refpect the ancient people in the modern, tho' the latter profefs a different religion, and are governed by different maxims.

It has been in all times obferved, that the influence of climate is ftronger than that of origin and blood.

[a] *Deliberant dum fingere nefciunt, conftituunt dum errare non poffunt.* TAC.

The

The Gallogrecians defcended from the Gauls who fettled in Afia, became in five or fix generations, as foft and effeminate as the Afiatics; tho' they fprung from warlike anceftors, who fettled in a country, where they had nothing to depend upon but their valor and arms. Livy, fpeaking of an event which happened at an almoft equal diftance of time from the eftablifhment of the Gallogrecian colony, and its conqueft by the Romans, fays of the Afiatic Gauls, *the Gallogrecians were a more warlike people at that time, not having yet degenerated from the fpirit of the ancient Gauls* [a].

People of all countries illuftrious for feats of arms, have grown effeminate and pufillanimous, after having been tranfplanted into lands, whofe climate foftens the native inhabitants. The Macedonians who fettled in Syria and Ægypt, grew in a few years time downright Syrians and Ægyptians, and degenerating from their anceftors valor, kept only their language and ftandards. On the contrary, the Greeks who went to Marfeilles, contracted the boldnefs and contempt of death, peculiar to the Gauls. But, as Livy fays [b],

[a] *Gallogræci ea tempeftate bellicofiores erant, Gallicos adhuc nondum exoleta ftirpe gentis geftantes animos.* LIV.

[b] *Sicut in frugibus pecudibufque, non tantùm femina ad fervandam indolem valent, quantùm terræ proprietas cælique fub quo aluntur mutant. Macedones qui Alexandriam in Ægypto, qui Seleuciam ac Babyloniam, quique alias fparfas per orbem terrarum colonias habent, in Syros, Parthos, Ægyptios degenerarunt. Maffilia inter Gallos fita traxit aliquantulum ab accolis animorum Tarentinis quid ex Spartana dura illa & horrida libertate manfit ? Generofiùs in fua quidquid fede gignitur ; infitum alienæ terræ, natura vertente fe, degenerat.* LIV. hift. l. 28.

relating

relating the facts here mentioned, 'tis the fame
" thing with fome men, as with plants and brutes.
" Now the qualities of plants do not depend fo
" much on the place from whence the grain has
" been borrowed, as from the foil in which it is
" fown ; in like manner the qualities of brutes de-
" pend lefs on their breed, than on the country
" where they are born, and grow up."

Thus the grains which fucceed very well in one
country, degenerate when fown in another. The
linfeed which comes from Livonia, and is fown
in Flanders, produces a very fine plant ; but
that which grows in Flanders, and is fown in the
fame foil, bears nothing but a baftard-plant. The
fame may be faid of the grain of melon, radifh,
and feveral other pulfe, which muft be renewed to
have them good, at leaft after a certain number of
generations, by fending for new grains to the country where they grow in full perfection. As trees
fhoot up, and produce fruit much flower than plants,
the fame tree gives different fruit, according to the
foil where it firft grew, and that to which it is tranfplanted. The vine tranfplanted from Champagne to
Brie, produces very foon a wine, which has none of
the qualities of the liquor it afforded in its primitive
foil. True it is, that brutes have not fo near a
relation to the earth, as trees and plants ; neverthelefs as the air makes animals live, and the
earth nourifhes them ; their qualities do not depend lefs on the places where they are bred, than
the qualities of the trees and plants on the country
where they grow. Let us go on with confulting
experience.

Since

Since Livy wrote his history, several nations in Europe have sent colonies into climates more remote and more different from that of their native country, than the climate of the Gauls was from that of Gallogrecia. It has happened also, that the change of manners, inclination, and spirit, which are unavoidable to those who change countries, has been more sudden and sensible in the new than in the ancient colonies.

The Franks who settled in the Holy Land, upon its being conquered by the first Crusade, became after a few generations, as pusillanimous and vicious as the natives of the country. The history of the latter Crusades abounds with bitter complaints against the treachery and effeminacy of the oriental Franks. The Sultans of Ægypt had no other method left of preserving the valor and discipline of their troops, than by recruiting them in Circassia, from whence their Mamelucks came. Experience had shewn them, that the children of the Circassians born and bred in Ægypt, had only the inclinations and courage of Ægyptians. The Ptolomys, and other sovereigns of Ægypt who were careful of keeping good troops, had always a standing army composed of foreigners. The natives of the country, who pretended to have performed such great exploits under Sesostris and their first kings, were very much degenerated at the time of Alexander the Great. Ægypt, since the conquest thereof by the Persians, has been always an easy prey to a handful of foreign soldiers. Since Cambyses's time, the natives have never, if I may say so, drawn an Ægyptian sword. Even at present an Æ-
gyptian

gyptian is not admitted into the troops maintained by the Grand Signor on the Ægyptian establishment : Thefe muft be compofed of foreign foldiers.

The Portuguefe eftablifhed in the Eaft-Indies are become as effeminate and cowardly as the natives of that country. Thofe invincible Portuguefe in Flanders, where they made up one half of the famous Spanifh infantry deftroyed at Rocrois [a], had near relations in the Indies, who let themfelves be beaten about like fheep. Thofe who can remember the particular events of the wars of the Low Countries, which gave birth to the republic of Holland, muft know that the Flemifh infantry could never ftand againft that which was compofed of native Spaniards. But fuch as have read the hiftory of the conquefts of the Dutch in the Eaft-Indies, muft remember on the other hand, that a handful of Dutchmen ufed to put whole armies of Indian Portuguefe to flight. I do not care to quote any odious writings, I fhall only appeal to the Dutch themfelves, whether their countrymen who are fettled in the Eaft-Indies, have preferved the manners and good qualities they had in Europe.

The court of Madrid, which has been conftantly attentive to the particular character and genius of the different nations it governed, has always placed a greater confidence in the children of Spaniards born in Flanders, than in the offspring of Spaniards born in the kingdom of Naples. The latter were not put upon an equal footing with the natives of Spain, as the others were. This wary court has

[a] in 1643.

made

made it always her maxim not to intruſt any employment of importance in the Weſt-Indies to the Creolian Spaniards, or ſuch as were born in America. And yet theſe Creolians are inhabitants born of Spaniſh parents, without any mixture of American or African blood. Thoſe that are deſcended of a Spaniſh Father and an American mother are called Meſtizo's; and when the mother happens to be a negro, they are called Mulattoes.

The incapacity of thoſe ſubjects has had as great a ſhare in this policy, as the fear of their revolting. 'Tis difficult indeed to conceive, how much the Spaniſh blood (a blood ſo brave and generous in Europe) has degenerated in ſeveral provinces of America. It would be abſolutely incredible, did not twelve or fifteen different relations of the expeditions of the Buccaneers to the new world, agree all of them in this point, and furniſh us with the moſt convincing circumſtances.

Brutes receive a different ſhape and conformation, in the ſame manner as men, according to the country where they are born, or bred. There was no ſuch things as horſes in America, when the Spaniards diſcovered that part of the world. 'Tis very likely that the firſt which were tranſported thither for breed, were the very fineſt of Andaluſia where the embarkation was made. As the expences of the freight amounted to upwards of two hundred crowns a horſe, 'tis likely the purchaſe money was not at all ſpared ; eſpecially as horſes were then exceeding cheap in that province. There are notwithſtanding ſome provinces in America where the breed of horſes has degenerated. The horſes of St
Domingo

Domingo and the Antilles are fmall, ill-fhaped, and have only the courage (if I be allowed to fpeak fo) of the noble animals from which they are defcended. There are indeed fome other provinces in America, where the Andalufian breed is rather improved. Thofe of Chili are as much fuperior in beauty and goodnefs to the Andalufian horfes, as thefe furpafs thofe of Picardy. The Caftilian and Andalufian fheep tranfported into other paftures, afford no longer fuch *precious* wool, as thofe mentioned by Juvenal,

———————— *Quas Bæticus adjuvat aer.*
Juv. fat. 12.

By noble fprings improv'd, and Bætic air.
POWER.

When the goats of Ancyra lofe their mountain pafture, they ceafe to have that hair fo vaftly efteemed in the eaft, and known even in Europe. [a] There are countries where a horfe is generally fo gentle an animal, as to let himfelf be led by children : In other places, as in the kingdom of Naples, he is almoft a favage animal, whom you muft take particular care of. Horfes even change their difpofition and temper, by altering their air and food ; hence thofe of Andalufia are much more tractable in their own country than in ours. In fine, moft animals ceafe to breed, when they are tranfported into a climate too different from their own : thus tigers, apes, camels, elephants, and feveral kinds of birds do not multiply in our countries.

[a] BUSBEQUIUS ep. 1.

CHAP.

CHAP XVI.

Objection drawn from the character of the Ro-
mans and the Dutch.   Anfwer to this ob-
jection.

IT will be objected here perhaps, that there are
two nations in Europe, whom the character given their anceftors by ancient writers do not fuit at
prefent.   The modern Romans, it will be faid, bear
no manner of refemblance to thofe ancient Romans
fo famous for their military virtues, and whom Tacitus, defcribes as a people who were profeffed foes
to all vain demonftrations of ceremonial refpect;
a people whofe fole occupation was to eftablifh and
extend their authority.   [a] Tiridates, brother of the
king of Parthia, who came to Rome in order to pay
homage (purfuant to our modern way of expreffing
it) for the crown of Armenia, would not have been
fo much afraid of the Roman ceremonial, continues
the abovementioned author, had he been a little better
acquainted with that nation.   The Batavians and ancient Frieflanders (it will be ftill objected) were two
warlike nations, who took up arms, as foon as the
Romans attempted to lay any other tribute upon
them, but that of military fervice.   The prefent
inhabitants of the province of Holland, which
includes the ifle of the Batavians, and a part of
the country of the ancient Frieflanders, are intirely addicted to commerce.   They furpafs all o-

---

[a] *Apud quos jus imperii valet, inania tranfmittuntur.*   TACIT.
Annal. lib 15.

ther

ther people in the regularity and order of their towns, and in their *municipal* government. The people are readier to pay the heavieft taxes that are raifed in Europe, than to enter into the fervice. *The Belgians are very unfit for land fervice, and a Dutchman on horfeback is a moft ridiculous fight*, fays Puffendorf [a], fpeaking of the prefent inhabitants of Holland, who are as willing to take foreign troops into their pay, as the Batavians were ready formerly to fight for foreigners.

With refpect to the Romans, my anfwer is, that when the reft of Europe will refolve to lay afide their ceremonies, the Romans will not be the laft to get rid of theirs. Ceremonies are the prefent fafhion ; for which reafon they endeavour to excel other nations in this refpect, as they were formerly fuperior to them in the military art. Perhaps the modern Romans would fhew us that moderation in fuccefs, and that intrepidity in danger, which formed the character of the ancient Romans, if their princes were not of a profeffion which forbids them to afpire to military glory. Muft people becaufe they have courage, get themfelves killed immediately in battle ; as thofe that are born poets fcribble verfes ? If the Romans have really degenerated, their degeneracy does not certainly extend to all forts of virtues. No nation underftands better how to behave refolutely, or to fhew a feafonable compliance in bufinefs ; and we may obferve even in the common people of Rome, that art of

---

[a] *Ad terreftrem militiam parum idonei funt Belgæ, & equo infidens Batavus ludibrium omnibus debet.* Puff. introd. ad hift. Europ.

in-

infinuating efteem for their fellow citizens; an art that has been always one of the principal caufes of a nation's reputation.

Befides, there has been fuch a prodigious change in the air of Rome and the adjacent country, fince the time of the Cæfars, that it is not at all aftonifhing there fhould be a difference between the prefent and ancient inhabitants: Nay, in our fyftem, this is the very thing that ought naturally to have happened, fince the alteration of the caufe muft be always fuppofed to alter the effect.

In the firft place, the air of the city of Rome, except the quarter of the Trinità di Monte, and that of the Quirinal, is extremely unwholfome during the dog-days, infomuch that it cannot agree but with thofe who are accuftomed to it gradually, as Mithridates was to poifon. People muft even renew every year the habit of fupporting the infected air, by beginning to breathe it the very firft days of its alteration: for 'tis mortal to thofe who breathe it the firft time, if it be at the height of its corruption. One is as little furprized to fee a perfon die, who upon coming from the country, goes to lodge where the air is corrupted, or even thofe who at that time fhould remove from a wholfome quarter of the town, as to fee a man expire when ftruck by a cannon-ball. The caufe of this corruption of the air is not a fecret to us. Rome was cut through as well under, as above ground, and every ftreet had a *cloaca* or common fhore under the pavement. Thefe common fhores met all at the Tiber by different channels, that were cleanfed continually by the waters of fifteen aque-

I   ducts,

ducts, which conveyed intire rivers to Rome ; and these rivers discharged themselves into the Tiber by means of the *cloacæ*. The buildings of this vast city having been destroyed by the Goths, by the Normans of Naples, and by time ; the ruins of the edifices erected on the seven hills have filled the adjacent valleys, insomuch that the ancient superficies of the earth lies frequently buried in these valleys full forty feet deep. This heap of rubbish has stopt up several branches, by which many of the lesser *cloacæ* communicated with the great ones, that terminated at the Tiber. The vaults being broken in by the fall of the neighbouring buildings, or thro' antiquity, consequently stopped several channels, and intercepted the course of the waters. But the greatest part of the sinks, thro' which the rain and the waters of the ancient aqueducts that are still subsisting, fall into the *cloacæ*, have continued to lye open. The water has therefore come constantly into these channels, without finding any out-let. Here it stagnates, and becomes infected to such a degree, that when the *rummagers* happen to dig one of these channels, the stink and infection which exhales from thence, strikes them frequently with mortal distempers. Those who have ventured to eat such fish as they have found there sometimes, have generally lost their lives for their rash curiosity. Now these channels are not so deep under ground, but that the heat, which is excessive at Rome during the dog-days, extracts from thence most pestilential exhalations, which break out so much the easier, as the chinks of the vaults are only stopt with rubbish and gravel, which are not so close a sieve for sifting

the

the exhalations, as that of the common earth or natural foil.

Secondly, the air of the level country about Rome, which extends twelve leagues in thofe places where the Appenine removes fartheft off from this city, reduces during the three hot months the very natives who are accuftomed to it from their infancy, to a ftate of languifhment and wearinefs almoft incredible to thofe that have not feen it. In feveral parts the religious are obliged to quit their convents to go and fpend the dog-days fome where elfe. In fine, the air of the country about Rome ftrikes a ftranger who expofes himfelf to its activity, in time of fleep, with as fudden and fure a death as the fword. This air is then always pernicious, from whatfoever quarter the wind blows, which is a convincing argument that the earth is in fome meafure the caufe of its alteration. The infection therefore fhews, that there has been fome confiderable change in the earth; whether this proceeds from its not being manured as in the time of the Cæfars; or whether it is to be attributed to the moraffes of Oftia and Ofanté [a], which are not drained as formerly; or whether in fine it arifes from the mines of alum, fulphur, and arfenic, which in fucceffion of time have been formed under the fuperficies of the earth, and emit at prefent, but efpecially in fummer-time, more malignant exhalations, than thofe which were emitted, before they had attained their prefent degree of maturity. We fee frequently in the country about Rome a phænomenon, which fhould

[a] *Pomptinæ paludes.*

induce

induce us to think, that the alteration of the air proceeds from a new cause, that is, from the mines
that have been perfected under the surface of the
earth. During the violent heats, exhalations rise
from the earth which lighten of themselves, and form
long ridges or columns of fire, with the earth for
their basis. Livy would have inserted a prolix recital of the sacrifices made for the expiation of these
prodigies, had these phænomena been seen in that
country when he wrote his history.

Another proof we have, that there has been a
physical alteration in the air of Rome and the adjacent country, is, that the climate is not so cold
as it was formerly in the time of the Cæsars, tho'
the country was better inhabited and cultivated
at that time, than it is at present. We are informed by the Roman annals, that in the year 480
of its foundation, the winter was so extremely cold,
that the trees were killed with the frost. The Tiber was frozen over at Rome, and the earth covered with snow during the space of forty days.
When Juvenal draws the picture of a super-
stitious woman, he says, that she causes the ice of
the Tiber to be broken, in order to make her
ablutions.

Hibernum fracta glacie descendet in amnem,
Ter matutino Tyberi mergetur, & ipsis
Vorticibus timidum caput abluet, inde superbi
Totum Regis agrum nuda & tremebunda cruentis
Erepet genibus.　　　　　　JUVEN. sat. 8.

Thro' ye they beat and plunge into the stream,
If so the God has warn'd them in a dream.

　　　　　　Weak

Weak in their limbs but in devotion strong,
On their bare hands and feet they crawl along
A whole field's length, the laughter of the throng.
DRYDEN.

Here he speaks of the Tiber's being frozen over, as of an ordinary event. Several passages of Horace suppose the streets of Rome full of ice and snow. We should have been better informed concerning this subject had the ancients understood the use of Thermometers ; but tho' their writers have not instructed us with respect to this point, they let us know enough to be convinced that the winters were formerly severer at Rome, than at present. The Tiber is no more frozen there, than the Nile at Grand Cairo. They think it a very rigid winter in Rome, when the snow lyes two days upon the ground, or when they can observe a thin bit of ice for two nights together in some fountain exposed to the north.

As for the Dutch, I answer that they do not live upon the same ground as the Batavians and ancient Frieslanders, tho' they inhabit the same country. The isle of the Batavians was indeed a low country, but it was covered with wood. With respect to the land of the ancient Frieslanders, which forms at present the greatest part of the province of Holland ; to wit, that which lies between the Ocean, the Zuiderzee, and the old bed of the Rhine which passes by Leyden, it abounded at that time with hills that were hollow withinside : This is expressed by the word *Holland* introduced in the middle age ; which signifies a hollow land in the language of
that

that country. Tacitus [a] informs us, that the a-bovementioned arm of the Rhine, which fepa-rated Friefland from the ifle of the Batavians, preferved the rapidity that river has in its courfe, an evident proof that the country was then mountainous. The fea having infinuated itfelf into thefe cavities was the caufe of the finking of the earth, which has raifed itfelf fince above the fur-face of the waters that covered it after its depref-fion, by the help of the fands which the waves of the fea brought thither, and of the flime which the rivers left behind them after frequent inunda-tions, before they were reftrained by dykes.

Another proof of what I have advanced is, that in that part of the province of Holland, which be-longed to ancient Friefland, they find frequently, upon digging foundations, trees which are faftened to the ground by their roots, fifteen feet below the level of the country. And yet this country which is as fmooth as a floor, is lower now than high water, and upon a level with very low water. This fhews that the earth which the abovementioned roots of trees are faftened to, is a foil that was formerly funk. Thofe that have a mind to be further informed with regard to the time and other circumftances of thefe inunda-tions, may read the two firft volumes of M. Al-ting's work, intitled, *Defcriptio agri Batavi.* 'Tis a work they will read with great utility, and not without regretting that this author died a-bout thirty years ago, before he could leave us his third volume. Holland having been drained and

[a] Tacitus Annal. l. 2.

P 2 peopled

peopled again, it is now an even pasture land, cut into a vast number of canals, and covered with some lakes and morasses. [a] The soil has changed its nature to such a degree, that the cows and oxen of that country are larger now than elsewhere, whereas formerly they were very small. In fine, a fourth part of its surface is covered with water, which was not the case perhaps of one twelfth part of it in former times. The people likewise having increased there more than in any other part of Europe, by means of events which are foreign to my present purpose; want and the facility of having pulse and milk-meats in a continued meadow, has accustomed the inhabitants to live upon this flegmatic diet; whereas the ancient inhabitants fed upon the flesh of their flocks, and of domestic animals that were grown wild, with which, pursuant to the observation of Tacitus and several other ancient writers, their woods abounded.

Sir William Temple, who was so much surprized at the difference of character between the Batavians and the Dutch, attempting to give the reason thereof, attributes it to their change of diet [b]. Such revolutions as these on the surface of the earth, which always cause a great alteration in the air, and have been also accompanied with so great a change in their ordinary aliment, that the modern inhabitants live like fishermen and gardeners, whereas the old ones lived like huntsmen; such revolutions, I say, could never have happened without altering the character of the people.

[a] TACITUS *Annal* l 4.
[b] *State of the United Provinces.* c. 4.

After

After all that has been hitherto faid, 'tis more than probable, that the particular genius of each nation depends on the quality of the air they breathe. One has reafon therefore to charge the climate, with that fcarcity of genius's and wits, which is obfervable in fome nations. *The temperature of hot climates*, fays Sir John Chardin, [a] *enervates the mind as well as the body, and diffipates that fire of imagination fo neceffary for invention. People are incapable in thofe climates of fuch long watchings and ftrong applications, as are requifite for the productions of the liberal and mechanic arts. 'Tis only towards the North we muft look for the arts and trades in their higheft perfection.* Our author fpeaks of Ifpahan ; and Rome and Athens are northern cities with refpect to the capital of Perfia. This is a fentiment founded on experience. Does not every body agree in attributing the ftupidity of the Negroes and the Laplanders to the excefs of heat or cold in their refpective countries ?

C H A P. XVII.

Of the extent of climates fitter for the arts and fciences, than others. And of the changes which thefe climates are fubject to.

IT may be here objected, that the arts and fciences have flourifhed under very different climates. Memphis, it will be faid, is eighteen degrees nearer the fun than Paris, and yet the arts and fciences have flourifhed in thefe two cities.

[a] Defcription of Perfia chap. 7.

I anfwer, that 'tis not every degree of heat or cold, that is contrary to the happy nourifhment of children, but only the very higheft excefs. Far from limiting the temperature of climate fit for the culture of arts and fciences, to four or five degrees, I am of opinion that this temperature may take in twenty or twenty five degrees of latitude. This happy climate may even extend itfelf and gain ground by the help of feveral favorable events.

For example, the extent of commerce may furnifh the northern nations at prefent with the means, which they had not formerly of making a part of their ordinary nourifhment of wines and other aliments which come from warm countries. Commerce, which has been furprizingly improved within thefe two laft centuries, has difcovered thefe things where they were before unknown ; and has even rendered them common in places, where they were formerly very fcarce. The increafe of trade has made wine as general a drink in feveral countries, where it does not grow, as in thofe kingdoms that have the pleafure of the vintage. It has put fugar and fpices in northern countries on the footing of provifions, that are for general confumption. Of late years, both fimple and compound brandy, coffee, chocolate, and other commodities that grow only in the very warmeft climates, are in general ufe, even among the common people, in Holland, England, Poland, Germany, and the North. The falts and fpirituous juices of thofe liquors throw a foul, or, to fpeak phyfically, an æthereal oil into the blood of the northern nations, which is not found in their own country food. Thefe juices fill the blood of a northern

thern inhabitant with fpirits formed in Spain and the very warmeft climates.   A portion of the air and fap of the land of the Canaries, is carried into England in the wines of thofe iflands, which are tranf-ported thither in fuch great quantities.   The frequent confumption therefore of the provifions and com-modities of hot countries, draws the fun, as it were, nearer to the provinces of the North, and infufes a vigor and delicacy into the blood and the imagina-tions of the inhabitants of thofe countries, which was unknown to their anceftors, whofe fimplicity was fa-tisfied with the productions of their own native foil. As people are fubject at prefent in thefe countries to diftempers, which they were ftrangers to, before the frequent ufe of ftrange aliments fo much prevailed, which are not perhaps juftly proportioned to the air of the country ; they ought for this very reafon to have a greater warmth and fubtlety in their blood.   Certain it is, that at the fame time that new diftempers appeared amongft them, or fome diftempers grew more frequent than formerly, o-thers difappeared, or became not fo common.   I have heard Monfieur Regis, a famous phyfician of Amfterdam, fay, that fince the ufe of thefe pro-vifions began to prevail generally among the inha-bitants of that city, they were not fubject to the twentieth part of the fcorbutic diftempers, with which they were formerly afflicted.

Tho' a country be at a certain diftance from the Line, this is not fufficient to render the climate fit for breeding men of wit and abilities. The air may happen to be contrary by its perma-nent qualities, to the phyfical education of children,

dren, who by the delicacy of their organs might have been defigned for men of wit and talents. The mixture of the corpufcles, which enter into the compofition of this air may happen to be bad by fome excefs of one of its good principles ; and the emanations of the earth may likewife chance to be heavy and coarfe in fome countries. All thefe defects, whereof we may conceive an infinite number, may be the occafion, that the air of a country, whofe temperature feems to be the fame as that of a neighbouring province, does not prove fo favorable to the phyfical education of children, as the air which they breathe in the latter. Two regions that are at the fame diftance from the Pole, may have a climate phyfically different. Since the difference of the air of two neighbouring provinces renders the inhabitants of the one taller than the others why may it not make them more ingenious and fenfible in one country than in another ? The fize of men fhould naturally be more difficult to vary, than the quality and fpring of the organs of the brain. The finer an organ is, the eafier the blood that contributes to its nourifhment, is able to change it. Now of all the organs of the human body, thofe are the moft delicate which ferve in the functions of the foul. What I have here faid, is only an explication of the general opinion, which has always attributed the difference obfervable between different nations, to the different qualities of the air. *The climate of each country is always, in my opinion, the principal caufe of the inclinations and cuftoms of men, which are not more different amongft themfelves, than the conftitution of*

the

the air varies in different places, fays a perfon [a] to whom we may apply the encomium which Homer beftows upon Ulyffes.

Qui mores hominum multorum vidit & urbes.

Hor. de art.

Who Troy once fall'n to many countries went,
And ftrictly view'd the men and government.

Creech.

C H A P. XVIII.

That we muft attribute the diverfity of the air of different countries, to the nature of the emanations of the earth which vary accord-ing to the difference of countries.

THE emanations of the earth are the only ap-parent caufe, to which we can attribute the fenfible difference, we obferve between the qualities of the air, in countries equally diftant from the Line. This opinion agrees very well with experience. The emanations, on which the qualities of the air depend, are themfelves dependent on the nature of thofe bo-dies from which they exhale. Now, when a per-fon comes to examine into the compofition of the terreftrial globe in two countries which have a dif-ference of air, he will find this compofition different. There is more water, for inftance, in a corner of Holland, than in the whole county of Kent. The

---

[a] Sir John Chardin, tom. 2. p. 4.

I

bofom

bofom of the earth does not include the fame bodies in France as it commonly contains in Italy. In feveral parts of the latter the earth is full of allum, fulphur, brimftone, and other minerals. Thefe bodies in France are not in the fame quantity in propoition to other bodies, as in Italy. We find thro' almoft all France that the gravel confifts of marl, or of a kind of a fat, whitifh, foft ftone, in which there is a vaft deal of volatile falts. 'Tis falt alfo that predominates in the foil of Poland ; infomuch that they find intire mines thereof in feveral parts of that kingdom. Thefe are fufficient not only for the confumption of the country, but moreover for that of feveral neighbouring provinces. 'Tis to this falt fo predominant in the foil of Poland, that philofophers attribute the furprizing fertility of the greateft part of its provinces, as likewife the extraordinary bignefs of its fruit, and if I be allowed to exprefs myfelf thus, the huge volume of the bodies born and nourifhed in that country. In England the gravel is compofed principally of lead, pewter, fea-coal, and other minerals, which vegetate and improve continually.

We may even venture to fay, that the difference of thefe emanations is obvious, in fome meafure, to our fenfes. The color of the ambient air, as alfo of the clouds which form a painted horizon at the fetting and rifing of the Sun, depend on the nature of the exhalations which fill the air, and mix with the vapors, of which thefe clouds are formed. Now every body may obferve, that the atmofphere and the clouds which glitter in the horizon, are not of the fame color in all countries. In Italy, for example, the

the atmofphere is of a greenifh blue, and the clouds of the horizon are of a very deep yellow and red. In the Netherlands the atmofphere is of a pale blue, and the clouds of the horizon are only tinged with a whitifh color. This very difference is obfervable in the painted *fkies* of Titian and Rubens, thefe two painters having reprefented nature fuch as it appears in Italy and the Low Countries where they copied it. I conclude therefore from what has been hitherto fet forth, that as the qualities of the earth decide the particular tafte of fruits in different countries, fo they determine alfo the nature of the air. The qualities and properties of the earth are alike the caufe of the diverfity there is in the air of two different countries, as they are the caufe of the different tafte of wines, which grow in neighbouring provinces.

Now this caufe is fubject by it's nature to a vaft number of viciffitudes and alterations. As the earth is a mixt body compofed of fluids and folids of different kinds and fpecies, they muft both of them inceffantly act, and produce continual fermentations, efpecially as the air and central fire contribute alfo to throw the matter into motion. As the leaven, as well as the mixture and proportion of this leaven, is not always the fame, the fermentations do not always terminate in the fame production. For which reafon the emanations of the fame foil cannot be always the fame in the fame country ; but muft be fubject to divers alterations.

Experience adds a great weight to this argument. Does the very fame earth emit every year the fame quantity of thofe exhalations, which form the matter

of

of thunder and lightning? As there are fome countries more fubject to thunder, than others, fo there
are fome years in which it thunders ten times oftner
than in others. There were hardly two claps of
thunder heard at Paris in the fummer of 1716; but it
thundered thirty times and upwards the fummer of
1717. The fame thing happens with refpect to
earthquakes. Are all years equally pluvious in the
fame country? 'Tis eafy to fee in the Almanacks of
the Obfervatory the difference there is in the quantity of rain which falls at Paris in the courfe of two
different years. This difference amounts fometimes
to very near two thirds. We cannot attribute the inequality which is obfervable in the eruptions of vul-
canos or fiery mountains, to any other caufe but to
the variety of fermentations which are continually
working in the bofom of the earth. 'Tis well known,
that thefe formidable mountains vomit more fire fome
years than others, and that they are fometimes a confiderable while without any eructations at all. In
fine, are all years equally wholfome, pluvious, win-
dy, cold, warm, in the fame country?

The fun and the emanations of the earth decide
in France, as well as elfewhere, the temperature of
different years; for we cannot affign any other
caufe, unlefs we fhould have recourfe to the influence
of the ftars. Now out of thefe two caufes, there is one
of them that never varies its action, that is the fun.
We muft therefore attribute the immenfe difference
we obferve in France between the temperature of two
different years, to the variation that happens in the
emanations of the earth. I fay that the action of the
fun does not vary. It mounts and defcends at Paris

ris every year at the fame height. If there be fome difference in its elevation, 'tis fenfible only to modern aftronomers, and it can produce nô other difference between the fummer of two years, than that which is obferved between the fummers of Senlis and Paris. The diftance there is between Paris and Senlis from North to South, amounts to the greater elevation which the fun may have one year at Paris, than another.

The difference in the temperature of years is quite another fort of variation. Some fummers at Paris are intolerably hot ; others are fcarce a degree different from cold weather. 'Tis frequently colder on midfummer day, than it was fix weeks before. The winter is fometimes very rigid in the fame city ; and the froft lafts forty days fucceffively. Other years the winter flides away without three confecutive days of froft. In fome years there falls twenty two inches of rain-water at Paris : [a] Other years there does not fall eight. Some years the winds are more frequent and violent than others : The fame may be obferved of every country : For all of them admit of a different temperature of years. 'Tis true that in fouthern climates, the feafons of rain and heat are not fo irregular as in our parts. Thefe heats and rains, more or lefs violent, generally come pretty near on the fame days ; wherefore the caufe varies indeed in thofe countries, but is not fo capricious as in France.

But, (fome will fay) tho' the fun afcends every year to the fame height, may not there be fome obftruction, fuch as a fpot, which may flacken his ac-

[a] *See the Almanacks of the Obfervatory.*

tion

tion in some years, more than in others? If so, he would have the greatest share in producing those variations, whose cause you go in search of into the bosom of the earth.

My answer is, that experience will not permit us to impute this variation to the sun. There would be a kind of rule in this irregularity, if it pro-ceeeded from the remisness of the action of the sun ; I mean that all countries would feel this irre-gularity in proportion to their distance from the line, and that the sun's elevation would constantly decide the degree of heat, let it be what it will in a parti-cular year. Thus a warmer summer than usual at Paris, would suppose a summer unusually warm at Madrid. A very mild winter at Paris, would sup-pose milder weather than usual at Madrid. But the thing is otherwise. The winter of 1699 and 1700 was very mild at Paris, and very rigid at Madrid. It froze fifteen days successively at Madrid, and not two days successively at Paris. The summer of 1714 was very dry and warm at Paris ; the same summer was exceeding rainy and tolerably cold in Lombardy. The day of the summer solstice is sometimes colder than the day of the equinox. Thus the variation of the temperature of years is such that it cannot be attributed to the sun. We must therefore impute it to a particular cause in each country, that is, to the difference of the emanations of the earth. 'Tis this also which renders some years more subject to distempers than others.

—— *Ipsâ sæpe coorta*
De terrâ surgunt. ——— LUCRET. l. 6.

There

There are fome epidemical diforders which rife infenfibly out of the ground, but there are others
which we fee ftatt up, as it were, of a fudden.
Such are the difeafes which break out in places, where
there have been lately great earthquakes, which
places were very wholefome before thefe fubterraneous
commotions.   The firft *ftratum* or cover of the earth
is compofed of common clay, ftones, flints, and
fand.   Thefe wife nature has employed to cover the
fecond *ftratum*, compofed of minerals and fat
earth, whofe juices contribute to the fecundity of
the outward foil.   Thefe juices either afcend into
the tubes of plants, or elfe they rife in the air, after
having been rarefied or filtered thro' the firft *ftratum*
of the earth, and there they form that aerial nitre,
which falling afterwards upon the ground, from
whence it fprung, contributes fo much to its fertility.   Now when there happens to be any of thofe
great earthquakes, feveral parts of this fecond *ftratum* are laid open, and expofed to the immediate action of the air and fun, which finding no interpofi-
tion, loofens and attracts too large a quantity of
molecula. Befides, thefe *molecula* being as yet too
coarfe, ought not to have rifen in the air, till
they had been rarefied by paffing thro' the firft *ftratum*, as thro' a fieve.   Thus the air of that part of
the country becomes infected, and continues fo till
the uncovered earth is exhaufted of a part of its
juices, or till the duft which is continually wafted by
the winds, has covered it with a new cruft.

But, as we have obferved already, there are fome
epidemical diftempers, which rife infenfibly, as it
were, out of the earth, without any perceptible
I   change.

change. Such are the peftilential maladies which break out fometimes in a country without being imported from other parts ; the caufe whereof can be nothing elfe but the alterations which happen in the emanations of the earth.

C H A P. XIX.

That the difference we obferve in the genius of people of the fame country in different ages, muft be attributed to the variations of the air.

I CONCLUDE therefore from what has been hitherto fet forth, that as the difference of the character of nations is attributed to the different qualities of the air of their refpective countries ; in like manner the changes which happen in the manners and genius of the inhabitants of a particular country, muft be imputed to the alterations of the qualities of the air of that fame country. Wherefore as the difference obfervable between the French and Italians, is affigned to the difference there is between the air of France and Italy ; fo the fenfible difference between the manners and genius of the French of two different ages, muft be attributed to the alteration of the qualities of the French air. As the quality of our air varies in fome refpects, and continues unvaried in others, it enfues that the French in all ages will have a general character which will diftinguifh them from other nations ; tho' this will not prevent a difference between

the

the French of different ages. 'Tis thus that wines have a particular tafte in each foil, which they always preferve, tho' they are not always of equal goodnefs. Hence the Italians, for inftance, will be evermore fitter for painting and poetry, than the inhabitants of the provinces bordering on the Baltick. But as the caufe which produces this alteration between nations, is fubject to feveral changes, it feems that fome generations in Italy muft have greater talents for excelling in thefe arts, than others.

The whole queftion concerning the pre-eminence between the ancients and moderns, fays the great defender of the latter [a], *being once rightly underftood, is reducible to this point; whether or no the trees which grew formerly in our fields, were larger than thofe in our days.* Methinks, continues he, *that the fureft way of deciding this point is to confult natural philofophy, who has the fecret of abridging a great many difputes which Rhetoric would protract to eternity.* Let us confult her, I freely give my confent. What anfwer does fhe give us ? She tells us two things. The firft is, that fome plants have in all times attained a greater perfection in one country than in another : The fecond, that even in the fame country trees and plants do not produce every year fruit of equal goodnefs.

We may apply to years what Virgil fays of countries, that all their productions are not alike excellent.

— *Non omnis fert omnia tellus.*

The caufe of this effect fhews an activity to which we may attribute the difference obfervable in

[a] FONTENELLE, Digreffion on the ancients.

the fpirit and genius of nations and ages.   Does it
not operate fenfibly on the fpirit of men, by rendering the temperature of climates as various as we
fee it in different countries and years ? Is not the
temperature of the climate either very prejudicial
to the phyfical education of children, or exceeding favorable ? Why fhould we not allow, that
children educated in France in a particular feries
of years, remarkable for a happy temperature,
have a better confttruction of brains, than fuch
as have been bred there during a fucceffion of
years, noted for intemperature ? Does not every
body attribute the capacity of the Florentines and
the ftupidity of the people of Bergamo, to the difference there is between the air of Bergamo and
Florence ?

   But (fome will object) if thefe changes which you
fuppofe to happen fucceffively in the earth, air, and
intellectual faculties, were real ; we fhould obferve in
the fame country fome alteration in the configuration
of human bodies. Wherefore the change you imagine happens within them, would be accompanied
with a fenfible alteration in their external parts.

   My anfwer is in the firft place grounded on all
that has been faid before, that the caufe which is
powerful enough to act on the brains, may not be fo
ftrong perhaps as to alter the ftature of the body.
Secondly, that were we to make in France, for inftance, an exact and continued obfervation on the fize
and ftrength of bodies, perhaps we fhould find, that
there are fome generations of men who are bigger
and robufter than others. Very likely we fhould difcover that there are fome ages, in which the human
fpecies

fpecies continually improves, and others in which it declines. When we obferve that our military people find the weight of a cuirafs and helmet an infupportable burthen, whereas a whole complete fuit of armour did not appear too great a weight to our anceftors ; when we compare the fatigues they muft have undergone in the wars of the Crufades, to the delicacy of our camps ; is it not very natural for us to fall into that opinion ?

It muft not be alledged, that 'tis the foftnefs of education which enervates the body: Is it only in our days that fathers and mothers are too fond of their children ? Have not children of all ranks and conditions been bred up by their parents in former times, as they are at prefent? Is it not becaufe children are born with a more delicate conftitution, that experience fupplies us with more fcrupulous precautions for their prefervation ? 'Tis natural for parents to have the fame care and attention in the phyfical education of their children, as they remember they themfelves ftood in need of: 'Tis natural for them to judge of their delicacy, by what they felt themfelves in their infancy. Experience alone, by fhewing us that thefe cares are no longer fufficient, can make us think, that we muft employ more attention and management for the prefervation of our children than was taken for ourfelves. Does not the impulfe of nature, which is very feldom refifted, render thofe exercifes that ftrengthen the body, amiable even in our days to fuch as have a fufficient fhare of health to go through them ? Why therefore does the generality of mankind in our days neglect them ? In fine, does

our

our foftnefs and effeminacy proceed from our kind of living ; or is it becaufe we are born with weaker ftomachs than our anceftors, that every one in his ftation feeks for new preparations of aliments, and eafier nourifhment ; and that the abftinences which thofe very anceftors found no great difficulty in obferving, are in our days abfolutely impracticable with refpect to one third of the world ? Why fhould we not think, that 'tis the phyfical part which prefcribes laws to the moral ? I am therefore apt to imagine, that the kind of life, for inftance, the cuftom of wearing more or lefs cloaths in particular feafons, which takes place fucceffively in the fame country, depends on the vigor of our bodies, which inables them to inure themfelves to more or lefs cold, according as they are more or lefs robuft. About fifty years ago, people were not fo warmly clad in France during the winter, as they are at prefent, becaufe their bodies at that time were generally more robuft and lefs fenfible of the injuries of the cold. *I have obferved*, fays Sir John Chardin [a], *in my travels, that as our manners follow the temperament of the body, purfuant to Gallien's obfervation, fo the temperament of the body follows the quality of the climate ; infomuch that the cuftoms or habits of people are not the effect of mere caprice, but of fome natural caufe or neceffity, which is not difcovered till after a very exact refearch.* When our bodies grow weaker and more fenfible of the injuries of the air, it follows of courfe, that people change fomething in their manners and cuftoms, as they would,

[a] Travels to Perfia, l. 2. p. 275.

were

were the climate to be altered : Their wants vary alike by either of the changes.

There are old folks in our days who affirm, that a certain court was composed of handsomer women and better built men, than another court peopled with the descendants of the former. Let us but enter into an exact inquiry of a hundred families in particular ages, and we shall find fourscore, in which the son is of an inferior size to that of his father. The race of mankind would degenerate in process of time into pigmies, if those days of decline and degeneracy of size, were not succeeded by times, in which the body is raised again to its former stature. Thus the weak and robust generations seem to have an alternate succession.

We can attribute likewise the difference which is observed between the behaviour and politeness of different ages, to no other cause, but to the changes which happen in the qualities of the air of the same country. There have been times, when it was an easy matter to prevail upon the principal men of a nation to quit their families. It was then no difficult task to persuade them to go in quest of military glory a thousand leagues from their own country, in contempt of the fatigues of a long journey, which to their soft posterity would appear like the labors of Hercules. 'Tis because (some will say) it was the fashion at that time to engage in such expeditions. But it would be impossible to introduce such fashions in our days : They cannot be established but by the help, as it were, of physical conjunctures. Can any one imagine, that were the most eloquent preacher in our times to announce

a cru-

a crufade, he would find a great many barons to follow him *beyond fea*.

C H A P. XX.

Of the difference of manners and inclinations
in people of the fame country in different
ages.

THERE are likewife ages, whofe events
make us imagine, that fome phyfical alteration has happened in the conftitution of mankind.
Such are thofe, wherein men, remarkable in other
refpects for politenefs and even learning, abandon
themfelves to moft unnatural actions with a fhock-
ing facility. This was the cafe of the French nation during the reigns of Charles IX and Henry III.
Every perfonage, that makes any thing of a figure
in the hiftory of Charles IX and in that of his brothers, even to the very clergy, died by a violent
death. The lords of that time, fuch as marfhal
St André, the conftable de Montmorenci, prince
Condé, and the duke of Joyeufe, were flain in battle, perifhed by affaffination and villany. The blows
were given by men that knew them, and who aimed
at their life in particular ; and we even know the
names of thofe that murdered them. I know not by
what fatality Henry II, the three kings his children,
and Henry IV, who fucceeded one another immediately, died all five by a violent death ; a misfortune
which happened not to any of our kings of the third
race, tho' moft of them reigned in very difficult

I   times,

times, and when men were more unpolished than in the sixteenth century. We have seen civil wars in France in the seventeenth century, and parties as much inflamed and animated against one another under Lewis XIII and Lewis XIV, as it was possible for the factions that followed the dukes of Guise or the admiral de Coligni in the preceding century ; and yet the history of the latter commotions has not been full of those poisonings, assassinates, and other tragic events so common in France under the latter princes of the branch of Valois.

Nor will it avail to say, that the motive of religion which influenced the civil wars during the reign of the Valois, poisoned people's minds ; a motive which did not affect our last civil wars. I should say for answer, that as the precept of loving one's enemies is not contested either by Rome or Geneva, it follows of consequence, that whosoever engages sincerely in either cause, ought to have a horror for murder or assassination. It was a wicked policy, seconded by the spirit of the age, which induced people whose whole religion (to make use of the expression of the times) consisted in a red or white scarf, to perpetrate such flagitious villanies. If any one should reply, that those wretches, tho sincere Catholics or Huguenots, were people of wild extravagant imaginations, and, in a word, honest fanatics ; this would be espousing my sentiment. As there were no such persons during the last civil wars, we must conclude, that there are times, in which men of this character, who always find occasions of running into the like excesses, are commoner than at other times. This

Q 4

is admitting of a difference of spirits in the same country, but in different ages.

In effect, were such rivers of blood spilt on account of the herefy of Arrius, which raifed fuch difputes and commotions in Chriftendom ? There had been feveral contefts in France in point of religion, before the Reformation ; but except the wars againft the *Albigenfes*, thofe difputes never occafioned the effufion of French blood ; becaufe there was not that fame acrimony in their humors, nor the fame inflammation in their minds.

Whence comes it, that men in fome ages are feized with an invincible averfion to all mental application, and have fo little an inclination to ftudy, that every method which is ufed in order to excite them to it, remains a long time ineffectual ? The moft painful exercifes of the body, and the greateft dangers, do not frighten them fo much as application. What privileges and advantages have not our kings been obliged to grant to graduates and the clergy in the twelfth and thirteenth centuries, in order to encourage the French to fhake off that extreme grofs ignorance, into which they had been plunged fo long by fome unknown fatality ? There was fo great a neceffity at that time for exciting people to ftudy, that in fome countries a part of the benefit of the clergy was extended to fuch as knew how to read. In fact, it was a common thing to fee great lords, who could not fign their own names, or who wrote them without knowing the power of the characters of which they were compofed, but copied only from the pattern fet before them. On the other hand, it was ufual to fee men, who were ready

ready to face the greateſt dangers, or to engage in the moſt laborious exerciſes. 'Tis upwards now of a century ſince people have had a ſtrong inclination for ſtudy, and for practiſing the liberal arts, tho' they have not had the ſame encouragement as formerly. Men of an indifferent ſhare of learning, and perſons who profeſs the liberal arts with ſlender or mean capacities, are grown ſo common, that ſome are whimſical enough to think, there ought to be as much care taken at preſent to limit the number of ſuch as profeſs the liberal arts, as there was formerly to augment it. Their number, ſay they, is increaſed too high, in proportion to thoſe who profeſs the mechanic arts ; and the diſproportion between them is become prejudicial to ſociety. *As we are ſo unfortunate*, ſays Seneca[a], *as to be luxurious in every thing elſe, ſo we are troubled alſo with an intemperance of letters.*

In fine, how comes it that we obſerve in the ſame country ſome ages ſo ſubject to, and others almoſt intirely exempt from, epidemical diſorders ; if this difference does not proceed from the alterations that happen in the qualities of the air, which varies in different ages ? We reckon four general plagues in France from 1530 to 1636. During the ſucceeding fourſcore years to 1718, very few cities in France have been viſited with this ſcourge. 'Tis upwards of fourſcore years ſince the Lazerettos of the greateſt part of this kingdom have not been opened. Strange diſtempers riſe in particular ages, and after ſhewing them-

[a] *Ut omnium rerum ſic litterarum quoque intemperantiâ laboramus.* SENECA epiſt. 106.

felves two or three times during a certain number of years, they difappear at laft for ever. Such were in France the *burning diftemper*, and the *cholic of Poitou*. When we fee fo many vifible effects of the alterations of the qualities of the air; when we have fo diftinct a knowledge that this alteration is real, and are even acquainted with the caufe thereof, can we forbear attributing thereto, the fenfible difference we obferve in the fame country between men of two different ages ? I conclude therefore with the words of Tacitus[a], " That the " world 'is fubject to changes and viciffitudes, " whofe periods are unknown to us; but their revolu- " tions bring back by an alternate fucceffion, po- " litenefs and barbarifm, as well as the talents of " mind, and the ftrength of body, and confe- " quently the increafe and decay of the arts and " fciences ; in the fame manner as the revolution " of the fun is attended with an alternate fuccef- " fion of feafons." 'Tis a confequence of the plan adopted by the Creator, and of the means he has chofen for its execution.

[a] *Rebus cunctis ineft quidam velut orbis, ut quemadmodum temporum vices, ita motum vertantur.* TACIT.

C H A P.

C H A P. XXI.

Of the manner in which the reputation of poets and painters is established.

I Intend to perform here the promise I made in the commencement of this work, to examine before I had done, the manner in which the reputation of painters and poets is established. Whatever my subject will oblige me here to say with respect to the success of verses and pictures, will serve for a further confirmation of what I have already observed relating to the most important and essential merit of these productions.

New performances are approved at first by judges of a very different character, that is, by men of the same profession, and by the public. They would be soon rated at their just value, were the public as capable of defending and maintaining their sentiment, as they know how to espouse the right party. But their judgment is easily perplexed by persons who make profession of the art, to whose jurisdiction the new production belongeth. Now these persons are frequently subject to make a false report of things, for reasons which we shall give hereafter. They therefore throw such a mist over the truth, that the public continues frequently for some time in a state of uncertainty or error. They do not know exactly what character the new work merits in a general consideration. They remain suspended with regard to the question, whether it be good or bad taken altogether, and they even sometimes give credit, but

only

only for a fhort time, to perfons of the profeffion that impofe upon them.

This firft time being elapfed, the public appraifes a work to its full value, and gives it the rank due to its merit, or condemns it to oblivion. 'Tis never deceived in this decifion, becaufe it judges difintereftedly, and likewife by a fenfible perception.

When I fay, that the public judgment is difintereſted, I do not pretend to affirm that one does not meet with fome whom friendfhip engages in favor of authors, and others who are prejudiced againft them by a particular averfion. But thefe are in fo fmall a number, in comparifon to difintereſted judges, that their prevention hath no great influence in the general fuffrage. A painter, and much more a poet (who generally is a great man in his own imagination, and frequently of that violent character of fpirit, as excludes any indifference of perfons) fancies to himfelf, that a great town, or a whole kingdom is peopled intirely with rivals or adorers of his merit. He has a notion that he has divided it into two factions, as much animated the one for him, and the other againft him, as the Guelfs and Gibellines were formerly for and againft the emperors; when actually there are not fifty who have declared either way, or who concern themfelves with any warmth in the fuccefs of his verfes. The greateft part of thofe whom he fuppofes to be abfolutely determined by fentiments of hatred or friendfhip, are very indifferent about the matter, and are difpofed to judge of the author by the comedy, and not of the comedy by the author.

They

They are ready to fpeak their opinion with as much freedom, as friends and fellow-boarders at the fame houfe give their fentiment with regard to a cook, whom the mafter of the houfe has a mind to make a trial of. This is a judgment which cannot be faid to be one of the leaft equitable in our country.

C H A P. XXII.

That the public judges right of poems and pictures in general. Of the fenfe we have to diftin-guifh the merit of thefe works.

THE public gives not only a difinterefted judgment of a work, but judges likewife what opinion we are to entertain of it in general, by means of the fenfe, and according to the impref-fion made thereon by the poem or picture. Since the chief end of poetry and painting is to move us, the productions of thefe arts can be valuable only in proportion as they touch and engage us. A work that is exquifitely moving, muft be an excellent piece, take it all together. For the fame reafon, a work which does not move and engage us, is good for nothing; and if it be not obnoxious to criticifm for trefpaffing againft rules, 'tis becaufe it may be bad, without any violation of rules; as on the contrary one full of faults againft rules, may be an excellent performance.

Now our fenfes inform us whether a work touches or makes a proper impreffion upon us, much better than all the differtations compofed by critics, to ex-

plain

plain its merit, and calculate its perfections and defects. The way of difcuffion and analyfis, which thofe gentlemen employ, is indeed very proper, when the point is to find out the caufes why a work pleafes or not; but this method is inferior to that of the fenfe, when we are to decide the following queftion: Does the work pleafe, or does it not? Is the piece good or bad in general? For thefe are both the fame thing. Reafon therefore ought not to intervene in a judgment which we pafs on a poem or picture in general, except it be to account for the decifion of our fenfes and to explain what faults hinder it from pleafing, and what charms are capable of rendering it engaging, Reafon will not permit us (if I may fay fo) to reafon on a queftion of this nature, unlefs it be defigned to juftify the judgment which the fenfe has paffed. The decifion of the queftion does not belong to the jurifdiction of reafon: This ought to fubmit to the judgment pronounced by fenfe, which is the competent judge of the queftion.

Do we ever reafon, in order to know whether a ragoo be good or bad; and has it ever entered into any body's head, after having fettled the geometrical principles of tafte, and defined the qualities of each ingredient that enters into the compofition of thofe meffes, to examine into the proportion obferved in their mixture, in order to decide whether the ragoo be good or bad? No, this is never practifed. We have a fenfe given us by nature to diftinguifh whether the cook acted according to the rules of his art. People tafte the ragoo, and tho' unacquainted with thofe rules, they are able to tell, whether

ther it be good or no.   The fame may be faid in fome refpect of the productions of the mind, and of pictures made to pleafe and move us.

We have a fenfe, which judges of the merit of works, that confift in the imitation of objects of a moving nature.   This is the very fenfe, which would have judged of the object, that the painter, poet, or mufician has imitated.   'Tis the eye, when we are to judge of the coloring of a picture.   'Tis the ear, when we are to decide, whether the accents of a recitative be moving, whether they agree with the words, and whether the mufic be melodious.   If we are to determine, whether the imitation we are entertained with in a poem or in the compofition of a picture, be capable of exciting our pity, and of moving us; the fenfe whofe province it is to judge thereof, is the very fenfe which would have been moved, and have judged of the object imitated.   'Tis that fixth fenfe we have within us, without feeing its organs.   'Tis a portion of ourfelves, which judges from what it feels, and which, to exprefs myfelf in Plato's words[a] determines, without confulting either rule or compafs. This is, in fine, what is commonly called fenfe or fenfitive perception.

The heart is agitated of itfelf, by a motion previous to all deliberation, when the object prefented is really affecting; whether this object has received its being from nature, or from an imitation made by art.   Our heart is made and organized for this very purpofe: Its operation therefore runs before our reafoning, as the action of the eye and ear

[a] De Repub. l 10.

precedes

precedes it in their fenfations. 'Tis as rare to fee men born without the fenfe here mentioned, as 'tis to meet with people born blind. *But it can be no more communicated by art,* fays Quintilian [a], *to thofe that have it not from nature, than the fenfe of tafte, or fmelling.* Wherefore imitations produce their effects, fo as to make us laugh or cry, and engage us, before our reafon has time to act or examine. We weep at a tragedy, before we have difcuffed whether the object which the poet prefents us, be naturally capable of moving, or whether it be well imitated. Our fenfe tells us its nature, before ever we have thought of inquiring into it. The fame inftinct which would force a figh from us, upon meeting a mother attending the funeral of an only fon, draws tears from us, when the ftage exhibits a faithful imitation of this melancholy event.

We know whether a poet has pitched upon a moving object, and whether he has properly imitated ; as we can tell, without reafoning, whether the painter has drawn a beautiful figure, or our friend's portrait be like the original. To judge whether this portrait has a likenefs, or no, muft we take the proportions of our friend's countenance, and compare them to thofe of the portrait ? The painters themfelves will acknowledge, that they have a fudden fenfe which goes before all examen, and that an excellent picture which they never faw before, makes fo quick an impreffion upon them, as enables them, before any difcuffion, to judge in general of its merit. This firft *Apprehenfion* is even fufficient to

---

[a] *Nec magis arte traditur, quam guftus aut adoratus.* QUINT. Inft. 1 5. c. 6.

give

give them a knowledge of the noble artift.

We are therefore in the right to fay, that if a perfon has but underftanding, he can judge of every thing, for here by underftanding we mean a juftnefs and delicacy of fenfe. Wherefore Monfieur Pafcal [a] had not properly digefted what he wrote, where he fays, *That thofe who judge of any work by rule, are with refpect to others, as a man, who has a watch, is with regard to the reft of the company that have none, when they want to know, what o' clock it is.* I fancy this is one of thofe thoughts which a little meditation would have made him explain; for every one knows that the work here mentioned is compofed of ideas, which Monfieur Pafcal committed to paper as they occurred to him, rather in order to examine than publifh them. After his deceafe they were printed juft in the condition in which they were found. When we are to decide the merit of a work that was made to move us, 'tis not the rules that are our watch, 'tis the impreffion we receive from the work. Our watch goes right, in proportion as our fenfe is delicate.

Boileau builds upon this reafon, when he affirms that the greateft part of profeft critics, who ftrive to fupply the defect of their fenfe by their knowledge of the rules, do not form as found a judgment of the merit of excellent works, as men of genius of the firft rank, who have not made fo exact a ftudy of thofe rules. *Give me leave to tell you,* fays he to Monfieur Perrault, *that even in our times, 'tis not, as you imagine, the Schrevelius's, the Pera-*

---

[a] P\fCHAL's *thou_h s.* chap 31.

redus's,

redus's, the Menagius's, nor, to express myself in Moliere's terms, the learned In I U S, who have the greatest relish for the beauties of Homer, Virgil, Horace, and Cicero. 'Tis your genius's of the first class, whom I have always seen most affected with reading those excellent authors: 'Tis your men of the most exalted situations. And if I were absolutely obliged to cite some of them, you would be surprized with the great names I should commit to paper: you would find among the rest not only the Lamoignons's, the Dagueffeaux's, the Trois-villes's, but likewise the Conde's, the Conti's and the Turenne's.

In effect, the ancient poets would be as much astonished to hear, what passages of their works the generality of their commentators are most displeased with, as if they were to know what Abbot de Marolles, and other translators of his rank, make them say sometimes. Are professors that have taught Logic all their lives, the propereft persons for knowing when a man speaks good sense, and reasons justly?

If the chief merit of poems and pictures were to consist in being conformable to written rules, one might then say that the best method of judging of their excellency, as also of the degree of esteem they ought to hold in the minds of men, would be certainly that of discussion and analysis. But the principal merit of poems and pictures is to please us. This is the chief end which painters and poets aim at, when they take so much pains to conform to the rules of their art. We are therefore able to judge whether they have succeeded, when we know whether their performance is affecting or no. One may

say

fay indeed, that a work, in which the effential rules are violated, cannot be pleafing. But this is better known, by judging from the impreffion made by that work, than by forming a judgment of it from the differtations of critics, who very feldom agree with refpect to the importance of each rule. Wherefore the public is capable of judging right with relation to verfes and pictures, without being acquainted with the rules of poetry and painting ; for, as Cicero [a] fays, *All men are capable of judging by the help of an inward fenfe, tho' unacquainted with rules, whether the productions of arts are good or bad, and whether the reafons they hear, be conclufive.*

Quintilian obferves in a work [b] which we have often cited, tho' not fo often as it deferves, *That 'tis not by reafoning we judge of works made to move and pleafe. We judge by an inward motion, which we know not how to explain : At leaft thofe who have hitherto endeavoured to explain it, have mifcarried in the attempt.*

The pit, without knowing the rules of dramatic poetry, forms as good a judgment of theatrical pieces, as thofe that belong to the profeffion. *The fame thing happens,* fays Abbot Aubignac, *with regard to the ftage as with refpect to eloquence ; the ignorant are as fenfible of their perfections as the learn-*

---

[a] *Omnes tacito quodam fenfu fine ulla arte aut ratione, quæ fint in artibus ac rationibus prava aut recta, dijudicant.* Cic. de orat. l. 3.

[b] *Non ratione aliqua, fed motu nefcio an inenarrabili judicatur. Neque hoc ab ullo fatis explicari puto, licet multi tentaverint.* Quint. Inft. 1 6.

R 2

ed, tho' they are not so well informed of the reason of these perfections.

Hence it comes that eminent artists think proper sometimes to consult persons, who are strangers to the rules of their arts, but are capable nevertheless of giving their decisions with respect to the effect of a work composed for moving mankind ; because of their being endowed with a very sensible disposition. Such people as these decide frequently even before they speak, and without thinking of passing a decision. But as soon as the motions of their heart, which operates mechanically, are manifested by their gesture and countenance, they become, as it were, a touch-stone, which distinctly indicates, whether the principal merit of a work that is shewn or read to them, be wanting or not. Wherefore tho' these persons are incapable of contributing to the perfection of a work by their advice, or of giving even a methodical account of their sentiment, their decision nevertheless may be safely depended upon. There are several examples of what I have here advanced ; and 'tis well known that Malherbe and Moliere used to read their verses to their servant maids, to try *whether they would take*, to use the favorite expression of our dramatic poets.

But there are some beauties (it will be objected) in works of this kind, whose value must absolutely lye hid from the ignorant. For instance, a person who does not know, that the same Pharnaces who joined with the Romans against his father Mithridates, was ignominiously stript of his territories some years after by Julius Cæsar, is not struck with the beauty

3

beauty of thefe prophetic verfes, which Racine puts into the mouth of Mithridates juft as he is expiring.

Tôt ou tard il faudra que Pharnace périffe,
Fiez-vous aux Romains du foin de fon fupplice.

At length Pharnaces muft receive his doom,
Th' avenging hand impends, I fee, from Rome.

Ignorant people cannot therefore judge of a poem in general, fince they underftand only a part of its beauties.

I intreat the reader not to forget the firft anfwer I am going to make to this objection. 'Tis that I do not mean the lower clafs of people by the public capable of paffing judgment on poems or pictures, or of deciding the meafure of their excellence. The word *public* is applicable here to fuch perfons only, as have acquired fome lights, either by reading or by being converfant with the world. Thefe are the only perfons who are capable of afcertaining the rank of poems and pictures ; tho' in fome excellent works one meets with beauties that are capable of making an impreffion upon the vulgar. But as they have no knowledge of any other works of the fame kind, they are unqualify'd to determine the degree of excellence of a poem that commands their tears, or of fixing the rank it ought to have among other poems. The public therefore here in queftion, is limited to perfons that read, and have a knowledge of theatrical entertainments, who fee or hear people talk of pictures, and who have acquired by fome means or other, that difcernment which is called the *Tafte of Comparifon,* whereof we fhall prefently have occafion to fpeak more at large. The reader, by attend-

ing

ing to times and places, as well as to the nature of
the work, which happens to be examined, will soon
conceive much better than I am able to explain, to
what ftage of capacity, to what degree of knowledge, and to what fituation or condition, the public here meant, ought to be reftrained. For example, every one that is able to pafs a found judgment on a French tragedy, is not equally capable of
forming a right opinion of the Æneid, or of
any other Latin poem. The public capable of
judging in our days with regard to the merit of
Homer, is not near fo numerous as the public that
is able to judge of the Æneid. The public judgment is therefore reftrained, according to the nature
of the work in queftion. The word *public* is likewife limited more or lefs, according to the times and
places fpoken of. There are fome ages and towns,
where the neceffary lights for judging properly of
a work by its effect, are more generally diffufed
than in others. A particular rank of citizens, who
have not the advantage of thefe lights in a country-
town, have them in a metropolis. A rank that was
deprived of them at the commencement of the fixteenth century, is favoured with them at the clofe of
the feventeenth. For inftance, fince the eftablifh-
ing of operas, the number capable of giving
their judgment on mufic, is confiderably increafed at
Paris. But as I have already faid, I am not afraid
that my reader will be miftaken with regard to the
extent, it will be proper to give the fignification of
the word *public*, purfuant to the occafions on which
I fhall employ it.

My

My fecond anfwer to the objection drawn from the verfes of Mithridates, is, that the public does not finifh in one day the trial of works that have real merit. Before verdict is given, they muft lie fome time, as it were, before the court. Now as foon as the merit of a work draws the public attention, thofe beauties which they cannot comprehend without the affiftance of fome explication, do not pafs unobferved. This explication is foon handed about, and defcends to the very loweft clafs, who account for them afterwards with the author, in giving a general definition of his work. Men have at leaft as ftrong a defire of telling what they know, as of learning what they know not. Befides, I do not imagine that the public would judge amifs of a work in general, were even fome of thefe beauties to efcape them. 'Tis not on beauties of this fort, that a fenfible author, who writes in a modern language, grounds the fuccefs of his poem. The tragedies of Corneille and Racine do not contain four fuch ftrokes as that juft now mentioned of Mithridates. If a piece is damned, we may venture to fay, it would have met with the fame fate, were every member of the public to have a thorough knowledge of thofe veiled beauties. Two or three paffages which they overlooked, and which would have pleafed them if they had rightly underftood their meaning, would not prevent their being tired with fifteen hundred others, which they underftood to perfection.

As the chief aim of poetry and painting is to move and pleafe us, every man who is not abfolutely ftupid, muft feel the effect of good verfes, and

R 4   fine

fine pictures. All men ought to be in possession of a right of giving their suffrage, when the question to be decided is, whether poems or pictures produce their proper effect. Wherefore, when the affair in hand is to judge of the general effect of a work, the painter and poet have as little right to object against those who are unpractised in their art, as a surgeon would be intitled to refuse the testimony of a person who had undergone an operation, when the point in dispute is only to know whether the operation had been painful ; merely under the pretext of the patient's ignorance in anatomy. What opinion should we have of a musician, were he to maintain, that such as do not understand music, are incapable of judging whether the minuet he has composed, be agreable or not? When an orator sets his auditory a yawning and sleeping, is it not agreed upon, that he made a bad discourse, without examining whether the persons he set asleep, understood any thing of rhetoric. Men convinced by instinct, that the merit of an oration, as well as of a poem or a picture, must come within the reach of sense, give credit to the auditor's relation, and depend upon his decision, as soon as they know him to be a sensible person. Were even one of the spectators of a decried tragedy, to give a bad account of the reasons of its being tiresome to him, this would not hinder us from paying a deference to the general sense of the public. We should still continue to look upon it as a bad performance, tho' the reasons of its badness were ever so ill explained. We believe the man, tho' we do not comprehend his arguments.

What

What is it but the general fenfe, which decides that fome colors are naturally gayer than others? Thofe who pretend to explain this truth by principles, advance nothing but what is very obfcure, and beyond the reach of moft capacities: And yet the thing itfelf is looked upon as certain all over the univerfe. It would be as ridiculous in the Indies, to maintain that black is a gay color, as it would be at Paris, to affert that a light green or pink were melancholy colors.

True it is, that with refpect to the merit of pictures the public is not fo competent a judge, as in relation to the merit of poems. The perfection of a great part of the beauties of a picture, for inftance, that of the defign, is not rightly perceptible but to painters, or *connoiffeurs* who have ftudied painting as much as the artifts themfelves. But we fhall inquire elfewhere, into the beauties of a picture that admit of the public for a competent judge, and thofe beauties that cannot be appraifed to their juft value, but by fuch as underftand the rules of painting.

C H A P.

C H A P. XXIII.

*That the way of difcuffion is not fo proper for
diflinguifhing the merit of poems and pictures, as that of fenfe.*

THE more we advance in years, and improve
in reafon, the lefs credit we are apt to give
to philofophical arguments, and the more confidence we have in fenfe and practice. Experience
teaches us, that we are very feldom deceived by a
diftinct report of our fenfes, and that the habit of
reafoning and judging from this report, leads us to a
plain and fure practice; whereas we are deceived
every day in philofophical operations, that is, in
laying down general principles, and in drawing
from thence a chain of conclufions. With refpect
to the arts, their principles are very numerous,
and nothing is eafier than to be miftaken in the
choice of that which we are willing to ftate as the
moft important. May not this principle change,
according to the kind of work we have a mind to
apply to? We may give alfo a greater extent to
a principle, than it ought naturally to have; and we
are apt very often to efteem an unprecedented thing
impoffible. This is enough to throw us out of the
right road, the very third fyllogifm: The fourth
therefore becomes a fenfible fophifm, and the fifth
contains a conclufion, whofe falfity ftrikes even
thofe who are incapable of making an analyfis of
the reafoning, and of tracing it to the very fource
of its error. In fine, whether it be that natural

I   philofo-

philofophers or critics ftate their principles wrong, or whether they do not infer their conclufions right, they find themfelves miftaken every day, tho' they give the ftrongeft affurances, that their method is an infallible guide to truth.

How many errors hath experience difcovered in philofophical reafonings, which were held in paft ages for folid arguments? As many as fhe will in future times difcover in thofe reafonings, which are fuppofed in our days to be founded on unconteftable truths. As we reproach the ancients for having believed the dreadful abfurdity of a vacuum and the influence of the ftars, our pofterity will object fome time or another againft the like errors, which reafon would attempt in vain to unfold, but experience and time will foon be capable of detecting.

The two moft illuftrious philofophical affemblies in Europe, the Academy of fciences at Paris, and the Royal fociety at London, have not thought proper to adopt, or build any general fyftem of phyfics. By conforming to the opinion of chancellor Bacon, they adhere to no fyftem, left the defire of juftifying it, fhould bewitch the eyes of the obfervers, and make them fee the experiments, not as they really are, but as they ought to be in order to add weight to an opinion which they have attempted to fpread for true. Thefe two famous academies are therefore fatisfied with verifying the facts and inferting them in their regifters, convinced that nothing is eafier for our reafon than to ftumble, as foon as it attempts to go two paces beyond the point, to which it has been conducted by experience. 'Tis therefore from the hands of

expe-

experience that thefe focieties expect a general fyftem. What fhall we think of thofe fyftems of poetic rules, which, fo far from being grounded on experience, attempt point-blank to contradict it, and
pretend to demonftrate to us, that works admired
by all who have been capable of underftanding them
thefe two thoufand years, are very far from deferving admiration ?

The more we know ourfelves and the reft of
mankind, the lefs, as I have already obferved,
we confide in fpeculative decifions, even in matters
that in rigor are fufceptible of geometrical demonftra-
tion. M. Leibnitz would never venture to let his
coachman drive thro' a place where the fellow
even when fafting affures him, that he muft abfolutely be overturned ; tho' a mathematician had
demonftrated to that learned man, by a geometrical analyfis of the declivity and height of the
way, as alfo by the weight of the vehicle, that
the thing could not happen. We are apt to believe our own common fenfe preferable to philofophy, becaufe the latter is eafier impofed upon than
the former.

If there is an art that depends on philofophical
fpeculation, 'tis that of navigation. Let us afk
our navigators, whether the old pilots, whofe whole
knowledge confifts in experience, and in what little
they have learnt by rote, do not give a better guefs
in a long voyage, what place or latitude the fhip actually fteers her courfe in, than your frefh-water
mathematicians, tho' the latter have ftudied for ten
years together, all the auxiliary fciences to the art of
navigation. They will anfwer, that they never faw
thefe

thefe mathematicians fet pilots right with regard to the eftimation, except in their printed relations ; on which occafion they may very well alledge the an-fwer of the lion in the fable, who was defired to take notice of a Low-relieve, where a man had flung a lion on the ground ; to which he replied that lions had no fculptors.

When archduke Albert undertook the famous fiege of Oftend, he fent for Pompey Targon, the greateft mathematician of his time, but without experience, to make him his principal engineer. But Pompey Targon was very far from anfwering the archduke's ex-pectation. Not one of his machines fucceeded, and they were obliged to difmifs him, after he had caufed an immenfe expence and effufion of blood to very little purpofe. They gave the direction of the fiege afterwards to the famous Ambrofe Spinola, who had only genius and experience, which however fucceeded. This great general had never ftudied any of thofe fciences that are requifite to form an engineer, when he took a difguft at feeing another noble Ge-noefe preferred to him in the purchafe of the palace Turfi at Genoa. This fet him upon going into the ar-my in the Spanifh Netherlands, at a very advanced period of life, in comparifon to the age in which people generally make their apprenticefhip in the art of war.

When the great prince Condé laid fiege to Thion-ville after the battle of Rocroi [a], he fent for Rober-val, the moft knowing perfon in the mathematics at that time, and who died royal profeffor in this fcience, as a perfon capable of advifing him with re-

[a] in 1643.

fpect

spect to the siege he was going to form. Roberval proposed nothing that was practicable; wherefore they were obliged to send him to Metz, to wait there till other engineers had taken the place. 'Tis plain from Boccalini's books, that he was acquainted with the moft ingenious obfervations the ancients and moderns have left us, on the great art of governing. Pope Paul V, from the notion he had of his fame and abilities, intrufted him with the government of a fmall town, which a man that did not underftand a word of Latin might very well know how to manage. The pontif was obliged after three months adminiftration, to recall the celebrated author of the political commentaries upon Tacitus, and of the famous book intitled the *Touch-ftone*.

A phyfician at twenty five years of age, is as well perfuaded of the truth of the phyfical reafonings, which pretend to unfold the manner of the operating of the bark in the cure of intermitting fevers, as he may be of the efficacy of the remedy. A phyfician at fixty is convinced of the truth of the fact which he has feen feveral times; but he gives no manner of credit to the explications of the effect of the remedy. Is it the knowledge in fimples, and fkill in anatomy, or is it the experience of a phyfician, that determines a perfon who has fome experience himfelf, in the choice of his phyfician? Charles II king of England ufed to fay, that of all the Frenchmen that ever he knew, Monfieur Gourville was the man of the beft fenfe. This Gentleman wanted a phyfician; and the moft celebrated members of the faculty made intereft to be admit-

ted

ted to affift him in that capacity. Without minding their recommendations he fent a trufty fervant to the door of the college one day when the faculty was affembled, with orders to bring him, without any further inquiry, the·phyfician whofe complexion he fhould judge to be moft like to that of his mafter. The fervant in conformity to his orders, brought him juft fuch a man as he wanted, and the fcheme anfwered his expectation. Monfieur Gourville's determination was in favor of experience, which with refpect to him was ftill more deferving of that appellation.

The late Monfieur de Tournefort, one of the worthieft members of the academy of fciences, fays, with refpect to a difficult pafs, which he got over[a], *For my part, I abandoned myfelf intirely to the guidance of my horfe, and found it anfwered better than if I had ftrove to manage him myfelf. An automaton that follows naturally the laws of mechanics, conducts itfelf much better on thefe occafions, than the moft knowing perfon in mechanics, who fhould attempt to practife the rules he has learnt in his cabinet, were he even a member of the academy of fciences.* Obferve, 'tis the experience of a horfe, that is, of a machine in the opinion of this author, which is preferred here to the reafonings of an academic. This horfe (give me leave to joke a little) carries us a great way. Tho' the counfellors are generally more learned than the judges, yet 'tis very common for the former to be miftaken in the conjectures they form of the iffue of a law-fuit. The judges who have read only a fmall number of books, but whofe daily experience ac-

[a] Voyage to the Levant, lett. 11.

quaints

quaints them with the motives that determine the tribunals in the trial of a procefs, are very feldom miftaken in their predictions with refpect to the event of a caufe.

Now if there is any fubject, in which reafon ought to be filent when oppofed to experience, 'tis certainly in thofe queftions which may be raifed concerning the merit of a poem. 'Tis when we want to know, whether a poem pleafes or not ; whether, generally fpeaking, it be an excellent or indifferent performance. The general principles we go upon, in reafoning confiftently with refpect to the merit of a poem, are exceeding few. There is fometimes room for exception againft a principle that feems the moft univerfal ; and a great many of them are fo vague, that one may maintain with equal probability, that the poet has either obferved or fwerved from them. The importance of thofe principles depends alfo on an infinite number of circumftances of times and places in which the poet has wrote. In fhort, as the principal aim of poetry is to pleafe, 'tis obvious that its principles are oftner arbitrary than thofe of other arts, becaufe of the various taftes of thofe for whom the poet compofes. Tho' the beauties of the art of rhetoric ought to be much lefs arbitrary than thofe of poetry, neverthelefs Quintilian [a] fays, *that it has never fubmitted but to a very fmall number of thofe principles and rules, which are called general*

---

[a] *Propter quæ mihi femper moris fuit quàm miminè alligare me ad præcepta quæ καθολικὰ vocantur, id eft, ut dicamus quomodo poffumus, univerfalia vel perpetualia. Raro enim reperitur hoc genus, ut non labefactari parte aliqua aut fubrui poffit.* QUINT. Inft. l. 2. c. 14.

and

and universal ; *for there are hardly any of them whose validity is not contested for very good reasons.*

: 'Tis therefore almoft impoffible to fet a juft value upon what may refult from the happy irregularities of a poet, as likewife from his attention to certain principles, and his negligence in deviating from others. In fine, what a vaft number of faults are generally forgiven becaufe of the beauty of his ftyle ? Another thing to be obferved is, that after having reafoned and concluded well for ourfelves, we fhould be liable to draw a bad conclufion for others, who might happen to be exactly the very perfons, for whom the poet compofed his work. Would a geometrical eftimation of the merit of Ariofto made by a Frenchman in our days, be of any weight with the Italians of the fixteenth century ? Would the rank which a French writer of differtations fhould chance to give Ariofto in confequence of a poetic analyfis of his poem, be acknowledged to be that which is due to *Meffer Lodovico* ? What a vaft number of calculations and combinations a perfon muft make before he is capable of drawing a juft confequence ! A great volume *in folio* would be fcarce fufficient to contain the exact analyfis of Racine's Phædra according to this method, and to eftimate this piece by way of examen. The difcuffion would be as much liable to error, as it would be tirefome to the writer, and difagreable to the reader. That which the analyfis in vain attempts to find, is immediately difcovered by our fenfe.

S The

The sense here spoken of, is in all men; but as they have not eyes and ears of equal goodness, so their sense is not equally perfect. Some have it better than others, either because their organs are naturally better compofed, or because they have improved it by frequent use and experience. Such as these ought naturally to difcern fooner than others the merit or infignificancy of a work. 'Tis thus a person, that is clear-fighted, difcovers people diftinctly a hundred yards off, when those who are juft clofe to him, can hardly difcern the color of men's drefs that are approaching towards them. Were we to be directed by our firft motion, we fhould judge of the extent of other men's fenfes by our own. It happens therefore, that fhort-fighted folks hefitate fometimes before they acquiefce to the fenfe of one that fees better than themfelves; but as foon as the perfon who is moving forward, comes within a proportionable diftance, they are all of one opinion.

In like manner all that judge by fenfe, agree at laft with refpect to the effect and merit of a work. If a conformity of opinion be not eftablifhed amongft them fo foon as it ought, 'tis becaufe men, in giving their opinion with refpect to a poem or a picture, do not confine themfelves always to fay what they think, and to relate fincerely the impreffion it makes upon them. Inftead of fpeaking fimply and according to their own *apprehenfion,* the merit of which they are frequently unacquainted with, they attempt to decide by principles; and as the greateft part are incapable of explain-

I

ing

ing themfelves methodically, they perplex their decifions, and difturb one another in their judgments.
A little time reconciles them again to themfelves, as
well as to one another.

C H A P.   XXIV.

*Objection againft the folidity of the public judge-
ments, and anfwer to this objection.*

I BEGIN already, methinks, to hear a long
citation of errors, into which the public in all
ages and countries have fallen with regard to the
merit of thofe who have been invefted with high
dignities, or have exercifed particular profeffions.
How can you pretend (fome will fay) to make us
imagine there is any infallibility in an *appraifer* of
merit, that has been fo often miftaken with regard
to generals, minifters, and magiftrates, and fo often
obliged to retract his judgment?

I fhall make two replies to this objection, which
in reality is more impofing than folid. In the
firft place, the public is feldom miftaken, in de-
fining in general the abovementioned perfons as
an example of injuftice, tho' it may commend or
blame them unreafonably fometimes with regard to
a particular event. Let us explain this propofition.
The public does not judge of the merit of a general
from a fingle campaign, nor of that of a minifter
from one fole negotiation, nor of a phyfician from
the treatment of a fingle diftemper. Its judgment

S 2   is

is formed from feveral events and fucceffes. Now as unjuft as it would be to judge of the merit of the perfons here mentioned from one fingle fuccefs ; fo reafonable, methinks, it is to form a judgment of them from repeated fucceffes, as well as by comparing them to thofe of perfons who have had the management of affairs of the like nature.

A fingle lucky fuccefs, or even two, may be the effect of the power of conjunctures. 'Tis rare that luck alone can produce three happy events ; but when thefe fucceffes amount to a certain number, it would be madnefs to pretend they are merely the effect of hazard, and that the ability of the general or minifter is not at all concerned in them. The fame may be faid with regard to unlucky adventures. A player of trick-track, who out of twenty games with the fame perfon wins nineteen, is always fuppofed to underftand the game better than his adverfary, tho' the caprice of the dice may make a bad player win two games running of a very good one. Now war and thofe other profeffions depend much lefs on fortune than trick-track, tho' fortune has fome fhare in the fuccefs of thofe who profefs it. The plan a general lays, after having examined his forces, his refources, and in fhort the means that are in the enemy's or in his own power, is not expofed fo often to be difconcerted as the project of a gamefter. Wherefore the public is in the right to think, that a general who is conftantly fuccefsful in his campaigns, underftands the art of war ; tho' a general may have a lucky event without merit, as he may lofe a battle or be obliged to raife a fiege, without being unfkilful in his profeffion. Cardinal Mazarin

Mazarin underftood as well as any man, what fhare capacity hath in events, which weak people imagine to depend almoft intirely on chance, becaufe they depend in part. For this reafon he never confided either armies or negotiations to any but lucky perfons, upon a fuppofition that one cannot fucceed often enough to merit the title of fortunate, without having great abilities. Now the public feldom retracts the general judgments it has paffed on the merit of generals and minifters, in the manner here explained.

My fecond anfwer is, that it would be wrong to conclude, the public may be miftaken with regard to a poem, or picture, becaufe it often praifes or condemns minifters and generals unreafonably with refpect to particular events. The public is never miftaken, for inftance, with regard to the praife or blame due to a general after winning or lofing a battle, but for paffing its judgment on an intire object, whereof it underftood only a part. When it is in the wrong, 'tis for having cenfured or commended, before it had been rightly inftructed in the parts which the general had in the good or bad fuccefs. The thing is, the public would fain judge, while it is mifinformed with refpect to the facts. It has paffed its judgment on the general, before it was rightly inftructed either concerning the conftraint he lay under from the orders of his prince or his republic, or with refpect to the croffes he met with from thofe whofe bufinefs it was to affift him, or in regard to his being difappointed of his promifed fuccours. The public does not know, whether he has not brought on the hazard which feems to have been the only caufe of his fuccefs, either by preffing the enemy clofe, or by giving him fome occafion of falling into a prefumptuous confidence ; and whether the benefit he draws from this hazard, be not due to the precautions he had taken beforehand to improve it to his advantage. It cannot tell, whether the general could remove, or at leaft whether he ought to have forefeen the unlucky accident which difappointed his enterprize, and has given it even an appearance of temerity, after it proved abortive. The fame may be faid of the public, when it commends or cenfures the minifter, the magiftrate, and even the phyfician, with regard to a particular event.

But the cafe is otherwife in praifing painters or poets, becaufe thefe are never happy or unhappy with refpect to the fuccefs of their productions, but in proportion to their merit. When the public decides of their works, its judgment is directed towards an object, which it knows and fees in all and every part. All the beauties and imperfections of thefe forts of works are laid open, and nothing that can render them worthy of blame or praife is concealed, but is known as much as is neceffary for forming a right judgment. A prince who has given his commiffion to a general, or his inftruction to a minifter, is not as capable of judging of their conduct, as the public is of judging of poems and pictures.

Painters and poets (fome will continue to object) are at leaft the unhappieft of all thofe whofe works are expofed to the eyes of the public. For every body has a right to arraign them, even without giving any

any reafon for fo doing ; whereas the learned in other arts or fciences are *judged only by their peers*, who are likewife obliged to convict them in form before they are intitled to proceed to fentence.

I do not imagine it would be any great advantage for painters and poets, to be judged only by their peers. But let us anfwer more ferioufly. When a work treats of fciences or fubjects that are merely fpe-culative, its merit is not difcernible to the fenfe. People therefore that have acquired a neceffary knowledge for diftinguifhing whether a work be good or bad, are the only perfons that are ca-pable of judging. Men are not born with a knowledge of aftronomy and phyfics, as with a fenfitive faculty. They cannot therefore judge of the merit of a phyfical or aftronomical piece, but by virtue of their acquired knowledge ; whereas they are able to form a judgment of verfes and pictures in confequence of their natural difcernment. Where-fore geometricians, phyficians, and divines, or thofe who without hanging out a fign of thefe fciences, are neverthelefs well acquainted with them, are the only perfons capable of judging of a work that treats of their refpective fciences. But every man may judge of verfes and pictures, becaufe every man has a natural fenfibility, and the effect of verfes and pic-tures falls under the fenfe.

Tho' this anfwer is irrefragable, yet I fhall ftill corroborate it with another reflection. As foon as the fciences abovementioned have operated by vir-tue of their principles, and produced fomething that muft be ufeful or agreable to mankind in ge-neral, we can tell then without any other light but

S 4   what

what comes from the fenfitive faculty, whether the learned author has fucceeded. People ignorant in aftronomy know as well as the learned, whether the aftronomer has foretold an eclipfe precifely, or whether the machine produces the effect promifed by the mathematician, tho' they can alledge no methodical proof, that the aftronomer and mathematician are in the wrong, nor are capable of telling in what they have been miftaken.

If there be any fuch thing as arts, that fall under the fenfe, painting and poetry muft certainly be of this number, fince their operation is defigned intirely to move us. The fole exception that can be made, is, that there are fome pictures and poems, whofe intire merit does not fall under the fenfe. We cannot determine by a fenfitive affiftance, whether truth be obferved in an hiftorical picture reprefenting the fiege of a place, or the ceremony of a confecration. Our fenfes alone cannot inform us, whether the author of a philofophical poem reafons juftly, and proves his fyftem with folidity.

Our fenfes, I allow, cannot judge of that part of the merit of a poem or picture, which may be diftinguifhed by the name of its extrinfecal merit; but this is becaufe the arts of poetry and painting themfelves are incapable of deciding of it. In this refpect painters and poets have no manner of advantage over the reft of mankind. If any of thefe artifts are capable of deciding with regard to what we have called extrinfecal merit in poems and pictures, 'tis becaufe they have the advantage of fome other knowledge, befides what they have received from the arts of poetry and painting.

When

When there happens to be a difpute concerning one of thofe mixt pieces, which fall within the infpection of different tribunals, each of them decides the queftion belonging to its jurifdiction. This gives rife fometimes to oppofite tho' juft fentiments concerning the merit of the fame work. Thus poets very juftly commend Lucretius's poem on the univerfe, as the production of an eminent artift ; when philofophers condemn it as a book ftuffed with falfe reafonings. 'Tis thus alfo hiftorians blame Varillas, becaufe of the miftakes he commits in almoft every page ; whilft thofe who feek for amufement only, commend him for his entertaining narratives, and for the graces of his ftyle.

But to return to Lucretius, the public is as much a judge of that part of the merit of his poem which belongs to the jurifdiction of poetry, as the poets themfelves. All this portion of the merit of Lucretius falls under the fenfe.

The true method therefore of diftinguifhing the merit of a poem, will be always to confult the impreffion it makes. Our age is too knowing, or, if you pleafe, too philofophical, to believe we muft learn of critics, what we are to think of a work compofed to move us, when we can read this work ourfelves, and there are multitudes that have actually read it. Philofophy, which teaches us to judge of things by their proper principles, informs us at the fame time, that in order to know the merit and excellence of a poem, we muft examine whether and how far it pleafes and engages its readers.

True it is, that perfons who are unacquainted with the art, are incapable of afcending as high as

the

the caufes, which render us tired with a bad poem, or of pointing out their particular faults. Wherefore I am far from pretending, that an ignorant perfon can tell precifely what the painter or poet has
failed in, and much lefs advife them with refpect
to the correction of each error; but this does not
debar him from judging by the impreffion made
by a work compofed on purpofe to pleafe and
engage him, whether and how far the author has
fucceeded in his enterprize. An ignorant perfon can
therefore affirm, that a work is good or bad; and
'tis even falfe that he gives no reafon for his judgment. The tragic writer, he will fay, has not
made him weep, nor the comic poet laugh. He al-
ledges, that he feels no pleafure in gazing at a picture,
for which he has no value or efteem. 'Tis the bufinefs
of the works themfelves to make their defence againft
fuch criticifms, and whatfoever an author may chance
to fay in order to excufe the weak parts of his poem, has no more effect, than the ftudied encomiums
which his friends beftow on the beautiful paffages. Scuderi's *tyrannical love* is ranked amongft
the bad performances, notwithftanding Sarrazin's differtation in its favor. In fact, all the critical arguments in the world are incapable of perfuading people that a work pleafes, when they feel it does not;
or that a work engages them, when they experience
the contrary.

C H A P.

CHAP. XXV.

Of the judgment of artifts.

AFTER having fpoken of the public judgment with refpect to a new work, 'tis proper we treat of fuch judgments as are paffed by the
artifts themfelves.   The greateft part of thefe
gentlemen are apt to judge wrong of works confidered in general ; for which there can be three
reafons alledged.   The firft is, that the fenfibility of artifts is blunted :   The fecond, they
judge of every thing by way of difcuffion :   The
third, in fine, they are prevented in favor of
fome part of the art, and in the general judgments they make, they fet a greater value upon
it, than it deferves.   Under the name of artifts I
include here, not only poets and painters, but likewife a great number of fuch as write concerning
poems and pictures.   What ! (fome will fay) the
more ignorant therefore a perfon is in poetry
and painting, the more capable he is of giving
a folid judgment of thefe arts.   Strange paradox !
The explication I am going to give of my propofition, joined to what has been already faid, will be a
fufficient reply to an objection fo proper for prejudicing the world againft my opinion.   There are
fome artifts much more capable than the generality of mankind, of paffing judgment on the
performances of their art.   Thefe are fuch as are
born with a genius which is always accompanied
with

with a more exquisite sense, than that of the common run of mankind. But the number of these is very inconsiderable ; and as for those without genius, I affirm that their judgments are less solid than those of the generality of people, or, if you will, of the vulgar. I am induced to think thus for the following reasons. The sensibility of an artist without genius wears off in time, and what little he learns by his practice, contributes only to deprave his natural taste, and incline him to the wrong side in his decisions. His sense has been blunted by the necessity of occupying himself with verses and painting, especially as he must have been frequently obliged to write and paint, as it were, against his will, in particular moments when he felt no inclination for his work. He is become therefore insensible to the pathetic of verses and pictures, which have no longer the same effect upon him, as they formerly had, and still have on men of his age.

'Tis thus an old physician, tho' born of a tender and compassionate disposition, is no longer moved as much as another man with the sight of a dying person, or as much as he would have been affected himself, if he had not practised physic. The surgeon is hardened in the very same manner, and acquires a habit of dissecting those wretches without repugnance, whose kind of death renders their bodies a stronger object of horror. The most doleful ceremonies make no impression on such, as by profession are obliged to assist at them. The heart grows *callous* in the same manner as the hands and feet ; as Cicero very
ingeniously

ingenioufly expreffes himfelf in giving a lively picture of the indolence of the republic.

Befides, painters and poets look upon imitations
as labor, whereas others confider them as interefting objects. Wherefore the fubject of imitation,
that is, the events of the tragedy, and the expreffions of the picture, make a very fuperficial impreffion upon painters and poets without genius,
fuch as are here confidered. They are accuftomed
to fo feeble an emotion, that they hardly perceive
whether a work moves them or not. Their attention is intirely fixt on the mechanic execution, from
whence they form a judgment of the whole. The
poetry of Coypel's picture reprefenting the facrifice
of Jephtha's daughter, does not ftrike them, and
they examine it with as much indifference, as if it
exhibited a ruftic dance, or fome other fubject incapable of moving us : Infenfible of the pathetic of
his expreffions, they arraign him only by confulting their rule and compafs, juft as if a picture
ought not to contain beauties fuperior to the decifion of thofe inftruments.

'Tis thus the greateft part of our poets would examine the Cid, if this piece were new. Painters and
poets who have no enthufiafm do not feel that of
others, and giving their fuffrage by way of difcuffion,
they commend or cenfure a work in general, and de-
fine it to be good or bad, according as they find it regular in their analyfis. How can they be good judges
of the whole, when they are bad ones of the invention, a part which conftitutes the principal merit of
works, and diftinguifhes the great genius from the
fimple artift ?

Wherefore

Artifts therefore judge ill in general, tho' their reafonings particularly examined prove tolerably juft ; but they apply them to a ufe for which they were never intended. To pretend to judge of a poem or of a picture in general by the way of difcuffion, is to attempt to meafure a circle with a rule : You fhould take a pair of compaffes, which is the proper inftrument for meafuring it.

In fact, we fee folks miftaken every day, in predicting the fuccefs of a dramatic piece, by reafon of their having formed their prognoftics by way of difcuffion ; who would form very folid judgments, were they directed by their fenfe. Racine and Boileau were of the number of thofe artifts, who are much better qualify'd than other men to judge of verfes and poems. Who would imagine, but that after having conferred and communicated their thoughts with one another, their judgments muft have been infallible at leaft with refpect to each fcene confidered in particular ? And yet Boileau has acknowledged, that the judgments which his friend and he frequently paffed after a methodical difcuffion on the different fuccefs, which fhould have attended the feveral fcenes of his friend's tragedies, happened frequently to be contradicted by the event, and that they had both of them been conftantly convinced by experience, that the public was always right in paffing a different judgment. Both of them, in order to be better able to judge of the effect of their verfes, made ufe of the fame method pretty near as that of Malherbe and Moliere.

We took notice, that artifts are likewife apt to fall into another error, in forming their decifion.

cifion. 'Tis their having too great a regard in
the eftimation of the work, for the capacity of
the attift in that part of the art, in favor of which
they are prevented. The fate of artifts without genius, is to apply themfelves principally to the ftudy
of a part of the art they profefs, and to imagine,
after having made fome progrefs therein, that 'tis
the only important branch. The poet, whofe principal talent confifts in his facility of rhiming, foon
imbibes the prejudiced notion, that a poem with
a neglected verfification muft of neceffity be an
indifferent piece ; tho' it be rich in invention, and
abounds with thoughts fo fuitable to the fubject, that
one is furprized at their being new. As his talent
does not lye in invention, thefe beauties have but
very little weight in his fcales. A painter, who of
all thofe talents fo neceffary to form the great artift,
has only that of coloring, decides of the excellence
or badnefs of a picture, in proportion to the artift's
abilities in managing the colors. The poetry of the
picture paffes for little or nothing in his judgment,
which is made without any regard to fuch parts
of the art as he is not mafter of. A poetic painter will fall into the fame error, by fetting a very
low value upon a picture, that fhould happen to be
defective in the ordonnance, and mean in the expreffions ; tho' the coloring may deferve to be admired.
By fuppofing that thofe parts of the art we are deficient in, are fcarce worthy of notice, we maintain,
without mentioning it directly, that we want nothing
to make us eminent in our profeffion. One may
apply to artifts what Petronius fays of men who
abound

abound in riches. *ᵃ Men are all defirous, that what-foever qualification they have themfelves fhould be the greateft merit in fociety.* The reader will pleafe to obferve, that what I have hitherto faid has been · in regard only to the general judgments by which artifts determine the merit of a work. That painters are more capable than others, of judging · of the merit of a picture with refpect to the coloring, the regularity of the defign, and fome other beauties in the execution, is what no body attempts to queftion, and what we fhall take notice of ourfelves in the twenty feventh chapter of this work.

'Tis manifeft that I have fpoken here in refpect to fuch painters and poets only, as are honeftly miftaken. Had I ftudied to render their decifions fufpected, what might not I fay concerning the injuftices they daily and purpofely commit, in characterifing the works of their competitors ? In other profeffions men are generally fatisfied with being the moft eminent among their cotemporaries : but in poetry and painting one can hardly fuffer the fhadow of a rival. Cæfar was contented to have an equal, but moft poets and painters, proud and haughty like Pompey ᵇ, cannot fo much as bear the thoughts of being approached. They are willing there fhould be a great diftance in the eyes of the public, between themfelves and fuch of their cotemporaries as feem to

---

ᵃ *Nihil volunt inter homines melius credi, quàm quod ipfi tenent.* PETRON. Satyr.

ᵇ *Nam neque Pompeius parem animo quemquam tulit, & in quibus rebus primus effe debebat, folus effe cupiebat.* PATERC. hift. l. 2.

I   tread

tread nearest their footsteps. 'Tis therefore very rare, that the principal men in these two professions condescend to do justice even to such of their cotemporaries, as are only just beginning their career, and who cannot of course be put upon a level with them, but in a future and very remote time. One has occasion frequently to reproach the great men here spoken of, with that touch of self-love, which Augustus was accused of: that is, with having chosen in the person of Tiberius, the properest successor to make him regretted. If great artists are so sensible of jealousy, what must we think of the indifferent ones?

C H A P. XXIV.

That the public judgments prevail at length over the decisions of artists.

WHAT has been above evinced by reason, is sufficiently confirmed by experience. Artists must certainly be often mistaken, since their decisions are commonly reversed by the public, on whose voice the fate of works has always depended. The public opinion carries it, when it happens to differ even with the most eminent artists, in respect to the merit of a new production. *'Tis to no purpose,* says Boileau [a], *for a work to be approved by a small number of connoisseurs; unless it has some attractive proper for exciting the general taste of mankind, it will never be able to pass*

[a] Preface to the edition of 1701.

for a good performance, and the connoisseurs themselves will be obliged to own, that they were mistaken in giving their approbation. The same thing happens, when the public gives its approbation to a work condemned by the connoisseurs. As the public will judge hereafter by their senses, in the same manner as those before them have judged, they will consequently be of one opinion. Posterity has never censured those poems which the cotemporaries of the author commended as excellent, tho' they may neglect to read them, in order to amuse themselves with better performances. On the other hand there is no instance of poems having been unacceptable to the cotemporaries of their author, and attaining in future times to any degree of reputation. *Posterity,* says a Roman writer, [a] *will believe as much, as the present age will warrant to be true.*

Party writings, and poems on recent events, have but a very short-liv'd fame, if they be indebted for their whole success to the conjunctures in which they are published. They are generally forgotten in six months, by reason that they are not considered so much in the light of poems, as in that of gazettes. 'Tis not at all surprizing, they should be ranked hereafter among those satyrical memoirs, which are curious only with respect to the facts of which they inform us, or in regard to the circumstances of those facts which they recal to our memory: The public had condemned them to this very fate six months after their birth. But those poems, and party-writings, which are esteemed

[a] *Tantumdem quoque posteri credunt, quantum præsens ætas spoponderit.* CURTIUS, lib. 8.

a year

a year after their firſt appearance, and without any reſpect to circumſtances, are tranſmitted with the ſame eſteem to poſterity. We ſet as great a value on Seneca's ſatyre againſt the emperor Claudius, as they could have done at Rome two years after the death of that prince. We have as great a regard for the Satyra Menippea, the provincial letters, and ſome other books of that kind, as they had a year after the firſt edition of thoſe writings. Thoſe ſongs which were compoſed ten years ago, and are ſtill retained, will be likewiſe ſung by our poſterity.

The faults which artiſts affect to obſerve in works eſteemed by the public, may retard indeed, but not obſtruct their ſucceſs. One may anſwer them, that a poem or a picture may be an excellent work, notwithſtanding its badneſs in ſome parts. It would be unneceſſary to explain here to the reader, that throughout this whole diſſertation the word *bad* muſt be underſtood in a relative ſignification. 'Tis plain, for example, that when 'tis ſaid, the coloring of a picture of the Roman ſchool is good for nothing, this expreſſion imports only that this coloring is inferior to that of ſeveral other pictures, whether Flemiſh or Lombard, whoſe reputation is notwithſtanding very indifferent. We ſhould not feel the force of the expreſſions of a picture, if the coloring were abſolutely falſe and bad. When we ſay that Corneille's verſification is bad in ſome places, we mean only that 'tis more neglected, than that of ſeveral poets, who are eſteemed indifferent artiſts. Were the verſification to be abſolutely bad, and to offend us at every line, the poem

T 2   would

would never be able to move us. For, as Quin‑
tilian obferves [a], *Phrafes that fet out by offending
the ear with their roughnefs, and ufher themfelves in,
as it were, with a bad addrefs, find the entrance into
our hearts obftruƈted.*

The decifions of artifts, notwithftanding their
being fubjeƈt to all the illufions here mentioned,
have a great fhare neverthelefs in the firft reputation of a new work. In the firft place, tho' they have
not influence enough to get a poem or piƈture condemned by thofe that know them; yet they may
hinder a great many from having any knowledge
of them, by diffuading them from going to fee,
or read them. Thefe prejudices, which fpread, have
an effeƈt for fome time. In the fecond place, the
public prejudiced in favor of the difcernment of
artifts, imagine for fome time that they have more
penetration and fagacity than themfelves. Wherefore as the work, to which they are willing to do juftice, attains quickly to the good or bad reputation
due to it; fo the reverfe falls out when they refufe
doing juftice to it, either thro' prevarication, or miftake. But when they are divided in their fentiments,
they invalidate their credit, and the public judges of
courfe without them. 'Tis by the help of this divifion that Moliere and Racine attained quickly to
fo high a degree of reputation.

Tho' the artifts cannot impofe on others, fo
as to make them take excellent things for bad,
yet they can make them believe that thofe excellent things are but indifferent with refpeƈt to

[a] *Nihil intrare poteft in affeƈtum, quod in aure velut quodam vef-
tibulo ftatim offendit.* QUINT. Inft. l. 9. cap 4.

others.

others. The error into which they throw the public by this means, with refpeƈt to a new performance, is a long while a removing. 'Till the work be-comes generally known, the prejudice which the decifion of the artifts has caufed in the world, ba-lances the fentiment of judicious and difinterefted perfons, efpecially if it be from the hands of an author whofe reputation is not yet eftablifhed. If the author be known already for an excellent artift, his work is fooner refcued from oppreffion. Whilft one prejudice combats againft another, truth efcapes, as it were, from their hands, and fhews itfelf.

The moft part of the prejudices which pain-ters and poets fpread againft a new work, pro-ceeds from this, that thofe who fpeak of a poem or of a piƈture on the credit of others, chufe to take and repeat the opinions of artifts, rather than to relate the fentiments of fuch as have not hung out their figns, as it were, in the profeffion to which the work belongs. In thefe kinds of things, in which men do not think they have an effential intereft to determine them to the right fide of the queftion, they let themfelves be im-pofed upon by an argument which has a very great weight with them. This is, that the artifts ought to have more experience than others. I fay, impofed upon ; for, as I have fhewn already, moft painters and poets do not judge by their fenfes, nor by paying a deference to their natural tafte improved by comparifons and experience ; but by way of analyfis. They do not judge like men endowed with the fixth fenfe abovementioned, but as fpeculative philofophers. Vanity contributes alfo

T 3

to make us efpoufe the opinion of artifts, preferable to that of men of tafte and fenfe. To embrace the fentiment of a perfon who has no more experience than ourfelves, is acknowledging in fome meafure that he is a man of better fenfe and underftanding. This is paying a kind of homage to his natural difcernment. But to believe the artift, and to pay a deference to the opinion of a man who is of a profeffion which we are not fo well acquainted with, is only fhewing a refpect to the art and paying homage to experience. The profeffion of the art impofes on a great many in fuch a manner, that they ftifle at leaft for fome time their own fentiment ; being afhamed, as Quintilian [a] obferves, to differ with others in opinion. We liften therefore with pleafure to artifts, who enter into a methodical examination of a tragedy, or picture, and we ftrive even to retain as much as we can of the very technical terms : but this is in order to gain the admiration and attention of others in repeating them.

[a] *Pudet enim diffentire, & quafi tacita verecundia inhibemur plus nobis credere.* QUINT. l. 10. cap. 1.

C H A P.

C H A P. XXVII.

That there is a greater regard due to the judg-
ments of painters, than to those of poets. Of
the art of discovering the hand of painters.

THE public seems to have more attention
to painters who are employed in examining a picture, than to poets taken up in criticis-
ing a poem : in which respect we cannot help
commending their judgment. The generality of
men are very far from having so much knowledge of the mechanic part of painting, as that of
poetry ; and, as we have shewn in the beginning of
these essays, the beauties of execution are much more
considerable in a picture, than they possibly can be
in a French poem. We have even seen that the
beauties of execution alone are capable of rendering a picture valuable. Now these beauties make a
sensible impression upon men, who do not understand the mechanic part of painting ; and yet they
are not capable to judge of the merit of a painter. To be able to judge of the commendation due
to him, one should know how near he has approached to those artists, who are most extolled for
having excelled in the parts, in which he has succeeded. These are some of the degrees more or
less, which form the difference between a great
and an ordinary artist : And this is what the artists are judges of. Wherefore the reputation of
a painter, whose talent consists in the chiaro-scuro or in the local colors, depends much more on

the

the *judgment of his peers*, than the fame of a perfon, whofe merit confifts in the expreffion of the paffions and in poetic inventions; things which the public underftands, compares, and judges of itfelf. We obferve alfo by the hiftory of painters, that the colorifts have not attained fo early to fo great degree of reputation, as painters famous for their poetry and defign.

'Tis obvious, that in purfuance of this principle, I muft acknowledge the artifts are the proper judges, when we want to know, as near as poffible, who drew the picture; but they are not for all this the only judges of the merit of the piece. As the greateft artifts have fometimes drawn very indifferently, we cannot infer the excellence of the picture from the knowledge we have of the author. It does not follow of courfe that it is a firft rate piece, from its being undoubtedly the production of one of the moft celebrated painters.

Tho' experience informs us, that the art of gueffing at the author of a picture, from the knowledge we have of the mafter's hand, is the moft fallible of all arts next to phyfic, it prejudices neverthelefs the public in favor of the decifions of thofe that practife it, even when they are made on other points. Men who are more ready to admire than to approve, hear with fubmiffion, and repeat with confidence, the judgments of a perfon who affects a diftinct knowledge of feveral things which they do not underftand. We fhall fee, from what I am going to fay concerning the infallibility of the art of defcerning the hands of great mafters, what bounds ought to be fet to the natural
prevention

prevention we have in favor of fuch judgments as are given by the profeffors of this art, and who decide with as much affurance as a young phyfician writes a prefcription.

Thofe that are expert in the art of diftinguifhing the hand of great mafters, are not well agreed among themfelves, but with refpect to fuch famous pictures, as have already eftablifhed, as it were, their credit, and made their hiftory known to the world. With regard to pictures whofe fame is not yet fixt by a conftant and uninterrupted tradition, there are none but our own and thofe of our friends, that have the names of their authors afcertained. As for the pictures in poffeffion of other perfons, and efpecially of fellow-citizens, they are doubtful originals. Some of thefe are objected againft for being only copies, and others *pafticci*. Intereft completes the uncertainty in the decifion of an art, which is fubject to miftakes, even when it proceeds ingenuoufly.

'Tis well known, that feveral painters have been miftaken with regard to their own works, and that they have frequently taken a copy for the very original they themfelves had painted. Vafari relates as an ocular witnefs, that Julio Romano, after having drawn the drapery of a picture done by Raphael, miftook a copy of this picture done by Andrea del Sarto for the very original. In fact, tho' it ought to be eafier at prefent to diftinguifh a man's pen than his pencil ; yet thofe who are fkilled in writing, are daily miftaken, and divided in their judgments.

The particular fhape of the ftroke, by which every man forms the four and twenty letters of

the

the alphabet, the connections of these characters, the figure and distance of the lines, the greater or lesser perseverance of the person that writes, in not precipitating, as it were, his pen in the heat of his motion, as most penmen do, who form the characters of the first lines better than those of the next; in fine, the manner in which he has held his pen; all this, I say, enables us better to distinguish people's hand-writing, than the strokes of a pencil qualify us to discern the hand of a painter. As writing flows from a rapid and continued movement of all the muscles of the hand, it depends intirely on their conformation and habit. A strained character is immediately suspected of being counterfeited, and we soon distinguish whether it be drawn with ease and freedom.

We cannot discern so well, whether the strokes drawn by a pencil are studied, or whether the copier has retouched and mended his stroke to give it a greater likeness to the natural touch of another painter. A person is as much master in painting to lick over his stroke several times, in order to give it its proper finishing, as the ancients were to mend their character, when they used to write on wax writing-tables. Now the ancients were so far convinced, that one might counterfeit another man's hand in his writing-tables, because the characters might be retouched without being discerned, that no public deed was esteemed valid unless the parties concerned set their seals to the contract. The perfection the ancients attained to in ingraving stones for seals, was owing to the care they had in making particular seals, such as could not easily be counterfeited. This care they

they had of having each a different feal, is the caufe of our finding at prefent fuch whimfical figures, and frequently the head of the owner of the feal, on the antique ingraved ftones.

But notwithftanding all the methods we have of difcerning men's hand-writing, this art is ftill fo very fallible, that thofe nations which are more careful in protecting the innocent than in punifhing the guilty, forbid their courts to admit the proof of hand-writing in criminal caufes: and in countries where this proof is received, the judges confider it rather as a probable circumftance, than as a complete evidence. What fhall we therefore think of the art, which boldly fuppofes it cannot be deceived by any counterfeit ftrokes in imitation of thofe of Raphael or Pouffin?

C H A P. XXVII.

Of the time when poems and pictures are appraif-ed to their full value.

THE time at length comes, when the public appraifes a work no longer by the relation of artifts, but according to the impreffion made by the work itfelf: Thofe who had judged differently from the profeffors of the art, by referring things to the decifion of their fenfes, communicate their opinions to one another, and the uniformity of their fenfation changes the opinion of every particular perfon into a perfuafion. New mafters rife up in the art, who form a juft and difinterefted judgment of injured works; and undeceive the world

I

metho-

methodically with regard to the prejudices fown by their predecefſors. People of themſelves obſerve, that thoſe who promiſed them ſomething better than the work whoſe merit had been conteſted, have not kept their word. On the other hand its profeſſed enemies drop off; by which means it is rated at length to its full value.

Such has been amongſt us the fate of the operas of Quinault. It was impoſſible to perſuade the public, that they were not moved with the repreſentations of Theſeus and Athys; but they were made to believe, that theſe pieces were full of groſs errors, which did not proceed ſo much from the vicious nature of the poem, as from the want of capacity in the poet. Thus it was thought an eaſy matter to write better than this poet, and if there occurred any thing that was good in his operas, a perſon was not allowed to be laviſh in commendations of the author, under the penalty of being reputed a ſhallow capacity. We have therefore ſeen Quinault pleaſe for ſome time, whilſt the very people he pleaſed, durſt not maintain that he was an excellent poet in his way. But the public being confirmed in their ſentiment by experience, have got rid of that conſtraint in which they had been ſo long confined, and plucked up at length a reſolution to ſpeak out their thoughts. There have been ſome later poets who have encouraged people to ſay, that Quinault excelled in that kind of lyric poetry to which he applied himſelf. La Fontaine and other choice wits have done ſomething more to convince us, that ſome of Quinault's operas are as excellent as thoſe poems really can be. They have wrote operas themſelves, that are vaſtly inferior to ſe-

I

veral

veral of Quinault's. Sixty years ago it was treafon
to fay that Quinault was an excellent poet in his way ;
and no body now durft fay the contrary. Among
the prodigious number of operas which have been
wrote fince his time, there are none but Thetis and Pe-
leus, Iphigenia, the Venetian Feafts, and Europe in
Gallantry, that are ranked in the fame clafs with
thofe of this excellent poet.

Were we to examine the hiftory of fuch poets
as have been an honor to the French Parnaffus, we
fhall find none but what are indebted to the public
for the fuccefs of their works ; none but what have
had the profeffors of the art a long while their declared enemies. The public admired the Cid a confiderable time, before poets would allow this piece
to be filled with moft exquifite beauties. How many
forry criticifms, and wretched comedies, have not
Moliere's rivals wrote againft him ? Did Racine ever
publifh a tragedy, without expofing it to fome critical piece, which reduced it upon a level with the
moft indifferent performance, and concluded with
ranking the author in the fame clafs with Boyer and
Pradon ? But Racine met with the fame fate as
Quinault. Boileau's prediction in favor of Racine's
tragedies is fully accomplifhed, and impartial pofterity has declared itfelf in their favor. The fame may
be faid of painters. Not one of them would have
attained after his death to the degree of diftinction due
to his merit, were his fate to be always in the power
of other painters. But by good luck his rivals are
mafters of his reputation but for a fhort time ; for
the public takes the caufe by degrees into their own
hands,

hands, and after an impartial inquiry, does every body juftice according to their merit.

But (fome will fay) if my comedy is damned by means of the hiffes and catcalls of an invidious party, how will the public be able to do juftice to this piece, if they never afterwards hear of it ? I anfwer in the firft place, that I do not apprehend that a party can damn a piece, let them hifs it ever fo much. The *Grumbler* was hiffed, but was not damned for all that. In the fecond place the play is printed, and thus remains under the eyes of the public. A man of fenfe, but of a profeffion too ferious to be prejudiced againft the merit of a piece by an event which he has never heard fpoken of, reads it without partiality or prevention, and finds it a good performance. This he tells to fuch as have an opinion of his judgment, who read it, and find his judgment exact. Thefe inform others of their difcovery, and the piece which I am willing to fuppofe had been funk, *begins to rife again above water*. This is one manner out of a hundred, whereby a good piece which had been wronged upon its firft appearance, may be raifed to the rank due to its merit. But, as I have already obferved, this is what never happens, and I do not really think that there can be one inftance given of a French piece rejected by the public, upon its firft appearance, which has been afterwards approved, when the conjunctures, that firft oppreffed it, were removed. On the contrary, I could name feveral comedies and operas, that have been damned upon their being firft reprefented, which have had the fame fate when they have

have been brought twenty years afterwards upon the ftage.   And yet the parties, to which the author and his friends imputed its firft fall, were quite difperfed, upon their being revived a fecond time. But the public never changes its fentiment, becaufe it efpoufes always the right fide of the queftion.   A piece appears ftill an indifferent performance upon its revival, if it was judged fuch at its firft reprefentation.   If one fhould afk me, what time the public takes to be able to know a work, and to form its judgment of the merit of the artift ; I anfwer, that the length of this time depends on two things ; that is, on the nature of the work, and on the capacity of the public before whom it is exhibited.   A theatrical piece, for inftance, will be fooner appraifed to its juft value, than an epic poem. The public is affembled to pafs judgment on the pieces of the theatre, and thofe who are there convened, foon communicate their fentiments to one another. A painter who paints the cupola's and vaults of churches, or who makes large pictures defigned for places where public affemblies are held, is fooner known than one that works on eafel-pieces deftined for private apartments.

C H A P.

C H A P. XXIX.

That there are some countries in which the value of works is sooner known, than in others.

IN the second place, as the public is not equally knowing in all countries, there are some parts where artists can keep them longer in the dark, than in others. For instance, pictures exposed at Rome, will be sooner appraised to their just value, than if they were to be exposed at London or Paris. The inhabitants of Rome are almost all of them born with a very great sensibility for painting, and their natural taste has likewise frequent occasions of improving and perfecting itself by the help of those excellent works, which they meet with in their churches, palaces, and almost every house they enter. The customs and manners of the country leave a great vacancy or leisure in every body's daily occupations, even in those of such artists as are condemned elsewhere to as uninterrupted labor as that of the Danaids. This inaction, together with the continual opportunities they have of seeing fine pictures, and perhaps the greater sensibility also of the organs in that country than in cold climates, produces so general a taste for painting at Rome, that 'tis a common thing to see some valuable pictures in barbers shops, where they explain their beauties most emphatically to their customers, to comply with the necessity of entertaining people, which even in Horace's time seemed to be a duty of their profession. In fine, in an industrious nation,

capable

capable of taking all forts of pains to get a livelihood, without being fubject to regular labor, a
peculiar fet of people have been formed, who fubfift by means of a traffick in pictures.

Thus the public in Rome is almoft intirely compofed of connoiffeurs in painting. 'Tis true, they
are but indifferent connoiffeurs ; yet they have at
leaft a comparative tafte, which hinders the profeffors of the art from impofing upon them fo eafily
as in other places. If the inhabitants of this
city are not learned enough to refute methodically their falfe reafonings, they are capable
at leaft of perceiving the fallacy, and of informing
themfelves of what they muft fay in order to refute it. On the other hand, artifts become more
circumfpect, when they find they have to do with
men that underftand fomething of the matter. 'Tis
not among divines that your reformers undertake to
make fincere profelytes to their doctrines.

A painter therefore who works at Rome attains
quickly to the degree of reputation he deferves,
efpecially if he be an Italian. The Italians, almoft
as fond of the glory of their nation as the ancient
Greeks, are very jealous of the fame which a nation acquires by fciences and the polite arts.
With refpect to the fciences, all the Italians muft
certainly agree to what fignor Ottieri has wrote
in the hiftory of the war which broke out in confequence of the difputes concerning the fucceffion
of Charles II king of Spain [a]. This author after
obferving, that the Italians ought not to give any
longer the name of Barbarians to the inhabitants of

[a] Printed at Rome in 1728

provinces fituated to the north and weft of Italy, but only to call them *Ultramontanes* ; becaufe of the politenefs they have acquired in thefe latter ages, adds[a] ; *and our Italians, tho'. endowed with as great a fhare of fenfe and capacity as other nations, are for this and feveral other reafons, fallen into a very great degeneracy with refpect to real. and folid learning.* But this nation thinks differently in regard to the polite arts.   Every Italian : becomes therefore a painter, when he is to give his opinion of a foreign picture.   He even complains, as: it were, that the ideas capable of being an honor to the inventer, fhould occur to any but his own countrymen. A friend of mine was eye-witnefs to the following ad- venture.

Every one knows the misfortunes of Belifarius, reduced to afk charity on the highway, after having frequently commanded with the moft fignal fuc- cefs the armies of the emperor Juftinian.   Vandyke has drawn a large eafel-piece, in which this unfortu- nate general is reprefented in the pofture of a beg- gar ftretching out his hand to the paffengers. Each perfon that ftands gazing at him, feems moved with a compaffion which expreffes the character of his age and condition.   But our attention is particularly engaged by a foldier, whofe countenance and attitude expreffes a perfon plunged into the deepeft medita- tion, at the fight of this great warrior precipitated

---

[b] *E i noftri Italiani benchè forniti di fenno e capacità non infe- riore all. altre nazioni, fono rimafti per quefta, e per altre cagioni avvilti, e preffo che abjetti nel preggio dell' eccellentè-litteratura.* fag. 296.

Into the loweſt miſery, from a rank which is the higheſt aim of military ambition. This ſoldier is ſo extremely well done, that one ſeems to hear him ſay, *behold what muſt perhaps be my fate after forty campaigns !* An Engliſh nobleman happening to be at Rome, where he brought this picture, ſhewed it to Carlo Maratti. What a pity it is (ſays this painter, with one of thoſe ſallies which with a ſingle ſtroke gives a deſcription of the bottom of the heart) that an *Ultramontane* ſhould have prevented us in this beautiful invention ? I have even heard from perſons worthy of credit, that among the common people at Rome, ſome of them were ſuch declared enemies to the reputation of our French painters, as to tear the prints ingraved from Sueur, le Brun, Mignard, Coypel, and ſome other painters of our nation, which the Carthuſians of that city had placed together with prints ingraved from Italian artiſts in the gallery over the cloyſters of their monaſtery. The compariſons made there every day between the French and Italian maſters, provoked our jealous Romans, as much as the parallels made at Paris about fourſcore years ago, between the pictures drawn by Sueur in the little cloyſter of the Carthuſians, and thoſe by le Brun, irritated the eleves of the latter. As the Carthuſians at Paris were obliged to hide Sueur's pieces, to prevent them from being expoſed to the inſults of le Brun's eleves ; ſo the Carthuſians at Rome were forced to hinder ordinary people from coming into the gallery where the prints of French painters are expoſed.

The

The French are generally prepoffeffed in favor of foreigners, where the queftion does not relate to cookery and drefs ; but the Italians on the contrary are prejudiced againft the *Ultramontanes.* The Frenchman at firft fuppofes the foreign artift to be more fkilful than his countryman, nor is he difabufed of his error, till after having made feveral comparifons. He finds fome difficulty in allowing an artift born in the fame country with himfelf, to be as knowing in his profeffion as one born five hundred leagues from France. On the contrary, the prepoffeffion of the Italians is feldom in favor of a ftranger who profeffes the liberal arts ; and if ever they do him juftice, 'tis as late as poffible. Thus after having neglected Pouffin for a confiderable time; they have acknowledged him at length for one of the moft eminent mafters that ever handled a pencil. In the fame manner they have done juftice to Monfieur le Brun's genius ; for after having made him prince of the academy of St Luke, they mention his merit with refpect, tho' they take too much notice of the weak coloring of this great poet, notwithftanding it is preferable to that of feveral of the great mafters of the Roman fchool. The Italians in general may boaft of their circumfpection, and the French of their hofpitality. M. Algarotti fays in the epiftle of his book on Sir Ifaac Newton's philofophy, addreffed to M. Fontenelle : *Were it not for the tranflation of fome French books, we fhould fee nothing new in Italy, but collections of verfes and fongs, with which we fwarm* [a].

[a] *Algarotti, epiftle on the Newtonian philofophy, dated the 24th of Janury,* 1736.

The

People are not fo knowing in painting at Paris, as at Rome ; and the French in general have not their inward fenfe fo lively as the Italians. The difference between them is already vifible in thofe who dwell at the foot of the Alps on the fide of France and Italy ; but it is ftill greater between the natives of Paris and Rome. Befides, we are far from cultivating as much as they, the common fenfibility of man for painting ; nor do we, generally fpeaking, acquire the comparative tafte as well here as at Rome. This tafte is formed within us, even without thinking of it : By dint of beholding pictures during our youth, the idea and image of eleven or twelve excellent pictures is ingraved and imprinted deeply in our yet tender imagination. Now thefe pictures, which are always prefent to us, and have a certain rank, and fixt merit, ferve, if I may fay fo, for pieces of comparifon, which inable us to judge folidly, how near a new work approaches the perfection which other painters have attained, and in what rank it deferves to be placed. The idea thefe twelve pictures prefent to our minds, produces part of the effect which would have proceeded from the pictures themfelves, were they placed next to that whofe merit and rank we want to difcern. The difference obfervable between the merit of two pictures fet oppofite to one another, is obvious to every body that is not either ftupid or blind.

But to acquire this comparative tafte, which inables us to judge of a prefent by an abfent picture, a perfon muft have been bred in the very

U 3 center

center of painting. He muſt have frequent opportunities, eſpecially in his younger days, of beholding ſeveral excellent pictures in perfect eaſe and tranquillity. Liberty of mind is as neceſſary, in order
to be ſenſible of the intire beauty of a work, as to
compoſe it. To be a good ſpectator, one muſt
have that peace of ſoul, which riſes not from the
exhauſting, but from the ſerenity of the imagination.

Phædri libellos legere ſi deſideras,

Vaces oportet, Eutyche, a negotiis,

Ut liber animus ſentiat vim carminis.

PHÆD. lib. 3. prolog.

Now we ſpend our lives in France in a continual
ſeries of pleaſures or tumultuary occupations, which
leave hardly any void ſpace in our time, but keep us
in a conſtant hurry and fatigue of ſpirit. One
may apply to us, what Pliny ſaid formerly of the
Romans of his time (who were a little more occupied than the preſent Romans) when he complains
of the ſlender notice they took of the magnificent
ſtatues, with which ſeveral porticos were adorned[a].
The great multitude and hurry of buſineſs and em-
ployments diverts every one from the contemplation of
theſe objects ; a contemplation ſuited to thoſe only,
who have leiſure and tranquillity of mind. Our life
is a perpetual ſcene of trouble and embarraſment,
either to make a fortune capable of ſatisfying our

[a] *Magni negotiorum officiorumque acervi abducunt omnes a con-*
templatione talium, quoniam otioſorum & in magno loci ſilentio apta
admiratio talis eſt. PLIN. hiſt. l. 36. cap. 5.

boundleſs

boundlefs defires, or to preferve it in a country, where it is not lefs difficult to keep than to acquire. Pleafures which are brifker and more repeated here than in other countries, lay hold of the little time left us by the occupations which either fortune has laid out for us, or our own inquietude of mind has procured us. A great many courtiers have lived thirty years at Verfailles, walking to and fro regularly five or fix times a day in the great apartment, whom you might eafily perfuade, that the pilgrims of Emaus were done by le Brun ; and the Queens of Perfia at Alexander's feet, by Paolo Veronefe. My French readers will find no difficulty in believing me.

Hence it is, that Sueur deferved his fame fo long before he enjoyed it. Pouffin, whom we extol fo much in our days, was in no great efteem with the public, when in his very beft days he came to practife in France. But difinterefted perfons, who are directed in their fentiments by truth, recover themfelves, tho' fomewhat late ; and laying a ftrefs upon an opinion which they obferve has been embraced by the majority, they oppofe thofe who would attempt to put two very unequal artifts upon a level. One of them afcends a ftep higher every year, while the other defcends a ftep lower, till at length they come to be fo diftant from one another, that the public being difabufed, is furprized to have feen them placed in the fame rank. Can we conceive, that Monfieur Mignard could have been compared for fome time to le Brun ? Perhaps we fhall be as much furprized twenty years hence, when we come to reflect on the parallels made in the prefent times.

The

The fame thing has happened at Antwerp, where the generality of people undeiftand no more of painting, than they do at Paris. Before Vandyke went to England, the other painters raifed him rivals, whom the deluded public imagined to have been his equals in merit. But now the diftance between them appears infinite, becaufe every day error lofes a partifan, while truth acquires one. When the fchool of Rubens was in its full prime, the Dominicans at Antwerp wanted fifteen large pictures to adorn the body of their church. Vandyke, fatisfied with the price, offered to do them all: But the other painters advifed thofe good fathers to divide the work, and to employ twelve of Rubens's eleves, who feemed to be pretty near in the fame clafs. They perfuaded thofe friars, that the difference of hands would render the order of thofe pictures more agreable, and that emulation would alfo oblige each painter to exert himfelf in a work deftined to be compared eternally to thofe of his competitors. Thus out of fifteen pictures Vandyke did but two, namely, the flagellation, and the carrying of the crofs. But the public cannot think at prefent of Vandyke's rivals without indignation and refentment.

As we have had a greater number of excellent poets than painters in France, the natural tafte for poetry has had therefore a better opportutunity of improving, than that for painting. If the fine pictures are almoft all of them fhut up at Paris in places where the public has not a free accefs, we have our theatres open to all the world, where we may venture to fay (without apprehending
the

the reproach of being led away by national prejudice, a thing almoft as dangerous as a party fpirit)
the beft theatrical pieces are reprefented, that have
been written fince the recovery of letters. Foreigners do not adopt the comedies and tragedies of
other nations with the fame readinefs, nor with
that refpeft for their authors, as they do ours.
They tranflate our tragedies ; while they are fatisfied with imitating thofe of other nations. Moft
young people frequent the playhoufes in France,
and, without reflection or defign, retain an infinite
number of comparative pieces and touchftones in
their memory. The women refort to our public
diverfions with as much freedom as the men, and
they all talk very frequently of poetry, and efpecially of the dramatic kind. Thus the public
knows enough to do juftice readily to bad pieces,
and to fupport the good ones againft the caballing
of parties.

The juftice rendered to works that are fent
abroad by means of the ptefs, may indeed be
fome months before it appears ; but performances
brought upon the ftage have their fate decided
much fooner. There would be nothing certain
in confequence of human knowledge, could four
hundred perfons, after communicating their thoughts
to one another, believe they are moved when
they are not ; or were they to be affected by
an object that has nothing engaging in its nature. Indeed the public cannot decide fo quickly
the difference between good and exquifite ; wherefore they cannot commend at firft a piece like
Phædra, as much as it deferves. They cannot
con-

conceive the full merit of a work, till they have
feen it feveral times, nor give it the preference it deferves, till after having compared for a while the
pleafure it gives them, with the fatisfaction they receive from fuch excellent works as have had a
long and eftablifhed approbation.

C H A P. XXX.

*Objection drawn from good works which have
been difapproved at firft by the public; as
alfo from bad ones that have been commended. Anfwer to this objection.*

IT will be objected here, that there have been
fome wretched farces, and pitiful comedies, which
have amufed the town for a long time, and have
fometimes drawn fpectators to the twentieth night.
But thofe who go to fee thefe farces while they are
new, will tell you themfelves they are not deceived, and that they are very fenfible of the little
merit of thofe Smithfield comedies. They will tell
you upon the very fpot, that they make an immenfe
difference betwixt thofe pieces and the Mifanthrope,
and that they come thither merely to fee an actor,
who fucceeds in fome odd character, or elfe a fcene
which bears a relation to a recent event, that is
very much talked of in the world. Wherefore
as foon as the time of their novelty is elapfed,
and the conjuncture which fupported them is over,
they are then intirely forgot, and the players

do not remember a word of them; which proves what Terence fays,

——————— *Olim cum ftetit nova,*
Actoris opera magis ftetiffe quàm fua.

TER. prolog. PHORM.

But (fome will continue to object) the fuccefs of the Mifanthrope was dubious for fome time.   Pradon's Phædra, which the public has now fo great a contempt for, and which, to fay fomething more, it has fo perfectly forgot, had at firft as great fuccefs as the Phædra of Racine.   Pradon had for fome time as many fpectators at the *Hotel de Guenegaud,* as Racine at the *Hotel de Bourgogne.*   In a word, thefe two tragedies, which appeared in the fame month, ftruggled for feveral days, before the good one obtained the victory.

Tho' the Mifanthrope is, perhaps, the beft comedy extant ; yet we are not furprized that the public hefitated a little before it acknowledged its excellency, and that the general fuffrage did not declare in its favor 'till after eight or ten reprefentations ; when we reflect on the circumftances in which it was firft exhibited.   The world was a ftranger at that time to that noble comic kind of writing, which fets true but different characters againft one another, fo as to caufe a refult of diverting incidents, tho' the perfonages never affect any pleafantry.   'Till then the public were hardly ever diverted with natural faces : Wherefore as they were accuftomed for a long time to a coarfe or *Romantic* comedy, which entertained them with low, or improbable adventures, and introduced none but

dawbed

dawbed or grotefque buffoons on the ftage, they were furprized to behold a mufe, which without putting any ridiculous mafks on the faces of the actors, exhibited neverthelefs moft excellent characters for comedy. Moliere's rivals fwore all this time from the knowledge they had of the ftage, that this new kind of comedy was good for nothing. Thus the public were in fufpence for a few days : They did not know whether they were in the wrong to believe that *Jodolet Mafter and Servant*, and *Don Japhet of Armenia* were in the right tafte ; or whether they were to blame for thinking that this tafte was to be found in the Mifanthrope. But after a certain number of reprefentations people began to fee, that the method of treating comedy as a moral philofopher, was much the beft ; and leaving the jealous poets (a fet of men who are as little to be credited with refpect to the works of their competitors, as women are to be believed with regard to the merit of their rivals) leaving them, I fay, to rail againft the Mifanthrope, they brought themfelves in a very little time to admire it.

Perfons of an exquifite tafte, faw from the very beginning which way the public would fhortly be determined. Every one knows the commendations the duke of Montauzier beftowed on the Mifanthrope upon its very firft reprefentation. Boileau, upon feeing the third, affured Racine, that he was not vexed at the danger to which Moliere's reputation was likely to be expofed, for this comedy would very foon meet with moft furprizing fuccefs. The public juftified the prediction of the author of the art of poetry, and the French for thefe many years have

cited

cited the Mifanthrope as the honor of their comic
ftage. In fact, this is, of all our French pieces, that
which our neighbours feem to be moft fond of.

As for Pradon's Phædra, we ftill remember that a
cabal formed of feveral partizans, among whom there
were perfons equally confiderable for their wit and
the rank they held in the world, had confpired to
raife Pradon's Phædra, and to humble that of Racine.
The confpiracy of the marquifs of Bedmar againft
the republic of Venice, was not conducted with
greater artifice, nor continued with more vigor. But
what was the effect of this confpiracy? It brought
a fuller houfe than there would otherwife have been
to Pradon's tragedy, merely to fee how Racine's
competitor had treated the fame fubject. But
this famous confpiracy could not hinder the public from admiring Racine's Phædra after the fourth
night.   When the fuccefs of thofe two tragedies
feemed pretty equal, reckoning the people who
took tickets at the *Hotel de Guenegaud* and the
Hotel de Bourgogne, one might eafily fee it was
quite the reverfe, upon hearing the fentiments
of thofe who returned from thefe Hotels, where
two feparate companies at that time acted the
French comedy. At a month's end this fhadow of
equality difappeared, and the *Hotel de Guenegaud*,
where Pradon's piece was acted, became a perfect
defert. Every one knows Boileau's verfes on the
fuccefs of Corneille's Cid:

En vain contre le Cid un miniftre fe ligue,
Tout Paris pour Chimene a les yeux de Rodrigue.

In

In vain the court against *the Cid conspires,*
While the whole town the fair Chimene admires.

I have already mentioned the operas of Quinault, and have said enough, methinks, to convince such of our dramatic poets as have miscarried in their plays, that the public proscribes none but bad performances. If we can apply the following verse of Juvenal to them,

Haud tamen invideas vati quem pulpita pascunt.
JUV. Sat. 7.

'Tis for other reasons foreign to my present subject.

It might be still objected, that the Greeks and Romans pronounced frequently unjust sentences in their theatres, which they afterwards retracted. Martial says, that the *men of Athens* denied Menander frequently the prize due to his comedies.

Rara coronato plausere theatra Menandro.

Authors cited by Aulus Gellius [a] have observed, that out of a hundred comedies written by Menander, there had been eight only which obtained the prize given by the ancients to poets, who were so lucky as to write the best piece among those that were represented on certain solemnities. We learn also from Gellius, that Euripides was crowned for five tragedies only out of seventy five which he composed. The public disgusted with Terence's *Hecyra,* when it was first acted, would not let the players go through with it.

I answer, that Gellius and Martial do not say, that the tragedies of Euripides, or Menander's co-

[a] AULUS GELLIUS. lib. 17. cap. 4.

medies

medies were condemned, tho' others might have been more entertaining. Were thofe victorious pieces extant, perhaps we fhould be able to unfold that which dazzled the fpectator : Perhaps we fhould even find, that the fpectator was right in his judgment. Tho' the great Corneille be, generally fpeaking, much fuperior to Rotrou, are there not feveral of the former's tragedies (I will not prefume to determine the number) which would lofe the prize when compared to Rotrou's Wenceflaus, in the judgment of an impartial affembly. In like manner, tho' Menander wrote fome comedies which rendered him fuperior to Philemon (a poet, whofe pieces frequently gained the prize over Menander's) might not Philemon have compofed feveral pieces which merited the prize in preference to fome of Menander's ? Quintilian fays, " that the Athenians " were miftaken in one thing only with refpect to " Philemon, which was, their preferring him too of- " ten to Menander. They would have been in " the right, had they been fatisfied to give him " the fecond place ; for in every body's judg- " ment, he deferved to be ranked immediately next " to Menander [a]." Apuleius fpeaks [b] of this fame Philemon in the fecond book of his *Florida*, as of a poet who had very great talents, and was particularly commendable for the moral excellence of his

---

[a] *Philemon, qui ut pravis fui temporis judiciis Menandro fæpe prælatus eft, ita confenfu omnium meruit credi fecundus.* QUINT. Inft. l. 10.

[b] *Sententiæ vitæ congruentes. Raro apud illum corruptilæ, & uti errores conceffi amores.* APUL. FLOR.

comedies.

comedies. He praises him for abounding in good maxims, for mixing very few dangerous paſſages in his plays, and for treating love as a treacherous and bewitching paſſion. Were not the Athenians in the right to have a regard to the morality of their comic poets, in diſtributing their prizes?

As for Euripides, the very beſt dramatic poets, of Greece were his cotemporaries, and 'tis ſuch pieces as theirs that have frequently obtained the prize in oppoſition to his. 'Tis therefore a wrong thing to place Euripides and Menander at the head of thoſe poets that have been diſregarded by the ſpeѐtators, in order to conſole by the likeneſs of their faces ſuch of our dramatic writers, as have had the misfortune of the public's being diſſatisfied with their performances.

I have ſtill another reaſon to produce in anſwer to the objeѐtion I am refuting. 'Tis that the theatre of thoſe days was not a tribunal comparable to ours. As the theatres of the ancients were very large, where people entered without paying, the aſſemblies degenerated into a multitude of careleſs people, who were conſequently ready to diſturb thoſe that ſhewed any attention. Horace informs us, that the bluſtering of the winds, locked up in the foreſts of Mount St Angel, and the roaring of the ſea, agitated by a tempeſt, did not raiſe a more frightful noiſe than thoſe tumultuous aſſemblies. "What " players, ſays he, have a voice ſtrong enough to " make themſelves heard?"

——Nam

————————*Nam quæ pervincere voces*
Evaluere fonum, referunt quem noftra theatra ?
Garganum mugire putes nemus aut mare Tufcum ;
Tanto cum ftrepitu ludi fpeEtantur.

HORAT. ep. 1. l. 2.

For who can judge, or who can hear the wit
When noife and ftrange confufion fills the pit ?
As when the winds dafh waves againft the fhoar,
Or lafh the woods, and all the monfters roar :
So great the fhout, when rich and ftrangely drefs'd
The player comes, they clap his gawdy veft.

CREECH.

The lower clafs of people who were foon tired, becaufe they could not be attentive throughout the
piece, called out fometimes with loud fhouts and
cries, even as early as the third act, for diverfions
more proportioned to their capacities ; and they even
infulted thofe who defired the comedians to proceed.
A defcription of one of thofe mobbifh uproars may
be feen in the fequel of the above-cited paffage of
Horace, and in the prologue of the *Hecyra*, the reprefentation of which was twice interrupted by the
heat and violence of the people. There were magiftrates indeed appointed to prevent thefe diforders ;
but they feldom did their duty, as is frequently the
cafe in matters of greater importance. At Rome and
under the reign of Tiberius (who of all the Roman
princes underftood beft the art of making himfelf
obeyed) fome of the principal officers of the emperor's guards were either killed or wounded at the theatre, attempting to hinder the diforder ; and the only fatisfaction obtained, was that the fenate gave the

prætors leave to banifh the authors of thofe tumults. The emperors who were defirous of ingratiating themfelves with the people, abolifhed even the cuftom of fending foldiers to mount guard at the play-houfes. Our theatres are not fubject to the like ftorms, but have the happinefs of enjoying a calm and order, which one would think it impoffible to eftablifh in affemblies, that fo lively a nation as ours forms for their diverfion, and where one part of the citizens comes armed, and the other difarmed. Here they liften very peaceably to bad plays, and fometimes to as indifferent players.

We have no public affemblies like the ancients to judge of poems that are not of the dramatic kind. Wherefore artifts are better able to favor, or decry thofe poems, whofe publication is made by means of the ptefs. They have it in their power to fet the fine paffages off, and to excufe the bad ones ; as they can diminifh the merit of the good ones, either by faying they were ftolen, or by comparing them to the verfes of another poet, who has handled the like fubject. When the public have been thus impofed upon in the general character of one of thofe poems, they cannot be undeceived in a day. There is fome time requifite for difinterefted perfons to be fenfible of their miftakes, and to confirm themfelves in the right opinion by the authority of numbers. The greateft proof we can therefore have of the excellency of a poem, upon its firft appearing, is its engaging us to continue the reading of it, and that thofe who have perufed it fpeak of it with a kind of affection, even when they cenfure its faults.

I am of opinion, that the time requisite for deciding the merit of a new poem, such as can be really called a good work, is confined to two years after its first edition. If it is a bad performance, the public does not take so much time to condemn it, let the professors of the art exert themselves ever so much to support its reputation. When the Maid of Orleans made its first appearance, it had the advantage of being encouraged by men of letters, as well French as foreigners. The great men of the nation had crowned it already with favors, and the world prepossessed by all these encomiums, waited for it with the censer in hand. And yet as soon as the Maid of Orleans was read, people shook off their prejudice, and despised it even before any critic had published the reasons of its being worthy of contempt. The premature credit of the work occasioned numbers to inquire into this affair with greater curiosity and spirit: and every one learnt from the first researches they made, that others yawned as well as themselves in perusing it, and that the maid was grown old in her cradle.

C H A P. XXXI.

That the public judgment is not recalled, but is every day more strongly confirmed.

THE judgment of the public receives an additional strength from time. The Maid of Orleans is continually more despised; whilst every day increases the veneration with which we look up-

on

on Polyeuctes, Phædra, the Misanthrope, and the Art of poetry. The reputation of a poet cannot reach during his life to its due point of elevation. An author, who is thirty years of age, when he publishes his best works, cannot live so many years longer as is necessary for the public to know, not only that his works are excellent, but likewise that they are of the same order as those Greek and Roman pieces, which have been so much extolled by those that understood them. 'Till the works of a modern author are placed in the abovementioned rank, his reputation may increase continually. Wherefore two or three years are sufficient to know whether a new poem be good, or indifferent; but perhaps an intire century is requisite to be able to judge of its whole merit, upon supposition of its being a work of the first order. Hence the Romans, who had Tibullus and Propertius's elegies in their hands, were some time before they ranked those of Ovid in the same class. Hence likewise that same people did not quit the reading of Ennius, as soon as Virgil's Eclogues and Bucolics made their first appearance. This is what the following epigram from Martial literally signifies, which is generally cited by poets, who are not so happy as to meet with success.

Ennius est lectus salvo tibi Roma Marone.

MART. 10. Epigr. lib. 5.

It would be so much the more ridiculous to pretend, that Martial meant here, that the Romans had placed Ennius's poems for some time in the same rank with the Æneid, as this epigram can relate only

to

to what paſſed at Rome in Virgil's life-time. Now every one knows that the Æneid was one of thoſe works which are called poſthumous, for being pub-liſhed after the death of the author.

I diſtinguiſh two ſorts of merit (If I may call them ſo) in a poem ; one real, and the other compara-tive. The firſt conſiſts in pleaſing and moving : The ſecond in moving as much or more than authors of a known character. It conſiſts in plea-ſing and engaging as much as thoſe Greeks and Romans, who are generally ſuppoſed to have attained to the higheſt pitch that human underſtanding can reach, becauſe we have not yet ſeen any thing that ſurpaſſes them.

Cotemporaries judge well of the real merit of a work, but they are apt to miſtake, when they judge of its comparative merit, or when they at-tempt to decide the rank due to it. They are ſubject in this caſe to fall into one of the following errors.

The firſt is to put a work too ſoon upon a level with thoſe of the ancients. The ſecond, to ſuppoſe a greater diſtance than there is in reality between it and the ancient pieces. I ſay therefore in the firſt place, that the public are miſtaken ſometimes, when too much charmed with ſuch new pro-ductions as move and pleaſe them ; they uſurp unſeaſonably the rights of poſterity, by decid-ing that theſe productions are of the ſame order as the claſſic, and, as we commonly call them, conſecrated performances of the Greeks and Ro-mans ; and that their authors will be always the principal poets in their language. 'Tis thus the

X 3   cotem-

cotemporaries of Ronfard and the French Pleiades
were miftaken, in pronouncing that the French poets would never be able to furpafs thofe new Prometheus's [a] who, to exprefs myfelf poetically, had no
other divine fire at their difpofal, but what they borrowed from the writings of the ancients.

Ronfard, the brighteft ftar of thofe pleiades, had
a great deal of learning, but very little genius. We
do not find in his verfes fuch fublime ideas, fuch
happy turns of expreffion, nor fuch noble figures, as
we obferve in the Greek and Latin authors. As
he had no enthufiafm, but was a mere admirer of
the ancients, the reading of them warmed him, and
ferved him inftead of Apollo's tripod. But as
he boldly adopts (which is his fole merit) the
beauties collected in his reading, without confining
himfelf to the rules of our fyntax, thefe beauties
feem to rife from his own invention. His liberties of
expreffion appear like fallies of a natural warmth of
vein, and his verfes compofed in imitation of Virgil
and Homer, have alfo the air of an original. The
ornaments therefore with which his works are ftrewed, were capable of pleafing readers, who did not
underftand thofe originals, or who were fo doatingly
fond of them, as to carefs even the refemblance
of their features in the moft disfigured copies. 'Tis
true, Ronfard's language is not French ; but people
imagined at that time, that it was impoffible to
write poetically and correctly in our tongue. Befides, poems in the vulgar languages are as neceffary
for polite nations, as thofe firft conveniences that are

---

[a] RONSARD, BELLEAU, JOACHIM DU BELLAY, JODELLE,
PONTUS DE THIART, DORAT, BAIF.

I   contrived

contrived by a growing luxury. When Ronſard and his cotemporaries, of whom he was the chief, appeared, our anceſtors had hardly any poems which they could read with pleaſure. The commerce with the ancients, which had been ſurprizingly increaſed ſince the recovery of letters, by the invention of printing, gave people a diſtaſte at that time for our old writers of romances. Hence Ronſard's cotemporaries looked upon his poems, as pieces dropt down from heaven. Had they been ſatisfied with ſaying, that his verſes were infinitely pleaſing to them, and that the images they abound in were vaſtly engaging, we ſhould have no reaſon to condemn them. But they ſeemed to claim a right which did not belong to them; and uſurped the prerogative of poſterity, by proclaiming him the greateſt French poet of their time, as well as of future ages.

There have been French poets ſince Ronſard, who had more genius, and beſides compoſed correctly. Hence we have laid Ronſard aſide, to make the works of the latter our preſent amuſement. We very juſtly prefer them to Ronſard; but thoſe who are acquainted with the latter, are not ſurprized that his cotemporaries found a pleaſure in reading his works, notwithſtanding the Gothic taſte of his images. I ſhall finiſh the ſubject of Ronſard with one remark. This is, that the cotemporaries of this poet were not miſtaken in their judgment with reſpect to his works, and ſuch others as were then extant. They did not prefer in earneſt the Franciad to the Æneid, when this French poem was firſt publiſhed. The ſame reaſons which hindered them from being miſtaken in this point, would

have

have likewife prevented them from preferring the Franciad to the Cinna and the Horatii, had thefe tragedies been then extant.

After what has been here faid, 'tis evident we muft leave to time and experience the determination of the rank, which the poets our cotemporaries are to hold among writers, who compofe that collection of books, which is raifed by men of letters of all nations, and may be called *the library of mankind.* Every nation has, 'tis true, a particular library of good books written in their own language, but there is befides a common one for all nations. We muft therefore wait 'till a poet's reputation has gradually increafed during a century, before we can decide, that he deferves to be ranked in the fame clafs with thofe Greek and Roman authors, whofe works are faid generally to be confecrated, becaufe they are of the number of thofe, which Quintilian [a] defines, *the monuments of the ingenious that have the approbation of a long fucceffion of ages.*

In the fecond place, I fay, that the public commits fometimes another fault, by fuppofing the works of their cotemporaries to be remoter than they really are, from the perfection to which the ancients attained. When we have as many poems in our hands as we can read, we are too difficult in doing juftice to feveral excellent productions, and for a long while we place them at too great a diftance from confecrated performances. But every one will make naturally of himfelf the reflections I fhould be capable of offering on this fubject.

a *Ingeniorum monumenta quæ faculis probantur.* QUINT. Inft. l 3. c 9.

Let

Let us fay fomething now of the prefages, by which we may promife to fuch works as have been pub- lifhed in our days and in thofe of the preceding ge- neration, the glory of being ranked by pofterity, in the fame order with the ancients. 'Tis a favor- able omen for a work of this kind, that its reputa- tion increafes every year. This happens, when the author has no fucceffor, and much more, when he has been dead a long time without having been re- placed. Nothing is a greater proof of his having been an uncommon perfon in the fphere in which he fhone, than the inutility of the efforts of thofe who have attempted to rival him. Thus fixty years which are elapfed fince the death of Moliere, with- out fubftituting a perfon of equal abilities in his room, add a luftre to his reputation, which it could not have acquired a year after his deceafe. The public have not ranked in the fame clafs with Moliere, the very beft of our comic writers who have appear- ed fince his death. This honor has not been done to Renard, to Bourfault, to the two authors of the *Grumbler* [a] nor to feveral other comic poets, whofe pieces have diverted the public, when well act- ed. Thofe even amongft our poets who are moft inclined to gafconading, never compared themfelves ferioufly to Moliere ; nor have they ever ranked the author of the *Philofopher married* above him. Every year that paffes without giving a fucceffor to the French Terence will add fomething to his reputation. But (fome will afk me) are you fure that pofterity will not contradict the encomiums, which have been

[a] The Abbot de BRUIEIS and PALAPRAT.

beftowed

beſtowed by cotemporaries on thoſe French poets, whom you conſider as placed already by future ages in the ſame rank with Horace and Terence ?

C H A P. XXXII.

That, in ſpite of critics, the reputation of our admired poets will always increaſe.

THE works of our eminent French poets have no reaſon, methinks, to apprehend the fate of thoſe of Ronſard. They have compoſed in the ſame taſte as the excellent authors of antiquity ; they have imitated them with judgment, and not as Ronſard and his cotemporaries, that is, ſervilely, and as Horace ſays that Servilius had imitated the Greeks,

⸺⸺ *Hoſce ſecutus,*
Mutatis tantum numeris. ⸺

This ſervile imitation of poets who have wrote in foreign languages, is the fate of authors who compoſe when their nation begins to ſhake off its barbarouſneſs. But our beſt French poets have imitated the ancients, as Horace and Virgil imitated the Greeks, that is, by following, as the others had done, the genius of the language in which they compoſed, and by taking nature for their firſt model. Good writers borrow nothing, but the manner of copying nature. The ſtyle of Racine, Boileau, La Fontaine, and our other illuſtrious countrymen, will never grow ſo old as to ſurfeit people with
the

the reading of their works ; no, it will be impoffible to read them without being ftruck with their beauties, becaufe they are copied from nature.

In faft, our language, methinks, attained feventy years ago to its higheft pitch of perfection. An author printed fixty years before Ablancourt, feemed in his time a Gothic writer. Now, tho' 'tis already upwards of fourfcore years fince Ablancourt wrote, his ftyle does not appear to us to have grown old. In order to write well, we muft always be direfted by thofe rules, which this author and his firft fucceffors have followed. Every reafonable change that may happen to a language, once its fyntax is become regular, can fall only upon words. Some wax old, or obfolete ; others become fafhionable ; fome new ones are coined ; and the orthography of others is altered, in order to foften the pronunciation. Horace has drawn the horofcope of all languages, where he fays of his own :

Multa renafcentur quæ jam cecidere, cadentque
Quæ nunc funt in honore vocabula, fi volet ufus,
Quem penes arbitrium eft & jus & norma loquendi.
                    Hor. de arte poet.

Some words that have, or elfe will feel decay,
Shall be reftor'd, and come again in play ;
And words now fam'd, fhall not be fancy'd long,
They fhall not pleafe the ear, nor move the tongue :
As ufe fhall thefe approve, and thofe condemn,
Ufe the fole rule of fpeech, and judge fupreme.
                    Creech.

Ufe

Ufe is generally the mafter of words, but very fel-dom of the rules of fyntax. Now old words never, make us grow tired of an author, whofe phrafes are laid out in a regular conftruction. Do we not still read Amiot with pleafure ? I fhall make one obfervation here by the way ; 'tis not becaufe the La-tin authors of the fecond and fubfequent centuries made ufe of new words, or becaufe the conftruction of their phrafes was not purfuant to the rules of grammar, that their ftyle appears to us fo inferior to that of Livy and his cotemporaries. The authors of the fecond and following centuries have, generally fpeaking, ufed the fame words as Livy. Their phrafes have been formed according to the fame rules of fyntax as his, at leaft the difference between them in this refpect was very inconfiderable. But vicious tranfpofitions were in fafhion in their times ; the cuftom of taking words in a tranflated fenfe that did not fuit them, was authorized ; and they were employed, without any regard to their proper fignification, either in foolifh epithets, or in thofe figures whofe falfe luftre prefents no diftinct image. 'Tis fo far true, that 'tis punning upon words, and the abufe of metaphors, which, for example, disfigure the profe of Sidonius Apollinaris, that the laws made by Majorianus, and the other emperors cotemporaries of this bifhop, are drawn up in as pure a ftyle as if they had been made in the time of the firft Cæfars, by reafon that the authors of thofe laws, reftrained by the dignity of their work from exceeding the limits of a grave and fimple ftyle, have not been expofed to the danger of making an abufe of figures, and of hunting after

points

points and falfe wit. But tho' the ftyle becomes corrupted, and the language adulterated, people will always
admire the ftyle of fuch authors, as have wrote when
the language was in its full force and purity. We
continue to commend their noble fimplicity, even
when we are incapable of imitating it ; for it is frequently our incapacity of performing as well as
they, that is the caufe of our undertaking to do
better. This tinfel and ftudy of points is fo often
fubftituted in the room of fenfe and energy of difcourfe, for no other reafon but becaufe it is eafier to
have fome fhare of wit, than to be both moving
and natural.

Virgil, Horace, Cicero, and Livy, were read
and admired, as long as the Latin was a living
language ; and the writers who compofed five
hundred years after thofe authors, and when the
Latin ftyle was already in a ftate of depravity, are
more liberal in their praifes upon them, than thofe
who lived in the time of Auguftus. The refpect
and veneration for the authors of the fame age as
Plato continued in Greece, notwithftanding the degeneracy of artifts. Thofe authors were admired as
great models, two thoufand years after they had
wrote, and at a time when they had fo few imitators. For the truth of this I appeal to the teftimony of thofe Greeks, who explained thefe authors to us after the taking of Conftantinople by the
Turks. The good writers of the age of Leo X, as
Machiavel and Guicciardin, are not grown obfolete,
with regard to the prefent Italians : Nay, fo far
from that, their ftyle is preferred to the moft florid
way of writing of later writers, becaufe the phrafe

I of

of the Italian tongue attained to its full regularity as early as the fixteenth century.

Whether therefore the ftyle, which our principal authors adopted under Lewis XIV, continues always in fafhio
which our poets and orators endeavour to compofe; or whether it has the lot of the ftyle in vogue under the two firft Cæfars, which began to degenerate in the reign of Claudius, when men of wit ufurped the liberty of introducing figures to excefs; and endeavoured to fupply with tinfel, that force of fenfe and fimple elegance which their genius could not reach to ; I maintain, that the celebrated poets of the age of Lewis XIV will be immortal like Virgil and Ariofto.

In the fecond place, our neighbours admire as much as we ourfelves, our celebrated French poets, and are as ready in repeating by heart thofe verfes of Boileau and la Fontaine, which pafs for proverbs. They have even adopted our beft works, by tranflating them into their own language. Notwithftanding the jealoufy of wit and learning, which reigns between nations as well as individuals, they rank fome of thefe tranflations above the works of the fame kind that have been compofed in their own country. Our good poems, like thofe of Homer and Virgil, are already placed in the abovementioned common library of nations. 'Tis as rare to find a cabinet in foreign countries without a Moliere, as without a Terence. The Italians, who avoid as much as poffible all occafions of giving us any fubject

charged with the care of our conduct) have done
juftice

juſtice to the merit of our poets. As we uſed to admire and tranſlate their poets of the ſixteenth century, they have paid the ſame honors to ours of the
ſeventeenth; and have rendered the beſt pieces of
our comic and tragic writers into Italian. Caſtelli,
ſecretary to the elector of Brandenburg, has tranſlated
Moliere's works into Italian, a verſion which has
gone thro' ſeveral editions. There are alſo ſome of
Moliere's pieces, which have not only been literally
tranſlated more than once into Italian, but have
been moreover found ſo pleaſing, as to deſerve to
be dreſſed and traveſted, as it were, into Italian comedies. There is an Italian comedy intitled, Don
Pilone[a], which Signor Gigli the author ſays he borrowed from Moliere's Tartuffe. To make a remark here
by the way, as Signor Gigli does not mention in his
preface what I remember to have read in ſome memoirs or other, viz. that the Tartuffe was origi-
nally an Italian comedy, and that Moliere had only
adapted it to the French ſtage; as, I ſay, Signor Gigli
makes no mention of it, we may very well queſtion
the truth of what the author of thoſe memoirs advances, who perhaps only heard it as a report. The
Italians laugh and weep at theſe pieces with more
earneſtneſs and paſſion, than at the repreſentation
of their own theatrical performances; and have been
ſo much affected with them, that even ſome of
their poets have complained of it. The abbot Gra-

---

[a] *Il Don Pilone overo il Backettone falſo, comedia tratta nova-
mente dal Franceſe da Girolamo Gigli, e dedicata all' Ill. Cont.
Flavia Theodoli Bolognetti In Luca per Mareſcardoli, con licenza
de' ſuperiori, l'anno 1711. Pref. il ſoggetto di queſta opera è
tirato dal celebre Tartuffo del Molier.*

vina,

vina, in his differtation on tragedy printed about five and twenty years ago[a], fays, that his countrymen adopt without judgment fome of our dramatic pieces, whofe faults have been cenfured by our nation, who has explained herfelf upon this head by the mouth of two of her ableft critics. He means here Rapin and M. Dacier, whofe judgments he produces on the French tragedies ; judgments which he adopts with fo much the more pleafure, as he had compofed his work principally to fhew the fuperiority of the ancient tragedy over the modern. But methinks it will not be amifs to give the abbot's own words, defiring my reader at the fame time not to forget that this gentleman was a poet himfelf, and had compofed feveral tragedies in imitation of the ancients[b]. *Thus we have feen with what feverity the French nation (a nation fo prodigioufly improved fince the time of Francis I) paffes her judgment on the merit of her own theatrical pieces by means of her moft learned critics ; and with what precaution and diftinction fhe propofes fuch, as are blindly and indifcriminately received and diffufed amongft our theatres, tranflated with the fringes of ridiculous points, romantic expreffions, and other fuch glittering*

[a] In 1715.

[b] *Or ecco quefta nazione dal tempo di Francefco primo fino à noftri giorni cultiffima, con che ferieta di giudicio per mezzo de i fuoi piu fini critici prononcia delle proprie opere teatrali, e con che diftintione propone quelle, che da noi ciecamente & fenza difcrezione alcuna fono ricevute e fparfe per tutti i teatri, e tradotte col fregio de i novi penfieri falfi ed efpreffioni piu Romanefche ed altre più belle pompe, le quali ftaccano per fempre la mente e la favella de gli uomini*

glittering tinfel, which never fail to alienate the minds and language of men from the rules of nature and rea-fon. If, as this author pretends, his countrymen dawb our pieces with points and romantic expreffions, the reproach does not relate to us.

Young people that have any thing of a polite education, are as well acquainted with Boileau as with Horace, and generally retain as many verfes of the French as of the Latin poet, at the Hague, Stockholm, Copenhagen, in Poland, Germany, and even in England. We need not be afraid of the partiality of the Englifh in our favor ; yet they admire Racine, Corneille, Boileau, and Moliere. They have fhewn the fame efteem for them as for Virgil and Cicero, by tranflating them into their language ; for as foon as a French piece fucceeds in France, it is almoft fure of attaining to this honor. I do not think that the Englifh have three different tranflations of Virgil's eclogues, and yet they have three different verfions of the tragedy of the Horatii by Corneille [a]. As early as 1675 they had a profe verfion of Racine's Andromache, revifed and fitted to the ftage by M. Crown. In 1712 Mr Philips publifhed a new tranflation in verfe of this fame tragedy, which has been alfo acted. 'Tis true, he has added three fcenes at the end of the fifth act, and as they are very proper for fhewing the tafte of Philips's countrymen, I will give here an extract of what they contain. In the firft of thefe additional fcenes, Phœnix appears with a numerous retinue,

mini dalle regole della natura, e della ragione. GRAVINA, p. 115.

[a] *That of Lower printed in* 1656 *That of Cotton printed in* 1671. *That of Mrs Philips finifhed by Sir John Denham, and printed in* 1678.

whom he commands to pursue Orestes. In the second, Andromache appears again upon the stage, not as M. Racine made her return in the first edition of his tragedy [a] that is, as a captive of Orestes, who is going to carry her with him to Sparta. But she comes back to offer to the body of Pyrrhus, which is brought upon the stage, all the attendance and care of a fond wife afflicted with the death of her husband. In the third scene, hearing a military sound which announces the proclamation of her son Astianax, she abandons herself to sentiments suitable to her character.

I speak here of those translations only which are published as such; for it frequently happens that English translators will not own themselves in that character, but attempt to give their copy for an original. How often has Mr Dryden [b], even in the judgment of his own countrymen, given nothing more than a mere translation of French authors in works, which he published for his own? But I should fatigue the reader, were I to enter too far into these particulars.

The Germans have rendered several of our French poets into their tongue, tho' they had less occasion for translations of this sort, than other nations, by reason that they have honored our language with making it familiar in their country. They write very frequently to one another in French, and several princes use this language in corresponding with their ministers, tho' they are natives of Germany.

[a] Done in 1668. p. 86.
[b] LANGBAINE's Lives of the dramatic poets. p. 131.

In Holland, thofe that have any thing of an education, fpeak French from their youth. The States ufe this language on feveral occafions, and even fix their great feal to acts drawn up in French. The Dutch neverthelefs have tranflated feveral of our beft works, efpecially our dramatic pieces; which they have naturalized as Dutchmen.

Count Ericeyra, the worthy heir of the Livy of his country, has tranflated Boileau's Art of poetry into Portuguefe. Now 'tis obfervable that our neighbours did not tranflate our old tragedies, fuch as thofe of Jodelle and Garnier. In Henry the IVth's time, there was no fuch thing, as companies of French comedians ftrolling about Holland, Poland, Germany, the North, and fome ftates of Italy, to act the pieces of Hardi and Chretien. But now there are companies of French comedians, that have fixt fettlements in foreign countries.

The fuffrage of our neighbours, which is as free and difinterefted as that of pofterity, appears to me as a fecurity of its approbation. The praifes which Boileau has beftowed upon Moliere and Racine, will procure them as much efteem in future times, as they have obtained amongft the Englifh and the Italians our cotemporaries.

It will not fignify to fay, that the vogue which the French language has had within thefe feventy years, is the caufe of the reputation which our poems have in foreign countries. Foreigners will tell us themfelves, that our poems and books have contributed more than any thing elfe to give the language, in which they are wrote, fo great a

currency,

currency, that it has almoſt deprived the Latin of the advantage of being a language, which moſt na-tions learn by a kind of tacit convention, to make themſelves underſtood. We may apply to the French tongue what Cicero ſaid of the Greek [a] : *Greek works are read by almoſt every nation ; but the Latin is confined within its own narrow bounds.* When a German miniſter has an affair to negotiate with an Engliſh or Dutch miniſter, there is no diſ-pute about the language they are to uſe in their con-ferences : It has been ſettled long ago, that they are to ſpeak French. Foreigners even complain that the French invades the rights, as it were, of living languages, by introducing its words and phraſes in-ſtead of their own expreſſions. The Germans and Dutch complain, that the uſe which their country-men make of French words, but eſpecially of the verbs, in ſpeaking Dutch and German, corrupts their languages, as much as Ronſard corrupted the French by the words and phraſes of the learned languages, with which he intermixed his verſes. The Examiner, the author of a political paper pub-liſhed periodically in London about thirty years ago, ſays that the French begins to be ſo vaſtly blended with the Engliſh phraſes, in ſpeaking of military affairs, that the common people in Eng-land are no longer able to underſtand the pre-ſent relations of ſieges and battles written by their countrymen. The abbot Gravina has made the ſame complaint with regard to the Italian in his

[a] *Græca leguntur in omnibus ferè gentibus. Latina ſuis finibus exiguis ſanè continentur.* CIC. orat. pro ARCHIA.

book

book upon tragedy. We have even reafon to think, that the writings of the great men of our nation bid fair for fecuring to our language the fate of the Greek and Roman tongues, that is of rendering it a learned language, if ever it happens to be a dead one.

But (fome will fay) may not future critics obferve fuch grofs miftakes in thofe admired writings, as will render them contemptible to pofterity?

I anfwer, that the moft fubtle remarks of the greateft metaphyficians will never be able to diminifh one degree of the reputation of our poets, be-caufe fuch remarks, were they even to be juft, will never ftrip our poems of thofe charms, by which they have a right to pleafe all readers. If the faults which thofe critics fhould happen to con-demn, are contrary to the art of poetry, they will only teach us to know the caufe of an effect, which was already felt. Thofe who faw the Cid, before the criticifms of the French academy were publifhed, were fenfible of fome defects in this poem, tho' incapable to tell diftinctly in what they confifted. If thefe faults fhould be contrary to other fciences, fuch as geography, or aftronomy, the public will be obliged to the critics who detect them; but ftill they will be incapable of diminifhing the reputation of the poet, which is not founded on this, that his ver-fes are free from the like miftakes, but that the read-ing of them is engaging. I faid, were even thofe remarks to be juft; for in all probability, for one good remark there would be a hundred bad ones.

'Tis undoubtedly much eafier to make well-grounded remarks on poems, when their authors

are

are known, and when they fpeak of fuch things as we have feen, or whofe explications or applications are preferved by a yet recent tradition ; than it will be hereafter, when all thefe lights will be extinguifhed by time and by revolutions to which human focieties are fubject. Now the remarks which are made at prefent againft our modern poets, and dwell upon errors into which, 'tis pretended, they have fallen, either with refpect to phyfics or aftronomy, are frequently a proof that the critics have a mind to find fault, not that the poets have committed fuch errors. Let us give one example.

Boileau compofed his letter to Monfieur de Guilleragues towards the year 1675, at a time when the new philofophy was the modifh fcience; for we have fafhions in fciences as well as in cloaths. Even the very ladies ftudied the new fyftems at that time, which feveral profeffors taught in our vulgar language at Paris. 'Tis very likely that Moliere, who wrote his *Learned Women* towards the year 1672, and who puts the dogmas and ftyle of the new philofophy fo frequently into the mouths of his heroins, attacked in 'that comedy the excefs of a reigning tafte, and that he expofed a ridiculous character which feveral perfons acted every day in private life. When Boileau wrote his epiftle to Monfieur de Guilleragues, the converfations on phyfics brought frequently upon the tapis the fpots of the fun, by the help of which aftronomers obferved that this planet turns on its own axis in about feven and twenty days. Some of thefe *maculæ* having difappeared, occafioned a great noife even upon Parnaffus. The wits on this occafion faid, that the fun, in order to attain to a greater refemblance

femblance to the late king, who had taken it for the body of his device, had got rid of his fpots.

In this juncture, Boileau willing to exprefs poetically, that notwithftanding the prevailing tafte he applied himfelf intirely to the ftudy of morals preferable to that of phyfics, (a fentiment very fuitable to a fatyric poet) writes to his friend, that he refigns feveral queftions, which the latter fcience treats of, to the refearches of other people. Let others, fays he, inquire,

Si le foleil eft fixe, ou tourne fur fon axe.
Does the fun ftand, or on its axis turn ?

Certain it is, that the poet means here to fpeak only of the queftion, whether the fun placed in the center of our vortex, turns on its axis, or not. Even the very conftruction of the phrafe is fufficient alone to prove, that it can have no other meaning, and this is the fenfe which offers itfelf at the very firft perufal. Neverthelefs feveral critics have explained this verfe, as if the author intended to oppofe the fyftem of Copernicus, which makes the planets whirl round the fun placed in the center of our vortex, to the opinion of fuch as maintain that the fun hath its proper motion, by which it turns on its own axis. If Boileau meant any fuch thing, he was certainly in the wrong. The opinion of thofe who affirm that the fun turns on its axis, and the fyftem of fuch as maintained before the late difcoveries, that it was immoveable in the center of the vortex, fuppofe both alike that the fun is in the middle of the vortex, where Copernicus has placed it. Monfieur Perrault objected againft Boileau upwards of thirty years ago, [a] *That thofe who maintain*

[a] Preface to the *Apology for women.* p. 7.

that

that the fun is fixt and immoveable, are the fame who hold that it turns on its own axis, and that they are not two different opinions, as he feems to infinuate in his verfes. True it is, continues Monfieur Perrault fome lines lower, *that it is not handfome for fo great a poet, to be ignorant of thofe arts and fciences he pretends to fpeak of.* But 'tis not Boileau's fault, if Monfieur Perrault mifunderdands him, and much lefs is it his fault, if other critics are pleafed to imagine that by the abovementioned words, he intended to oppofe the fyftem of Copernicus to that of Ptolomy, which fuppofes that the fun turns round the earth. Boileau has repeated it a hundred times, that his fole intention was to oppofe the opinion of thofe who made the fun turn on its own axis, to the fyftem of fuch as would not admit of this motion ; and the verfe itfelf points out this fenfe clear enough to want no explication.

Accufations of this nature have not leffened the reputation of our poets, fince the ancients never fuffered for the like injurious imputations, tho' far more confiderable in number. As they wrote in languages that are reckoned dead in our days, and as a great many things they fpoke of are but very imperfectly known by the moft learned ; we may without temerity believe, that their critics and commentators are frequently in the wrong, even on feveral occafions, where one cannot prove that they are not in the right.

We may therefore venture to predict, without any danger of prefumption, the fame fate as that of Virgil, Horace, and Cicero, to the French writers who have honoured the age of Lewis XIV, that

is

is of being confidered in all ages and nations, as upon a rank with thofe great men, whofe works are efteemed the moft valuable productions of the human underftanding.

C H A P.   XXXIII.

That the veneration and refpect for the excellent authors of antiquity will always continue. Whether it be true that we reafon better than the ancients.

BUT are not (fome will fay) thofe great men themfelves expofed to be degraded? May not our prefent veneration for the ancients be changed into a fimple efteem, in ages more enlightened than thofe which have fo much admired them? Is not Virgil's reputation in danger of the fame fate, as that of Ariftotle? Is not the Iliad expofed to the deftiny of Ptolomy's fyftem, with regard to which the world is at prefent undeceived? Our critics make poems and other works undergo a feverer trial, than they have been heretofore ufed to. They make analyfes of them, purfuant to the method of geometricians; a very proper method for difcovering the faults which efcaped the preceding cenfors. The arms of the ancient critics were not fo fharp as ours. 'Tis eafy to judge by the prefent ftate of the natural fciences, how much our age is more enlightened than thofe of Plato, Auguftus, and Leo X. The perfection to which we have brought the art of reafoning, which has led us into fo many difcoveries in the natural sciences, is a fertile source of new lights, which begin to spread themselves already over polite learning, and are likely to dispel the old prejudices from thence, as they have removed them from the natural sciences. These lights will communicate themselves likewise to the various professions of life, and we begin already to perceive their dawn in all states and conditions. Perhaps the next generation, shocked with the enormous blunders of Homer and his companions, will despise them, as a person who has attained to the use of reason, contemns the boyish stories which were the amusement of his infancy.

Our age may be perhaps more learned than the preceding ones ; but I deny that the human understanding has at present, generally speaking, more penetration, and justness, than in those times. As the most learned men have not always the most sense ; so one age, more learned than another, is not always the most rational. Now our present dispute relates to good sense, since the question is about judging. In questions where facts are generally known, a person does not judge better than another, because he is more learned, but because he has more sense and justness of mind.

It cannot certainly be proved, by the conduct of people in high or low stations of life, within these seventy years, in all those states of Europe, in which the study of sciences, that are so great an improvement to human reason, flourishes most, that the minds of men have been sounder and clearer within this period than in the preceding ages, and that during this time they have been more rational than their

their anceftors. This date of feventy years, which is given for an epoch to this pretended renovation of minds, is very ill chofen. I do not care to enter into odious details, with regard to nations and individuals, I fhall be fatisfied with faying, that this philofophical fpirit, which renders men fo rational, and as it were *fo conclufive*, will very foon reduce a great part of Europe into the fame ftate it was in under the Goths and Vandals, fuppofing it continues to make the fame progrefs, as it has done within thefe feventy years. I fee the neceffary arts neglected ; the moft ufeful fyftems for the prefervation of fociety abolifhed ; and fpeculative reafonings preferred to practice. We behave without any regard to experience, the beft director of mankind, and we have the imprudence to act, as if we were the firft generation that knew how to reafon. The care of pofterity is intirely neglected ; and the expences which our anceftors made in buildings and moveables, would have been loft to us, infomuch that we fhould not be able to find wood in our forefts for buildings or fire, had they been rational after our prefent manner.

Tho' kingdoms and republics (fome will fay) reduce themfelves to the neceffity of ruining, either their fubjects who lend them money, or the people who fupport thofe ftates by their labor which they will be no longer able to continue, after they are reduced to indigence ; tho' particulars behave, as if they were to have their enemies for their heirs, and the prefent generation acts, as if it were to be the laft fprig of mankind : this does not however hinder us from reafoning with refpect to fciences, better than our predeceffors.

predeceffors. They may have furpaffed us, if this expreffion be allowed me, in *practical reafon*, but we excel them in the *fpeculative.* One may judge of our fuperiority of wit and reafon over men of paft ages, by the ftate in which the natural fciences are at prefent, and that in which they were in former times.

I anfwer, that 'tis true the natural fciences, which cannot be too much efteemed, nor their depofitaries or truftees too much honored, are more perfect at prefent than they were in Auguftus's time or in that of Leo X. But this is not owing to our having a greater juftnefs and folidity of mind, nor to our knowing better how to reafon than the people of thofe days, nor to a kind of regeneration of minds : The only caufe of the perfection of natural fciences, or to fpeak more exactly, the only caufe of thefe fciences being lefs imperfect at prefent than they were in former days, is our knowing more facts than they were acquainted with. Time and chance have opened to us within thefe latter times an infinite number of difcoveries, in which I fhall prove, that reafoning has had very little fhare ; and thefe difcoveries have demonftrated the falfity of feveral philofophical dogmas, fubftituted by our predeceffors in ftead of truth, which men were before incapable of knowing.

And here, methinks, we have hit upon the folution of a problem that has been often propounded : Why fhould not our poets and orators furpafs thofe of antiquity, as 'tis certain that our learned in natural fciences excel the ancient natural philofophers ? We are indebted to time for whatfoever advantage we may chance to have over the ancients in natural fciences. Time has

has demonftrated feveral facts which the ancients were ignorant of, in whofe place they fubftituted erroneous opinions, which were the occafion of their making a hundred falfe reafonings. The fame advantage which time has given us over the ancients, our pofterity will have over us. 'Tis fufficient one age fucceeds another to excel the preceding in the natural fciences, unlefs there has happened fome revolution in fociety confiderable enough to extinguifh, to the prejudice of pofterity, the lights by which their anceftors were directed.

But has not reafoning, fay they, contributed very much to extend the new difcoveries ? I grant it ; moreover I do not deny but that we reafon with juftnefs. I only deny that we reafon with greater folidity than the Greeks and Romans ; and I am fatisfied with affirming, that they would have made as good a ufe as we, of the capital truths which hazard, as it were, has detected to us, had it difcovered the fame truths to them. I ground my fuppofition on this, that they have reafoned as well as we, on all thofe fubjects of which they could have as much knowledge ; and that we do not reafon better than they, except in things of which we are better inftructed, either by experience or revelation, that is, in natural fciences, and theology.

In order to prove that we reafon better than the ancients, it would be requifite to fhew, that it is to the juftnefs of our reafoning, and not to chance, or fortuitous experiments, we are indebted for the knowledge of fuch truths as we know and they did not. But far from being able to

evince

evince that we are under an obligation for our new difcoveries to philofophers who attained to the moft important natural truths by methodical refearches, and by the fo much boafted affiftance of the art of making a concatenation of conclufions ; the very reverfe of all this can be demonftrated. We can fhew that thefe inventions, and, as it were, original difcoveries, are intirely owing to hazard, and that we have benefited by them only in quality of laft comers.

In the firft place, I fhall not be cenfured for denying to philofophers and the learned who inveftigate methodically the fecrets of nature, all thofe inventions whereof they are not generally acknowledged the inventers. I can refufe them the honor of all the difcoveries made within thefe three hundred years, which have not been publifhed under the name of fome learned perfon. As philofophers, and their friends likewife write, the public is informed of their difcoveries, and quickly hears to what illuftrious perfon it owes the leaft obligation. Wherefore I may deny that philofophers are the inventers of fluices which have been difcovered within thefe two hundred years, and have been not only of infinite fervice in commerce, but have likewife furnifhed fubjects for fo many remarks on the nature and properties of water. I may deny that they were the inventers of water-mills or wind-mills, as alfo of weight or balance clocks, which have been fo ufeful in obfervations of all kinds, by enabling us to meafure time with exactnefs. I may deny likewife that they were the inventers of gun-powder, which has been the occafion of fo many obfer-

vations

vations on the air ; nor of feveral other difcoveries, whofe authors are not certainly known, tho' they have contributed very much towards the perfecting of the natural fciences.

Secondly, I can alledge fome pofitive proofs of my propofition. I can make it appear that me-thodical refearches had no fhare in the four dif-coveries, that have contributed the moft towards what fuperiority our prefent times may have over paft ages in the natural fciences. Thefe four difco-veries, namely, the knowledge of the weight of the air, the compafs, the art of printing, and the telef-cope, are intirely owing to experiments and hazard.

Printing, an art fo favorable to the advance-ment of fciences, which grow more perfect in pro-portion as knowledge is thereby extended, was dif-covered in the fifteenth century, and near two hun-dred years before Defcartes, who paffes for the father of the new philofophy, had publifhed his medita-tions. 'Tis difputed who was the firft inventer of printing [a], but no one attributes this honor to a philofopher. Befides, this inventer appeared at a time, when the moft he could know was the art of reafoning, fuch as was then taught in the fchools ; an art which our modern philofophers treat with fo much fupercilioufnefs and contempt.

It feems the compafs was known as early as the thirteenth century ; but whether the ufe of it was difcovered by John Goya a mariner of Melphi, or whether by fomebody older than him, its inventer is in the fame cafe as the inventer of printing. What lights have not been derived to thofe who ftudy

[a] POLYD. VIRGIL. de Inv. Rer. l. 3. c. 7.

phyfics,

phyfics, from the knowledge of the property of the loadftone in turning towards the North pole, and from the knowledge of the virtue it has to communicate this property to iron. Befides, as foon as the compafs was found, the art of navigation muft of neceffity have been perfected, and the Europeans muft fooner or later have made thofe difcoveries, which were abfolutely impoffible without fuch an affiftance, and which they have made fince the latter end of the fifteenth century. Thefe difcoveries, which have brought us acquainted with America, and fo many other unknown countries, have inriched botany, aftronomy, phyfic, the hiftory of animals, and in fhort, all the natural fciences. Have the .Greeks and Romans given us any reafon to believe they were incapable of diftributing the new plants (which would have been fent them from America, and from the extremities of Afia and Afric) into different claffes, and of fubdividing them into feveral kinds; or of diftributing the ftars near the Antarctic pole into conftellations ?

'Twas towards the commencement of the feventeenth century, that James Metius of Alcmaer, feeking for fomething elfe, found out the telefcope. It feems as if it had been the pleafure of fate to mortify the modern philofophers, by giving birth to the accident which was the caufe of the invention of telefcopes, before the time which thefe gentlemen mark as the epoch of the reftoration of human underftanding. Within thefe fourfcore years, fince men have begun to fhew themfelves fo exact and penetrating, there has been no fuch important difcovery made as that juft now mentioned.

The

The springs of natural knowledge concealed from the ancients, were discovered before the period, in which it is pretended that the sciences began to acquire that perfection which reflects so great an honor on those who have improved them.

James Metius, inventer of the telescope, was a very ignorant person, pursuant to Descartes's account [a], who lived a long time in the province where the fact here in question happened, and who committed it to writing thirty years after the event. Mere hazard gave him the honor of this invention, which alone has contributed more than all the speculations of philosophers to perfect the natural sciences ; and this in preference to his father and brother, who were great mathematicians. This man discovered the telescope not by any methodical research, but by a mere fortuitous experiment ; for he was then amusing himself with making burning glasses.

It was an easy matter to find the microscope, after the invention of the telescope. Now we may safely affirm, that it is by the help of these instruments so many observations have been made which have inriched astronomy and natural philosophy, and rendered these sciences so much superior to what they were in former times. We are indebted likewise to these instruments for several observations in which they are not used, because they never would have been attempted, if preceding observations performed by the instruments here mentioned, had not first raised the idea of the experiment.

[a] Dioptrics, chap 1.

The effects of such a discovery may be infinitely multiplied. After they improved astronomy, astronomy improved other sciences. It has improved, for example, geography, by giving the points of longitude with certainty, and with almost as much ease, as they could have given heretofore the points of latitude. As the progress of experience is not sudden, there was a necessity for an interval of very near fourscore years from the invention of the telescope to the planisphere of the observatory, and to Monsieur de Lisle's map of the world, the first in which the principal points of the terrestrial globe have been placed in their true position. Whatsoever facility was derived from the telescope towards ascertaining the breadth of the Atlantic ocean, since Galileo had applied it to the observation of the stars ; still all the geographers who published maps before de Lisle, have been mistaken here in several degrees. 'Tis not fifty years since this gross mistake, with regard to the distance of the coasts of Afric and South America, countries discovered two hundred years ago, has been corrected. Within this very space of time a true discovery has been also made of the real breadth of the interjacent sea between Asia and America, commonly called the South-Sea. The philosophical spirits, or your speculative naturalists, had made no use of all those facts ; when there started up a man whose profession it was to make prints and maps, who benefited by these experiments. Perhaps the Greeks and Romans would have improved by the telescope, sooner than we ; for the distance and positions of places which they have left us, intitle us to make this supposition. Monsieur

de

de Lifle, who detected more faults in the modern geographers, than thefe have difcovered in the ancients, has fhewn, that it was a miftake of the moderns, when they cenfured the ancients with refpect to the diftance they fixed between Sicily and Afric, as likewife with regard to fome other points of geography.

The laft of thofe difcoveries, which have fo vaftly contributed to inrich the natural fciences, is that of the weight of the air. This refcues our philofophers from fuch errors, as thofe, who were ignorant of it, gave into, by attributing the effects of the weight of the air to the horror of a vacuum. It has likewife given birth to the invention of the barometer, and to all the other inftruments or machines, that produce their effect by virtue of the weight of the air, and by which fo great a number of philofophical truths have been demonftrated.

The celebrated [a] Galileo had obferved indeed, that the attracting pumps raifed the water thirty two feet high ; but he attributed this elevation, fo oppofite to the motion of heavy bodies, to the horror or dread of a vacuum, in the fame manner as his predeceffors had done, and as the prefent philofophers would likewife do, were it not for the fortuitous difcovery I am going to fpeak of. In 1643 Torricelli, mechanic profeffor of the great duke Ferdinand II, obferved in fome experimental effays, that when a tube ftopt at the upper orifice, and open underneath, was kept ftanding upright in a veffel full of quickfilver, the quickfilver remained fufpended to a certain heigth in the tube, and thus fufpended

[a] Deceafed in 1642.

fell

fell directly into the veffel, if the upper orifice were opened. This was the fitft experiment made on this fubject, and was called the experiment of the vacuum ; but the confequences that attended it, have rendered it famous. [a] Torricelli finding his experiment very curious, communicated it to his friends, but without referring it to its real caufe, which he had not yet difcovered.

Father Merfenne, a Minim of Paris, celebrated among the philofophers of that time, was informed of this experiment by letters from Italy as early as 1644, upon which he made it public in France. Monfieur Petit, and M. Pafcal, the father of the author of the provincial letters, made feveral experiments in confequence of that of Torricelli. M. Pafcal, junior, made his likewife, and publifhed them in a treatife printed 1647. No one had yet thought of explaining thefe experiments by the weight of the air. This is an unconteftable proof that the learned did not proceed from one principle to another, and in a fpeculative way to the difcovery of this truth. Experiments gave a fortuitous knowledge of it to philofophers, who fo little dreamed of the gravity of the air, that they handled it, as it were, for a long time, without being able to comprehend it. This truth fell in their way by chance, and it feems alfo, that by mere chance they took notice of it.

We are pofitively affured by ocular witneffes who have written on this fubject, that M. Pafcal [b] had no knowledge of the idea of the weight of the air,

[a] *Saggi d'efperienze fatte nell Academia del Cimento, pag,* 23.
[b] *Preface to his treattfe on the equilibrium of liquors.*

which

which Torricelli hit upon at length by dint of repeating his experiment, till after he published the above-
mentioned treatise.   M. Pafcal found this explication very pleafing ; but as it was only a fimple conjecture, he made feveral experiments to know the
truth or falfity of it, and one of thofe was the famous
experiment made in 1648 on the *Puis de Domme*, a
very high mountain in France.   At length he compofed his treatifes of the equilibrium of liquors, and
of the weight of the air, which have been printed feveral times.   After that M. Guericke, burgo-mafter
of Magdeburg, and Mr Boyle found out the pneu-
matic machine, and others invented thofe inftruments
that mark the different changes which the variations
of the weather produce in the weight of the air.   The
rarefactions of the air have given likewife fome infight into thofe of other liquids.   Let the reader
judge therefore by this recital, the truth of which
no one can difpute, whether it was the learned
doubts and fpeculations of philofophers, that led
them on from one principle to another, to the experiments which difcovered the weight of the air.
In reality, the fhare which reafoning had in this difcovery, does no great honor to it.   I fhall not
fpeak here of inventions unknown to the ancients,
but whofe authors are known to us, fuch as that of
cutting the diamond, which was found out by a
goldfmith of Bruges under Lewis XI[a], before which
time they ufed to prefer coloured ftones to diamonds.
None of thefe men were philofophers, not even of
the peripatetic fchool.

[a] *The hiftory of precious ftones*, by BERQUEN, *p.* 15.

'Tis

'Tis therefore evident from what has been here mentioned, that the knowledge we have in the natural sciences, and which the ancients had not, and that the truth likewise which is found in our reasonings on several physical questions, and could not be found in theirs, are all owing to hazard and fortuitous experiments. The discoveries that have been made by this means, have, if I may say so, been a long time a shooting up. It was necessary that one discovery should wait for another, to produce all the fruit it was able to give. One experiment was not sufficiently conclusive without another, which was not made till a long time after the first : And the last inventions have thrown a surprizing light upon the knowledge which preceded them. Happily for our age, it has found itself in the maturity of time, when the natural sciences were making the most rapid progress. The lights resulting from the preceding inventions, after having made separately a certain progression, began to combine about fourscore or a hundred years ago. We may say of our age what Quintilian said of his [a] *Antiquity has instructed us by so many precepts and examples, that no other age seems to have been so happy as ours, for whose improvement the learned of past ages have so carefully laboured.*

For example, the human body was well enough known in Hippocrates's time, to give him a vague notion of the circulation of the blood, but was not as yet sufficiently laid open to let this great man into a

---

[a] *Tot nos præceptoribus, tot exemplis instruxit antiquitas, ut possit videri nulla forte nascendi ætas felicior quam nostra, cui docendæ priores laboraverunt.* QUINT. Inst. l. 12. c. 11.

clear

clear knowledge of that truth [a]. It appears by his writings, that he has rather gueſſed than underſtood it, and that far from giving a diſtinct explication to his cotemporaries, he had not a clear idea of it himſelf. Servetus, a perſon ſo well known for his impiety and his puniſhment [b], coming ſeveral ages after Hippocrates, had a much diſtincter notion of the circulation of the blood, and has given a very clear deſcription of it in his preface to the ſecond edition [c] of the book, for which Calvin had him burnt at Geneva. Harvey coming ſixty years after Servetus, has been able to give us a more diſtinct explication of the principal circumſtances of the circulation. The greateſt part of the learned of his time were convinced of the truth of his opinion, and they even eſtabliſhed it in the world, as much as a phyſical truth, which does not fall under the ſenſes, can be eſtabliſhed ; that is, it paſſed for a more probable ſentiment than the contrary opinion.

The public aſſent to philoſophical reaſonings cannot go further ; for mankind either by inſtinct, or principle, place always a great difference between the certainty of natural truths, known by means of the ſenſes, and the certainty of ſuch as are known only by the way of reaſoning. The latter appear to them as mere probabilities. 'Tis neceſſary to place at leaſt ſome eſſential circumſtance within the reach of their ſenſes, in order to convince them fully of theſe truths. Wherefore, tho' the greateſt

[a] *Almelozeen Invent. Nov. ant.*

[b] *He was executed at Geneva in 1553.*

[c] W o t t o n *preface to reflections upon ancient and modern learning.*

part

part of the natural philosophers, as well as of the public, were convinced in 1687 of the certainty of the circulation of the blood, yet there were still a great many learned men who had drawn a confiderable party into their opinion, that this circulation was a mere chimæra. In the medical fchool of the univerfity of Paris, thefes were held at that very time againft this opinion. At length the microfcopes were perfected to that degree, that by their affiftance one might fee the blood run with rapidity thro' the arteries towards the extreme parts of the body of a fifh, and return more flowly thro' the veins towards the center ; and this as diftinctly, as we can fee from Lyons the Rhone and the Saone run within their banks. No body would attempt now to write or maintain a thefis againft the circulation of the blood. 'Tis true, that thofe who are perfuaded at prefent of this circulation, have not all of them feen it themfelves ; but they know it is no longer proved by arguments, but by ocular demonftration. Men (I repeat it again) are more apt to give credit to thofe who tell them, *I have feen it*, than to fuch as fay, *I have concluded.* Now the doctrine of the circulation of the blood, by the lights it has given with regard to the circulation of other liquors, and by the difcoveries it has been the caufe of, has contributed more than any other obfervation, to improve anatomy. It has even improved other fciences, fuch as botany. Can it be denied, but that this doctrine gave great lights to Monfieur Perrault the phyfician, with regard to the circulation of the fap in trees and plants ? I leave it to any man to judge, what fhare the philofophi-

cal

cal fpirit born within thefe hundred years, could have had in the eftablifhment of this dogma.

The truth, or opinion, of the motion of the earth round the fun, has had the fame fate as that of the circulation of the blood. Several ancient philofophers were acquainted with this truth, but as they had not the fame means in hand as we have, to prove it, it remained a dubious point, whether Philolaus, Ariftarchus, and other aftronomers, were in the right to make the earth turn round the fun ; or whether Ptolomy and his followers had reafon to make the fun turn round the earth ? Ptolomy's fyftem feemed to prevail, when Copernicus undertook, in the fixteenth century, to maintain Philolaus's opinion with new proofs, or at leaft feemingly fuch, which he drew from obfervations. The world was divided once more, and Tycho Brahé fet up a middle fyftem, to reconcile the aftronomical facts which had been at that time demonftratively fhewn, to the opinion of the immobility of the earth. About that time navigators began to fail round our globe, and foon after it was known that the eafterly winds blew continually between the tropics in both hemifpheres. This was a phyfical proof of the opinion which makes the earth turn on its axis, from weft to eaft in four and twenty hours, and finifh its courfe thro' the Zodiac in a year. Some time after this the telefcope was invented ; and by the help of this inftrument fuch evident obfervations were made on the appearances of Venus and the other planets, fuch a refemblance was difcovered between the earth and thofe planets,

which

which turn on their axis and round the fun, that the public is at prefent convinced of the truth of Copernicus's fyftem. About fixty years ago, there was not a profeffor in the univerfity of Paris, that would venture to teach this fyftem. At prefent almoft every body teaches it, at leaft as the only hypothefis, that can explain the aftronomical phænomena of which we have a certain knowledge. Before thefe principal truths were fet in a proper light, the learned, inftead of going from this point to make new difcoveries, loft their time in wrangling. They fpent it in maintaining the opinion which they embraced either thro' choice or hazard, by proofs that could never be good or folid when fupplied by argumentation alone ; whilft the natural fciences made no manner of progrefs. But as foon as thefe truths were demonftrated, they led us, as it were, by the hand to an infinite number of other difcoveries ; and enabled philofophers, that had any fenfe, to employ their time ufefully in compleating their knowledge by experiments. If our predeceffors therefore had not the fame knowledge, as we have, 'tis becaufe they had not the clue which guides us thro' the labyrinth.

In fact the fenfe, penetration, and extent of mind, which the ancients fhew in their laws, their hiftories, and even in their philofophical queftions, where (thro' a weaknefs fo natural to man and into which we fall every day) they have not given their own reveries for truths, which they could have no knowledge of in their days, as the accident to which their difcovery was owing had not yet happened : All this together, I fay, induces us to think that their

3

reafon

reafon was capable of making the fame ufe as ours of the great truths, which experience has revealed to us within thefe two centuries. Not to ftray from our fubject, did not the ancients know as well as we, that this fuperiority of reafon, which we call the philofophical fpirit, ought to prefide over all arts and fciences? Have not they acknowledged that it was a neceffary guide? Have not they faid in ex-prefs terms, that philofophy was the mother of the polite arts? *Nor are you ignorant*, fays Cicero [a] to his brother, *that philofophy fo called by the Greeks, is by the learned efteemed the fource and parent, as it were, of all commendable arts.*

Let thofe who attempt to anfwer me, reflect fe-rioufly on this paffage, before they conclude I am in the wrong : For one of the defects of our critics is to reafon before they have reflected. Let them recol-lect alfo (a thing they feem to have forgot) what the ancients have obferved with refpect to the ftudy of geometry, *which improves even thofe who do not in-tend to profefs it* [b], and that Quintilian has wrote a whole chapter on the utility which even orators them-felves may draw from the ftudy of this fcience. Does not he fay there in exprefs terms, " There is this " difference between geometry and the other arts, " that thefe are of no fervice 'till after they " are learnt, but the ftudy alone of geometry is " of great utility, by reafon that nothing is more " proper for opening, extending, and giving ftrength

<hr>

[a] *Neque enim te fugit, laudatarum omnium artium procreatricem quandam & quafi parentem, eam quam philofophiam Græci vocant, ab omnibus doctiffimis judicari.* Cic.

[b] *Quæ inftruit etiam quos fibi non exercet.*

" to

" to the mind, than the method of geometri-
" cians [a]."

Indeed, to conclude that our reason is of a different stamp from that of the ancients, or to affirm
that it is superior to theirs, because we are more
learned than they in the natural sciences, is the same
as if we were to infer that we had more understanding than they, because we know how to cure intermitting fevers with the bark, which they could not ;
when all our merit in this cure is owing to our
having learnt of the Indians of Peru, the virtue of this
medicine which grows in their country.

If we excel the ancients in some sciences independent of the fortuitous discoveries made by hazard
and time, this superiority proceeds from the same
cause, which makes a son die richer than the father, on
supposition that their conduct has been equal, and
fortune has favored them both alike. If the ancients had not cleared away the weeds, as it were,
from geometry, the moderns born with a genius
for this science would have been obliged to employ their time and talents in grubbing them up ;
and as they would not consequently be so much advanced upon their first setting out, they would never
be able to reach as far as they have done. The marquifs de l'Hopital, Mr. Leibnitz, and Sir Isaac Newton, would never have pushed geometry so far, had
they not found this science in a state of perfection,
which was owing to its having been cultivated by a

---

[a] *In geometria partem fatentur esse utilem teneris ætatibus, agi-
tari namque animos & acui, & ingenia ad percipiendi facilitatem
venire inde concedunt : sed prodesse eam non ut cæteras artes cum per-
ceptæ sint, sed cum discatur, existimant.* QUINT. Inst. l. 1. c. 18.

I

great

great number of ingenious men, who had improved succeſſively by the lights and diſcoveries of their predeceſſors. Had Archimedes appeared in the time of Newton, he would have done as much as Newton, as the latter would have done the ſame as Archimedes, had he appeared in the time of the ſecond Punic war. We may likewiſe preſume, that the ancients would have made uſe of algebra in their geometrical problems, if they had had as convenient cyphers for arithmetical calculations as the Arabic; by the help of which Alphonſus X, king of Caſtile, made his aſtronomical tables in the thirteenth century.

'Tis alſo certain, that we are frequently miſtaken, when we accuſe the ancient philoſophers of ignorance; for the greateſt part of their knowledge was loſt with the writings that contained it. As we have not the hundredth part of the books compoſed by Greek and Roman authors, we may be eaſily miſtaken in fixing the limits as we do to their progreſs in the natural ſciences. The critics bring charges very often againſt the ancients merely thro' ignorance. Has not our preſent age, by its ſuperior knowledge over the preceding generations, juſtified Pliny the elder with regard to ſeveral reproaches of error and falſity which were brought againſt him a hundred and fifty years ago.

But (ſome will be apt to reply) it muſt be allowed at leaſt, that logic or the art of thinking is much completer in our days than in former times, and that it muſt follow of neceſſity, that the moderns who have learnt this logic, and have formed themſelves by its rules, reaſon on all ſubjects with greater exactneſs than the ancients.

I

I anſwer in the firſt place, 'tis not abſolutely certain that the art of thinking is completer in
our days than in former ages. Moſt of the rules
which are looked upon as new, are implicitely
contained in Ariſtotle's logic, where we find the
method of invention, and that of doctrine. Beſides, had we the explication of the rules which the
philoſophers delivered to their diſciples, perhaps we
ſhould find there what we imagine we have invented, as it has happened to famous philoſophers to
find in manuſcripts a part of the diſcoveries, of
which they fancied themſelves the principal authors.
Were we even to grant that logic is ſomewhat more
perfect at preſent than it was formerly, yet the learned, generally ſpeaking, would not reaſon better now
than in thoſe times. The juſtneſs with which a perſon
lays down his principles, draws conſequences, and
proceeds from one concluſion to another, depends
more on the character of his mind, whether volatile
or ſedate, raſh or circumſpect, than on the logic
he has learnt. 'Tis imperceptible in practice, whether he has ſtudied Barbey's logic, or that of Port
Royal. The logic he chanced to learn, does not
make as much difference perhaps, with reſpect to
his manner of reaſoning, as ariſes from the weight
of an ounce taken from or added to a quintal. This
art rather ſerves to ſhew us how we reaſon naturally, than to influence the practice, which, as
I have already obſerved, depends on each perſon's
particular character of mind. Is it obſerved, that
thoſe who are beſt verſed in logic, I mean in that
of Port Royal, and even whoſe profeſſion it is to
teach it, are the people who reaſon moſt conſequen-
tially,

tially, and make the moſt judicious choice of principles proper for laying the baſis of their concluſions? Does a young man of eighteen years of age, who knows by heart all the rules of ſyllogiſm and method, does he, I ſay, reaſon more juſtly, than a perſon of forty, who never knew them, or has in-tirely forgot them? Next to the natural character of the mind, 'tis experience, or the extent of diſ-coveries, and the knowledge of facts, which ena-ables one man to reaſon better than another. Now the ſciences in which the moderns reaſon better than the ancients, are exactly thoſe wherein the former know ſeveral things, which the latter born before the fortuitous diſcoveries abovementioned, could not poſſibly have been acquainted with.

In effect, (and this is my ſecond anſwer to the objec-tion drawn from the perfection of the art of think-ing) we do not reaſon better than the ancients in hiſtory, politics, or morals. Not to mention remoter writers, have not Commines, Machiavel, Mariana, Fra Paolo, Thuanus, D'Avila, and Guic-ciardin, who wrote when logic was not in a more perfect ſtate than in former ages, have not they, I ſay, penned their hiſtories with as much method and good ſenſe, as all thoſe hiſtorians who wrote within theſe ſixty years? Have we ever an author to compare to Quintilian for the order and ſolidi-ty of his reaſonings? In fine, were it true that the art of reaſoning is more perfect in our times than it was formerly, our philoſophers would agree bet-ter with one another than the ancient philoſophers.

It will be here objected, that 'tis no longer al-lowable to lay down principles but ſuch as are clear

and

and well proved. 'Tis no longer permitted to draw a confequence from thence, unlefs it is clearly and diftinctly deducible. A confequence of a greater extent than the principle from whence it was drawn, would be immediately obferved by every body, fo as to be treated as a ridiculous conclufion. I anfwer, that a Chinefe who had no other knowledge of our age but from this picture, would imagine that all our learned are of one opinion. Truth is one, he would fay, and 'tis impoffible now to miftake it. All the ways by which a perfon may be led aftray, are ftopt up. Thefe ways are to lay down wrong principles of an argument, or to infer a wrong confequence from juft principles. How then is it poffible to err? All the learned therefore, of whatever profeffion, muft be at length of one opinion. They muft all agree what are thofe things whereof men cannot as yet difcover the truth; they fhould likewife be all of the fame fentiment where the truth of things can be known: And yet people never difputed more than they do at prefent. Our learned, as well as the ancient philofophers, are agreed only in refpect to facts, and they refute one another upon every thing that cannot be known but by way of argumentation; treating each other as perfons who are wilfully blind, and refufe to fee the light. If they do not difpute any longer with regard to fome thefes, 'tis becaufe facts and experience have obliged them to agree in refpect to thofe points. I embrace here fo many different profeffions under the name of philofophy and fciences, that I dare not name them all. All of them, tho' guided by the fame logic, muft be fometimes miftaken with

refpect

respect to the evidence of their principles ; or else they must chuse such as are improper for their subject, or in fine they must sometimes infer wrong consequences. Those who extol so highly the lights which the philosophical spirit has shed on our age, will answer perhaps, that they understand by our age only themselves and their friends, and that we must look upon such as are not of their opinion in every thing, as people like the ancients, who understand nothing of philosophy.

We may apply the emblem of time, which discloses the truth only by slow degrees, to the present state of the natural sciences. If we see a greater portion of truth than the ancients, 'tis not because we are clearer sighted, but time has discovered more. I conclude therefore that those works whose reputation has maintained itself against the remarks of past critics, will always preserve it, notwithstanding the subtle observations of future censors.

C H A P. XXXIV.

That the reputation of a system of philosophy may be ruined. And that this cannot happen to a poem.

THO' the physics of the schools and Ptolemy's system are now exploded, it does not from thence follow that Homer's Iliad, or Virgil's Æneid can meet with the like treatment. Those opinions whose extent and duration are founded on sense, and on the inward experience, as it were, of such as have always adopted them, are not subject to be exploded, like philofophical opinions, whofe extent and continuance are owing to the facility with which they are received upon other men's credit and authority. As the firft authors of a philofophical fyftem may be miftaken, fo they may impofe upon their followers fucceffively from generation to generation. Pofterity may therefore rejeft at length, as an error in philofophy, what their anceftors looked upon a long time as truth, and which even they themfelves imagined to be fuch upon the authority of their mafters.

Men, whofe curiofity extends much further than their lights, are always defirous of knowing what opinion they fhould be of with refpeft to the caufe of feveral natural effeets; and yet the moft part of them are incapable of examining or difcovering by themfelves the truth of thefe matters, fuppofing it even within the reach of their eye. On the other hand there are always reafoners amongft them, vain enough to imagine they have difcovered thefe phyfical truths; and others fo infincere as to affirm they have a diftinft knowledge of them by principles, tho' they are fenfible that their light is mere darknefs. As both the one and the other fet themfelves up for mafters, what is the confequence? The fmatterers receive as a ceitain truth, whatever is delivered to them as fuch by perfons in whofe favor they are prejudiced thro' different motives, without knowing or even examining the merit and folidity of thofe proofs with which they fupport their philofophical dogmas. The difciples are perfuaded that thofe perfons are better acquainted with the truth than others, and that they have no defign to de-

ceive

ceive them. Their firft followers contrive afterwards to get new eleves, who imagine frequently that they are ftrongly convinced of a truth, of which they do not underftand one fingle proof. Thus it is, that an infinite number of falfe opinions on the influence of the ftars, the ebbing and flowing of the fea, the prefage of comets, the caufes of diftempers, the organifation of the human body, and on feveral other phyfical queftions, have been eftablifhed. 'Tis thus the fyftem taught in the fchools under the title of Ariftotle's phyfics, was generally received.

The great number therefore of fuch as have followed and defended an opinion in phyfics eftablifhed by authority, or by a confidence in other people's knowledge, the number alfo of ages in which this opinion prevailed, prove nothing at all in its favor. Thofe who adopted this opinion received it without inquiry ; or, if they inquired, they were not fo fuccefsful in their refearches, as perfons who having examined it after them, improved by the new difcoveries, or even by the faults of their predeceffors.

It follows therefore, that with refpect to phyfics and other natural fciences, pofterity are very much in the right not to depend on the fentiments of their anceftors. Hence a man of fenfe and learning may impugn feveral principles of chymiftry, botany, phyfics, medicine, and aftronomy, which during the fpace of many centuries, were regarded as unconteftable truths. He is allowed (efpecially when he can alledge fome experiment in favor of his fentiment) to attack thefe principles with as little reftraint and ceremony, as if he were to fight only againft a fyftem of four days ftanding, fuch as one of thofe fyf-

A a 2

tems

tems which are not as yet believed but by the author and his friends, who ceafe to give their affent to it, as foon as they begin to quarrel with him. No man can eftablifh an opinion fo well by reafoning and conjecture, but another with more penetration or good luck may fubvert it. Hence it is, that the prepoffeffion of mankind, in favor of a philofophical fyftem, does not even prove it will continue thirty years. Men may be difabufed by truth, as they may pafs from an ancient error to a new one more capable of deceiving them than the firft.

Nothing therefore is more unreafonable, than to lay a ftrefs on the fuffrage of ages and nations, in order to prove the folidity of a philofophical fyftem, and to maintain that the vogue it has at prefent will laft for ever ; but 'tis prudent to lay a ftrefs of this fort to evince the excellence of a poem, or to maintain that it will be always admired. A falfe fyftem may, as I have already obferved, furprize the world, it may prevail for feveral ages ; but this cannot be faid of a bad poem.

The reputation of a poem is determined by the pleafure it affords the reader, and eftablifhed by the fenfes. Wherefore as the opinion of this poem's being an excellent work, cannot be riveted nor fpread but by means of an inward conviction arifing from the very experience of thofe who receive it, we may alledge the time it has lafted, for a proof that this opinion is founded on truth itfelf. One has even good grounds to maintain that future generations will be moved with reading a poem, which has af-fected all thofe in paft ages that have been able to read it in the original. There is only one fuppofition

pofition admitted in this reafoning, which is, that men of all ages and countries refemble one another with refpect to the heart.

People are not therefore fo much expofed to be duped in point of poetry, as with refpect to philofophy ; and a tragedy cannot, like a fyftem, make its fortune without real merit. Befides, we fee that perfons who are not agreed with regard to thofe things, whofe truth is examined by way of argumentation, are neverthelefs of one opinion in refpect to matters decided by the fenfe. No body complains of thefe decifions ; that Raphael's transfiguration, for inftance, is an admirable picture, and that Polyeuctes is an excellent tragedy. But philofophers rife up every day in oppofition to thofe who maintain, that *the fearch after truth* is a work in which the truth is taught. Philofophers in general do juftice to the perfonal merit of Defcartes, yet they are divided with regard to the goodnefs of his philofophical fyftem. Befides, men, as we have before obferved, frequently adopt the fyftem they profefs, upon other people's credit ; and the public voice, which declares in their favor, is thus compofed of echoes, that repeat only what they have heard. The fmall number that chance to tell their own fentiments, mention no more than what they have feen amidft their prejudices, the influence of which is as ftrong in oppofition to reafon, as it is weak in oppofition to fenfe. Thofe who fpeak of a poem, fay what they felt themfelves while they were reading it ; and thus each perfon gives the judgment he has formed on his own experience. Now we are feldom deceived with refpect to truths that fall under the fenfes, as we are with regard to things that cannot be decided but by way of reasoning.

We are not only right in deciding things which can be judged by the senses, but moreover 'tis impossible for others to deceive us in these matters. Our senses oppose a person, who would attempt to make us believe that a poem which we found insipid is capable of engaging us; but they do not contradict a person who endeavours to make us take a bad argument in metaphysics for a good one. 'Tis only by an effort of mind, and by reflections which some for want of lights, and others thro' laziness, are incapable of, that we are able to know its falsity, and unravel its error. We know without meditating, nay, we even feel the contrary of whatever a person says, who intends to persuade us, that a work which gives us a vast deal of pleasure, violates those rules that have been established in order to render a work capable of pleasing. If we are not learned enough to answer his reasonings, at least an inward repugnance hinders us from giving any credit to them. Men are all born with a conviction, that every argumentation which tends to persuade them to think the contrary of what they feel, can be nothing but a sophism.

A poem therefore which has pleased in all ages and nations, is really worthy of pleasing, notwithstanding what defects may be observed in it; and consequently it ought always to be agreeable to such as understand it in the original..

Prejudice (some will here say) is almost as capable of seducing us in favor of a poem, as in favor of a
system.

fyftem. For example, when thofe who are
charged with the care of our education, admire
the Æneid, their admiration caufes a prejudice,
which makes us think it a better work than it
really is. They engage us by the influence they
have over us, to think as they do. Thus we are
taught to embrace their fentiments ; and 'tis to
prejudices like thefe that Virgil and the authors
who are commonly called *claſſics,* are indebted for
the greateft part of their reputation. Critics may
therefore caft a blemifh upon this reputation, by
fapping the foundation of thofe prejudices which
exaggerate the merit of Virgil's Æneid, and make
his eclogues appear fo fuperior to others, which in
reality do not fall very fhort of them. This argument may be enforced with a methodical differtation on the force of prejudices which mankind im-
bibe in their infancy ; a common place well known
to all the world.

My anfwer is, that fuch prejudices as thefe here
in queftion, would never be able to fubfift long in
the minds of fuch as had imbibed them, unlefs they
were founded on truth. Their very experience and
fenfes would foon difabufe them. Upon fuppofition that during our infancy, and at a time when we
have no knowledge of other poems, they had infpired us with a veneration for the Æneid which it did not
deferve, we fhould fhake off this prejudice as foon
as we began to read other poems, and to compare
them with the Æneid. In vain we fhould have been
told a thoufand times during our infancy, that the
Æneid charms all its readers, we fhould not be im-

pofed

pofed upon any longer, if it afforded us but very little pleafure, when we became capable of underftanding it of ourfelves. 'Tis thus the difciples of a profeffor, who had taught that the declamations which go by Quintilian's name, are fuperior to Cicero's orations, would throw off this prejudice, as foon as they attained to a fufficient maturity to be able to diftinguifh between thefe performances. The errors in philofophy which we have brought away with us from the college, may always ftick to us, becaufe we cannot be undeceived but by a very clofe meditation, which we are often incapable of making. But it would be fufficient to read thofe poets, whofe merit had been exaggerated, to get rid of our prejudice, unlefs we were abfolute fanatics. Now, we not only admire the Æneid as much in our full maturity of judgment, as during our infancy, and when the authority of our mafters might impofe upon our tender reafon; but moreover our admiration continually increafes, in proportion as our tafte improves, and our lights become more extenfive.

Befides, 'tis an eafy matter to prove hiftorically and by a deduction of facts, that Virgil and the other excellent poets of antiquity, are not indebted to colleges, nor to early prejudices, for their firft admirers. This opinion cannot be maintained except by a perfon who does not carry his reflections beyond his own time and country. The firft admirers of Virgil were his own countrymen and cotemporaries; among whom there were numbers of women, and men engaged in the hurry and occupa-

I   tions

tions of life, lefs learned perhaps than thofe who
fabricate the reputation of poets after their own
fancy, inftead of fearching for it in the writings
of the ancients. When the Æneid firft appeared,
it was rather an affembly-book, if I may fay fo,
than a work defigned for the ufe of a college.
As it was written in the living language of
that time, women therefore as well as men, the
ignorant as well as the learned, perufed it, and
paffed their judgments according as it affected
them. The name of Virgil was not impofing ; but
his book was expofed to all the affronts to which a
new performance can be fubject. In fhort, Virgil's
cotemporaries judged of the Æneid, as our fathers
judged of Boileau's fatyres, or of La Fontaine's fables upon the firft publication of thefe works. It
was therefore the impreffion which the Æneid made
upon the public, and the tears which the women fhed
upon the reading of it, that gave it the character of
an excellent poem. This approbation was changed into admiration as early as Quintilian's time, who
wrote about ninety years after Virgil. Juvenal, Quintilian's cotemporary, informs us, that even in his time
children were taught already to read Horace and
Virgil.

Dum modo non pereat totidem olfeciffe lucernas,
Quot ftabant pueri, cum totus decolor effet
Flaccus, & hæreret nigro fuligo Maroni.

                                    Juv. fat. 7.

Then thou art bound to fmell on either hand
As many ftinking lamps, as fchool-boys ftand ;

                                    Where

Where Horace *could not read in his own fully'd book :*

And Virgil's *facred page is all befmear'd with fmoke.* Mr. CHARLES DRYDEN.

This admiration has always continued to increafe. Five hundred years after Virgil, and at an age when the Latin was ftill a living language, people mentioned this poet with as much veneration, as his greateft admirers can fpeak of him in our days. Juftinian's inftitutes [a] the moft refpectable of all profane books, inform us that the Romans always meant Virgil when they faid the word *poet* abfolutely, and by way of preference, as the Greeks conftantly underftood Homer when they ufed the fame expreffion.

Virgil therefore is not indebted to tranflators or commentators for his reputation. He was admired before there was any neceffity for tranflating him, and 'tis the fuccefs of his verfes that was the firft occafion of his being honored with commentators. When Macrobius and Servius commented or explained him in the fourth century, according to the moft probable opinion, they could not beftow much greater encomiums upon him than thofe which he received from the public. Otherwife thefe encomiums would have been contradicted by every body, as the Latin was ftill the living language of thofe for whom Servius and Macrobius wrote. The fame may be faid of Euftatius, Afconius Pedianus, Donatus, Acron and other ancient commentators, who

[a] *Cum poetam dicimus nec addimus nomen, fubauditur apud Græcos egregius Homerus, apud nos Virgilius.* Inft. l. 1. tit. 2.

1   publifhed

publifhed their comments, when people ftill fpoke the language of the Greek or Roman author, who was the fubject of their labors.

In fine, all the modern nations that were formed in Europe after the deftruction of the Roman empire by the Barbarians, have fet a value upon Virgil's writings, in the fame manner as the cotemporaries of that poet. Thefe people, fo different from one another with regard to language, religion, and manners, united all of them in their fentiments of refpect for Virgil as foon as they began to be polifhed, and became capable of underftanding him. They did not look upon the Æneid as an excellent poem, becaufe they had been taught at an univerfity to admire him ; for they had no univerfities at that time ; but becaufe they found it an excellent poem upon the reading of it, they all agreed to make the ftudy thereof a part of the polite education of their children.

As foon as the northern nations acquired fettlements in the territories of the Roman empire, and learnt the Latin tongue, they began to have the fame tafte for Virgil as the cotemporaries of that amiable poet. I fhall be contented with producing only one example. Theodoric, the firft king of the Vifigoths eftablifhed in Gaul, and cotemporary of the emperor Valentinian III, ordered his fon Theodoric II to apply himfelf to the ftudy of Virgil. The latter Theodoric, writing to the celebrated Avitus, who was proclaimed emperor in 455, and who preffed him to make up matters with the Romans, fays to him as follows :

Par

—————— *Parvumque edifcere juffit*
Ad tua verba pater, docili quo prifca Maronis
Carmine molliret Scythicos mihi pagina mores.

SID. Apoll. carm. fept.

" I have too many obligations to you, to refufe
" any thing you demand. Was it not you that
" had the care of inftructing me in my youth, and
" that explained Virgil to me, when my father in-
" fifted upon my applying myfelf to the ftudy of
" this poet ? " Sidonius, who relates this fact,
was fon-in-law to Avitus.

'Tis the fame with refpect to the other famous
poets of antiquity. They wrote in the vulgar language of their country, and their firft admirers
gave them an approbation which was not fubject to error. Since the fettlement of the modern nations in Europe, not one of them has
preferred the poems compofed in their own language to the works of thofe ancient poets. Thofe
who underftand the poetry of the ancients, are all
agreed as well in the north as the fouth of Europe,
in catholic as in proteftant countries, that they are
more moved and taken with them, than with poems
compofed in their own native language. Can it be
fuppofed that the learned of all ages entered into a
whimfical confpiracy to facrifice the glory of their
countrymen, moft of whom they had no knowledge of but by their books, to the fame of Greek
and Roman writers, who had it not in their power
to requite them for their prevarication ? The perfons here mentioned could not be ingenuoufly miftaken, becaufe they were to give an account of their
own

own fenfe and feeling. The number of thofe, who have expreffed themfelves differently, is fo inconfi-derable, as not to merit the name of an exception. Now if there can be any difpute with refpect to the merit and excellence of a poem, it ought to be de-cided by the impreffion it has made on all men during the courfe of twenty centuries.

The philofophical fpirit, which is nothing but reafon ftrengthened by experience, whereof the name alone would be new to the ancients, is of great fer-vice in compofing books which inftruct people to avoid miftakes in writing, as alfo in detecting thofe that have been committed by an author ; but it mif-guides us in judging of a poem in general. Thofe beauties in which its greateft merit confifts, are bet-ter felt than found out by rule and compafs. Quin-tilian did not make a mathematical calculation or a metaphyfical difcuffion of the real and relative faults of thofe, on whom he has paffed a judgment adopted by all ages and nations. 'Tis by the im-preffion they make on the reader, that this great man has defined them ; and the public, which has conftantly ufed the fame method of judging, has al-ways conformed to his opinion.

In fine, in things which belong to the jurifdic-tion of the fenfe, fuch as the merit of a poem ; the emotion of all men who have and ftill do read it, as well as their veneration for the work, amount to as ftrong a proof as a demonftration in geome-try. Now 'tis on the ftrength of this demonftra-tion, that people are fo paffionately fond of Virgil and other poets. Wherefore men will not change their opinion on this point, till the fprings of the
human

human machine are altered. The poems of thofe great authors will not appear indifferent perform-ances, till the organs of this machine be fo chang-ed, as to find a bitternefs in fugar, and a fweet-nefs in wormwood. People will anfwer the cri-tics, without entering into a difcuffion of their re-marks, that they are already fenfible of the faults of thofe poems they admire ; but ftill they will not change their opinion, tho' they were to fee fome more. They will anfwer, that the countrymen of thefe great poets muft have obferved feveral faults in their works, which we are incapable of difcover-ing. Their works were written in a vulgar lan-guage, and their countrymen knew an infinite number of things that are now forgot, which might have afforded fubject for feveral well-grounded criticifms. And yet they admired thofe illuftrious authors as much as we do. Let our cri-tics confine themfelves therefore to write againft fuch commentators as would fain make beauties of thofe faults, of which there is always a large num-ber in the very beft performances. The ancients are no more anfwerable for the puerilities of thefe commentators, than a fine woman ought to be ac-countable for the extravagancies into which the blindnefs of paffion throws her unknown admirers.

The public has a right of leaving fuch reafonings as conclude contrary to their experience, to be dif-cuffed by the learned, and to ftick to what it cer-tainly knows by way of fenfation. Their own fenfe, confirmed by that of former ages, is fufficient to perfuade them, that all thofe reafonings muft be falfe, and they continue very quietly in their opi-nion,

nion, waiting till fomebody takes the trouble of giving us a methodical account of their errors. For
inftance, a phyfician, who is a man of parts and a
great logician, writes a book to prove, that vegeta-
bles and fiih are as wholefome nourifhment as flefh
in our country and climate. He lays down his
principles in a methodical manner ; his arguments
are well drawn up, and feem conclufive ; and yet
no body is convinced of the truth of his propofition. His cotemporaries, without giving themfelves the trouble of detecting the fource of his error, condemn him upon their own experience,
which fenfibly convinces them, that flefh is with us
an eafier and wholefomer food than fifh and vegeta-
bles. Men know very well, that 'tis eafier to daz-
zle their underftanding, than to impofe upon their
fenfes.

A perfon who attempts to defend an eftablifhed fyftem or opinion, undertakes a fubject that
does not excite greatly the curiofity of his
cotemporaries. If this author writes ill, no body thinks him worth mentioning ; if he writes
well, people will fay, that he expofed in a fenfible
manner what they knew already. But to attack an
eftablifhed fyftem, is the thing which prefently
diftinguifhes an author. 'Tis not therefore in
our days only that men of letters have endeavoured, by attacking received opinions, to acquire the reputation of men of a fuperior knowledge, born to prefcribe and not to receive laws
from their cotemporaries. All the eftablifhed opinions in literature have fuftained repeated attacks.
There is not fo much as one celebrated author but
what

what some critic has attempted to degrade ; and we have seen writers maintain, that Virgil **was** not the author of the Æneid, and that Tacitus did not write the hiftory and annals that go under his name. Whatever can be alledged to diminifh the reputation of the excellent works of antiquity, has already been wrote, or at leaft afferted : And yet they continue in the hands of all mankind ; no more expofed to be degraded than to perifh, a misfortune which great part of them has fuffered by the devaftations of Barbarians. The art of printing has multiplied too many copies, and were Europe to be fo ravaged as to lofe them all, ftill the libraries of the European colonies in America, and the remote parts of Afia, would preferve thofe precious monuments to pofterity.

But to return now to the critics. When **we** obferve any defeats in a book which is generally acknowledged to be an excellent piece, **we** muft not imagine ourfelves the firft that have defcried them. Perhaps the ideas that occur to us then, prefented themfelves before to feveral others, who at the firft motion would have been willing to have publifhed them the very fame day, in order to undeceive the world immediately of its old errors. A few reflections made them defer attacking the general opinion fo very foon, which to them appeared a mere prejudice ; and a little meditation made them fenfible, that their imagining themfelves more clear fighted than others, was owing to their own ignorance. They were convinced at length, that the world had fome reafon to think as it did for fo many ages ; that if the reputation of the ancients could have been poffibly

fibly

fibly diminished, the duft of time would have fullied it long ago ; and in fhort, that they had been impofed upon by an inconfiderate zeal.

A young man who enters upon a confiderable employment, fets out with cenfuring the adminiftration of his predeceffor. He cannot comprehend how people of fenfe and prudence could have commended him ; wherefore he propofes to put a ftop to vice, and to promote virtue in a more effectual manner. The ill fuccefs of his endeavors to reform abufes, and to eftablifh that order and regularity of which he had formed the idea in his cabinet, the knowledge alfo which experience furnifhes him, by which alone he can be inftructed, will foon convince him that his predeceffor managed right, and the public had reafon to applaud him. In like manner our firft meditations prejudice us fometimes againft the received opinions of the republic of letters ; but a courfe of more ferious reflections on the manner in which thefe opinions were eftablifhed, likewife a more extenfive and diftincter knowledge of what men are capable of doing, and in fine, even our own experience reconciles us to thefe opinions. A French painter of twenty years of age, who goes to Rome to ftudy, does not fee at firft in Raphael's works a merit equal to their great reputation. He is fometimes fo volatile and unguarded as to publifh his fentiment ; but within the fpace of a year, when a little reflection has brought him over to the general opinion, he is vexed for having expreffed himfelf in that manner. 'Tis owing to ignorance, that people recede fometimes from the common opinion in things, the merit of which may be known by all mankind. *No-*

thing, says Quintilian [a], *is more odious than thofe who knowing only fomething more than the firft elements of letters, are puffed up with a vain and conceited notion of learning.*

C H A P. XXXV.

Of the idea which men have of the writings of the ancients, when they do not underftand the originals.

AS for thofe who are not acquainted with the languages, in which the poets, orators, and even the hiftorians of antiquity have wrote, they are incapable of themfelves to judge of their excellency; wherefore if they are defirous of having a juft idea of the merit of thofe works, they muft take it from the relation of perfons who have and do underftand thefe languages. Men cannot judge right of an object, when they are not able to form their judgment by the report of the fenfe deftined to know it. We cannot give our opinion of the goodnefs of a liquor 'till after we have tafted it, nor of the excellence of a tune, 'till we have heard it. Now a poem written in a language we do not underftand, cannot be known to us by the report of the fenfe appointed to judge of it. 'Tis impoffible for us to difcern its merit by means of that fixth fenfe we have fpoken of. 'Tis the bufinefs of this

---

[a] *Nihil eft pejus iis qui paululum aliquid ultra primas litteras progreff, falfam fibi fcientiæ perfuafionem induerunt.* QUINT. l. 1. c. 2.

fenfe

fenfe to know whether the object prefented to us, be moving and capable of engaging us ; as it belongs to the ear to judge whether the founds are pleafing, and to the palate, whether the tafte is agreable.

All the critical difcourfes in the world are no more capable of conveying a juft idea of the merit of Horace's odes to a perfon that does not underftand Latin, than a relation of the qualities of a liquor which we had never tafted, would be able to give us a right notion of the tafte of that liquor. Nothing can fupply the report of the proper fenfe for judging of the thing in queftion. The ideas which we form to ourfelves from other people's reafoning and difcourfe, refemble the notion a blind man has formed to himfelf of colors : Or we may compare them to the ideas which a perfon who had never been fick, may have formed of a fever or cholic.

Now, as a perfon who has never heard a particular air or tune, is not admitted to difpute with regard to its excellence, againft thofe who have heard it ; and as a man who never had a fever, is not allowed to conteft the impreffion made by this diftemper, with thofe who have been afflicted with it ; in like manner he who does not underftand the language in which a poet has wrote, ought not to be allowed to difpute with fuch as underftand this poet, concerning his merit and the impreffion he makes. To difpute with regard to the merit of a poet and his fuperiority over other writers, is it not difputing in relation to the different impreffion which their poems have on their readers, and to the emotion they caufe? Is it not difputing of the truth of a natural fact, a queftion on which people will always give credit to ocular witnelles who are uniform in their report, preferable to all thole who fhould attempt to contest the poffibility thereof by metaphyfical arguments?..

Since men therefore, who do not underftand the language the poet has writ in, are incapable of paffling a judgment upon his merit, and upon the rank due to him ; is it not more reafonable they fhould adopt the judgment of fuch as have and do underftand him, than embrace the opinion of two or three critics who affirm that the poem does not make fuch impreffion upon them, as every body elfe fays it does? I take no notice here but of the fenfitive decifions of critics, for I reckon analyfes and difcuffions for nothing in a fubject which fhould not be determined by the way of reafoning. Now thofe critics who fay, that the poems of the ancients do not make the fame impreffion upon them, as upon the reft of mankind, are one againft a hundred thoufand. Should we take any notice of a fophift, who would attempt to prove, that thofe who feel a pleafure in wine, have a depraved tafte, and would corroborate his arguments by the example of five or fix abftemious perfons, that have an averfion to this liquor? Thofe who are capable of underftanding the ancients, without relifhing them, are in as fmall a number with refpect to their admirers, as men who have a natural averfion to wine are in comparifon to fuch as love it.

We muft not be impofed upon by the artifices of the *defpifers of the ancients*, who ftrive to juftify their difrelifh by the authority of fuch learned men, as have obferved miftakes in the fineft works

of

of antiquity. Thefe gentlemen, fo dextrous in the art of falfifying the truth without lying, would fain make us believe that the learned are of their party. Here in one fenfe they are in the right; for in queftions relating to matters of fact, as that of knowing whether the reading of a particular poem be engaging or not, men judge commonly according as the courts of judicature are accuftomed to determine; that is, they pronounce always in favor of a hundred witneffes, who depofe they have feen a fact, in oppofition to all the arguments of a fmall number who fay they have not feen it, and even aver it to be impoffible. The *defpifers of the ancients* are intitled to appeal to the authority of thefe critics only, who have advanced, that the ancients were indebted to old miftakes and grofs prejudices, for a reputation of which their defects rendered them undeferving. Now the catalogue of thefe critics might be comprifed in two lines, while whole volumes would fcarce contain the lift of critics of the oppofite tafte. In fact, to attack fo general a confent, and to give the lye to fo many paft ages, nay, even to our own, one muft fuppofe that the world has but juft got over its infancy, and that we are the firft generation of rational men that the earth has yet produced.

But fome will afk me, whether the tranflations made by learned and able writers, do not enable thofe, for example, who do not underftand Latin, to judge of themfelves and even by their fenfes of Virgil's Æneid?

I anfwer, that Virgil's Æneid done into French, falls, as it were, under the very fenfe which would

have

have judged of the original poem; but the Æneid in French is not the fame poem as in the Latin. A great part of the merit of a Greek or Latin poem confifts in the numbers and harmony of the verfes; and thefe beauties, tho' very fenfibly felt in the originals, cannot be tranfplanted, as it were, into a French tranflation. Even Virgil himfelf would be incapable of tranfplanting them, efpecially as our language is not fo fufceptible of thofe beauties as the Latin, purfuant to what we have obferved upon this fubject in the firft part of this work. In the fecond place, the poetic ftyle (of which we have difcourfed at large alfo in the firft part, and which decides almoft intirely the fuccefs of a poem) is fo disfigured in the very beft tranflation, that it has fcarce any traces left to diftinguifh it.

'Tis difficult to tranflate an author with purity and fidelity, even an author who relates nothing but facts, and with the greateft fimplicity of ftyle, efpecially when he has compofed in a language more favorable for nervous and accurate expreffions, than that into which we attempt to tranflate him. 'Tis therefore vaftly difficult to render any writer into French, who compofed in Greek or Latin. Let the reader therefore judge whether it be poffible to tranflate the figurative ftyle of thofe poets who have wrote in Greek or Latin, without enervating the force of their ftyle, and ftripping it of its greateft ornaments.

Either the tranflator takes the liberty of changing the figures, and of fubftituting others which are ufed in his own language, inftead of thofe employed by the author; or elfe he renders thofe figures word for word, and preferves the very fame images in his copy, which

which they reprefent in the original. If he changes the figures, 'tis no longer the original author but the tranflator that is fpeaking to us. This muft certainly be a great lofs, even were the tranflator (which very feldom happens) to have as much fenfe and genius as the original author?

'Tis natural for us to exprefs our own idea better than that of another perfon. Befides, 'tis very rare, that the figures which are confidered as relative in the two languages, have exactly the fame meaning ; and even when they have the fame meaning, they may happen not to have the fame dignity. For example, to exprefs a thing that furpaffes the power of man, the Latins would fay, *Clavam Herculi extorquere*; but the French would fay, *Prendre la Lune avec les dents* [*]. Is the fimplicity and grandeur of the Latin proverb, fo well expreffed by the French figure ?

The lofs is every bit as great, at leaft to the poem, when the tranflator gives the figures word for word. In the firft place, 'tis impoffible for him to render the words exactly, without being frequently obliged to ufe epithets either to reftrain or extend their fignification. Words which neceffity makes us oftentimes confider as fynonymous, or relative in Latin and French, have not always the fame propriety, nor the fame extent of fignification ; and 'tis this propriety which frequently forms the exactnefs of the expreffion, and the merit of the figure which the poet has employed. The French tranflate generally the Latin word *Herus* by that of *Maitre*, tho' the latter does

[*] That is, *to lay hold of the moon with one's teeth.*

not

not include exactly the fenfe of the Latin, which properly fignifies a mafter with regard to his flave. The tranflator is therefore obliged fometimes to ufe a circumlocution, in order to convey the fenfe of a fingle word, which drawls out the expreffion, and renders the phrafe languid and heavy in the verfion, tho' it might have been very lively in the original. The fame may be faid of Virgil's phrafes, as of Raphael's figures. Alter but ever fo little of Raphael's contour, and you take away the energy of the expreffion, and the noble air of the head. In like manner, if Virgil's expreffion be ever. fo little changed, his phrafe affumes fo different a form, that we find no longer the expreffion of the original. Tho' the French word *Empereur* is derived from that of *Imperator*, are we not obliged by the different extent of the fignification of thefe two words, to employ frequently a circumlocution to point out precifely the fenfe in which we ufe the word *Empereur*, in tranflating *Imperator?* Some of our beft tranflators have even chofen to adopt in a French phrafe the Latin word *Imperator*.

Befides, may not a word, which bears exactly the fame fignification in the two languages, be nobler in one than in the other, when confidered as a fimple found, and taken independent of the idea fixt to it ; infomuch that one fhall find a low word in the tranflation, when the author ufed a graceful one in the original. Is the word *Renaud* in French as graceful as *Rinaldo* in *Italian?* Does not *Titus* found better than *Tite ?*

Again, words tranflated from one language into another, may be degraded and fuftain fome damage,

as

as it were, with refpect to the idea affixed to the word. Does not the word *Hofpes* lofe a part of the dignity it has in Latin, (where it fignifies a man unit-ed to another by the ftrictelt ties of friendfhip, a man fo clofely connected with another as to be able to make the fame ufe of his friend's houfe as of his own) when it is rendered into French by the word *Hôte*, which commonly fignifies a perfon who enter-tains or is entertained by others for the fake of mo-ney ? 'Tis the fame with words, as 'tis with men. To imprint veneration, 'tis not fufficient to fhew themfelves fometimes in honorable fignifications or functions, 'tis neceffary moreover that they never appear in low functions, or mean fignifications.

In the fecond place, fuppofing a tranflator has fucceeded fo as to render the Latin figure in its full ftrength, yet it will frequently happen that this figure will not make the fame impreffion upon us, as it did upon the Romans for whom the poem was compofed. We have but a very imperfect know-ledge of things whofe figures are borrowed. Were we even to have a compleat knowledge of them, ftill we fhould not, for reafons I am going to lay down, have the fame tafte for thofe things as the Romans had ; wherefore the image that repre-fents them, cannot affect us as much as it did the Romans.

Thus the figures borrowed from the arms and military machines of the ancients, cannot make the fame impreffion upon us as they did upon them. Can the figures drawn from the combat of gladia-tors ftrike a Frenchman who knows nothing of, or at leaft who never faw the combats of the amphitheatre,

as

as much as the Romans, who were fo taken with thofe fpectacles as to be prefent at them feveral times in a month ? Is it to be fuppofed, that the figures borrowed from the orcheftra, from the chorufes and dances of the opera, could affect fuch as never faw this fpectacle, as much as they ftrike thofe who go to the opera every week ? Does the figure, *to eat his bread under the fhade of his fig-tree,* make the fame impreffion upon us, as it does upon a Syrian almoft continually tormented by a fcorching fun, and who finds an infinite pleafure in laying himfelf down to reft under the fhade of the large leaves of this tree, the beft fhelter he can find amongft all the trees in the fruitful plains of his country ? Can the northern nations be as fenfible of all the other figures which defcribe the pleafure of a cool fhade, as the people who live in hot countries, and for whom thefe images were invented ? Virgil and the other ancient poets would have employed figures of an oppofite tafte, if they had wrote for the northern nations. Inftead of drawing the greateft part of their metaphors from a brook whofe cool ftreams quench the traveller's thirft, or from a grove fpreading a delightful fhade on the brink of a fountain, they would have taken them from a good warm ftove, or from the effects of wine and fpirituous liquors. They would have chofen to defcribe the fenfible pleafure which a man, who is almoft ftiff with cold, feels upon approaching the fire ; or the flower but more agreable fenfation he finds in putting on a coat lined with good comfortable fur. We are much more affected with the defcription of fuch

pleafures

pleafures as we feel every day, than with the picture
of pleafures we have never or but feldom tafted.
As we are indifferent in refpect to delights which
we never wifh for, we cannot be fenfibly affected by
the defcription of them, were it drawn even by
Virgil. What charms could a great many people
of the north, (who never drank a drop of pure water, and who have only an imaginary knowledge of
the pleafure defcribed by the poet) what charms, I
fay, could they find in the following verfes of Virgil's fifth eclogue, which entertain us with fo delightful an image of the pleafure a man feels, when
oppreffed with toil, he compofes himfelf to fleep on
the green turf; or of the fweet fenfation a traveller
who is burnt with thirft, finds in quenching it with
the cool waters of a cryftal fountain?

Quale fopor feffis in gramine, quale per æftum
Dulcis aquæ faliente fitim reftinguere rivo.

Virg. eclog. 5.

As to the weary fwain with cares oppreft,
Beneath the fylvan fhade, refrefhing reft :
As to the fev'rifh traveller, when firft
He finds a cryftal ftream to quench his thirft.

Dryden.

This is the fate of moft of thofe images, which the
ancient poets adopted with fo much judgment, to
engage their cotemporaries and countrymen.

Befides, an image that is noble in one country,
may be low and mean in another. Such is that
which a Greek poet gives us of the afs, an animal
which in his country is fmooth and well made, whereas
in ours 'tis a wretched creature. Befides, this animal

mal is in thofe parts faddled and mounted by the principal people of the nation, and frequently honored with gold trappings ; whereas among us it is always miferably harneffed, and abandoned to the meaneft drudgery of the populace. Let us hear, for inflance, what a miffionary writes with relation to the opinion they have of affes in fome parts of the Eaft-Indies'. *We meet with affes here as well as in Europe. You would not imagine, madam, that we have here an intire breed, which is pretended to defcend in a right line from one afs, and is even very much honored upon that account. You will fay, perhaps, that this breed muft be one of the very meaneft. Not at all, madam, 'tis the king's.* Would it be right to pafs judgment on a poet of that country, by the ideas we have formed of him from a French tranflation ? Had we never feen any other horfes but thofe of the peafants in the ifle of France, fhould we be fo affected as we are, with all thofe figures which give a pompous defcription of a courfer ? But, you'll fay, one ought to allow a poet, who is criticized in a tranflation, all the figures and profopopæias that are founded on the cuftoms and manners of his country. I anfwer in the firft place, that this is never done. I do not think that it proceeds from prevarication, and I accufe the critics only of not having a fufficient knowledge of the manners and cuftoms of different people, to be able to judge what figures are authorized or not in a certain poet. In the fecond place, thefe figures are not only excufable, but they are beautiful in the original.

ᵃ Lettres Edif. t. 12. p. 96.

In

In fine, let us only inquire of thofe who know how to write in Latin and French. They will anfwer, that the energy of a phrafe, or the effect of a figure, are fo inherent, as it were, in the words of the language in which one has invented or compofed, that they are incapable of tranflating their own writings to their mind, or of giving the original turn to their own thoughts, when tranflating them from French into Latin, and much lefs when they render them from Latin into French. Images and ftrokes of eloquence lofe always fome part of their beauty and ftrength, when tranfplanted from the language in which they had their origin.

We have as good tranflations of Virgil and Horace, as tranflations can be. And yet thofe who underftand Latin, never fail to tell us, that thefe verfions do not give us an idea of the merit of the originals; and their teftimony is ftill corroborated by the general experience of people who are led by the agreablenefs of books in their choice of reading. Thofe who are verfed in the Latin tongue, are never fatiated with reading Horace and Virgil; while fuch as cannot read thefe poets but in tranflations, find fo little entertainment, that they have occafion for a great deal of refolution to read the Æneid thro'; and cannot help being furprized that the originals are read with fo much pleafure. On the other hand, perfons who are aftonifhed, that works which charm them fo much in the originals, fhould be fo tirefome to fuch as perufe the tranflations, are as much in the wrong as the former. They ought both to reflect, that thofe who read Horace's odes in French, do not read the fame poems as people who read

them

them in Latin. My reflection is fo much the more juft, as one cannot learn a language, without picking up at the fame time a knowledge of feveral things relating to the manners and cuftoms of the people who fpoke it, which gives us an infight into the figures and ftyle of the author, of which thofe who have not fuch lights, muft be deprived.

How comes it, that the French have fo little relifh for the tranflations of Ariofto and Taffo, tho' the reading of the *Rolando Furiofo*, and the *Gieru-falemme liberata*, juftly charms fuch Frenchmen, as have a fufficient knowledge of the Italian, to underftand without difficulty the originals? What is the reafon that the fame perfon who has read Racine's works fix times over, cannot go thro' with the tranflation of Virgil, notwithstanding thofe who underftand Latin have read the Æneid ten times, for thrice they have perufed the tragedies of the French poet? 'Tis becaufe it is natural for every tranflation to give a bad copy of the greateft beauties of a

plan and characters. The merit of things in poetry

preffion) with the merit of the expreffion.

Thofe who read hiftory for inftruction, lofe only the beauties of the hiftorian's ftyle, when they read him in a good tranflation. The principal merit of an hiftorian does not confift like that of a poet, in moving; nor is it his ftyle that chiefly engages us to his work. Events of importance are interefting of themfelves, and truth alone furnifhes them with the pathetic. The chief merit of hiftory is to inrich our memory, and to form our judgment; but

that

that of a poem confifts in moving us, and 'tis the very charm of the emotion that makes us read it. Wherefore the principal beauty of a poem is loft when we do not underftand the poet's own felect expreffions, and when we do not behold them in the order in which he ranged them to pleafe the ear, and to form images capable of moving the heart.

In effect, let us change the words of the two following verfes of Racine which we have already cited.

Enchaîner un captif de fes fers étonné,
Contre un joug qui lui plait vainement mutiné.

To lead a captive at his chains furpriz'd,
Rebelling vainly 'gainft a pleafing yoke.

And let us fay, ftill keeping to the figure : *To lay a prifoner of war in irons, who is furprifed thereat, and afts in vain the mutineer againft an agreable yoke* ; the verfes would lofe the harmony and poetry of their ftyle.   The fame figure prefents no longer the fame image ; and the painting exhibited in Racine's verfes is dawbed over, as it were, as foon as the terms are difplaced, and the definition of the word is fubftituted inftead of the word.   Thofe who want to be further convinced how far one word taken for another enervates the vigor of a phrafe, even without going out of the limits of the language in which it was compofed, let them read the twenty third chapter of Ariftotle's art of poetry.

. The French tranflators of Greek and Latin poets are obliged to deviate a great deal more from the expreffions of the original than I have done in thofe verſes of Phædra. Perſons of the greateſt capacity and application are tired with the unſuccefsful efforts they make in order to inſpire their tranſlations with as much energy as the original, where they find a ſtrength and exactnefs which they cannot tranſfuſe into their copy. They let themſelves at length be led away with the genius of our language, and ſubmit to the fate of tranſlations, after having ſtruggled againſt it for ſome time.

Since therefore a tranſlation does not give us the author's ſelect words, nor the arrangement in which he placed them in order to pleaſe the ear and to move the heart, we may ſay, that to judge of a poem in general from the verſion, is to form a judgment of the picture of a great maſter, celebrated chiefly for his coloring, from a print in which the ſtrokes of his deſign are quite loſt. A poem loſes by a tranſlation its harmony and numbers, which I compare to the coloring of a picture ; as alſo the poetry of the ſtyle, which may be compared to the deſign and the expreſſion. A verſion is a print, in which nothing remains of the original picture, but the ordonnance and attitude of the figures ; and even this is frequently altered.

To judge therefore of a poem by tranſlations and criticiſms, is judging of a thing deſigned to fall under a particular ſenſe, without having any knowledge of it by that ſenſe. But to form an idea of a poem from the unanimous depoſition of perſons acquainted with the original concerning the impreſſion it makes on them, is the beſt way to judge, when we do not underſtand it ourſelves. Nothing is more reaſonable than to ſuppoſe, that the object would make the

ſame

fame impreſſion upon us, as it does on them, were we as ſuſceptible of this impreſſion. Is it likely we ſhould liſten to a man, who ſhould attempt to prove by plauſible arguments, that the picture of the marriage of Cana, done by Paolo Veroneſe, which he never ſaw, cannot be ſo agreable, as people ſay it is, who have ſeen it ; by reaſon that it is impoſſible a picture ſhould pleaſe, when there are ſuch a number of defects in the poetic compoſition of the work, as are obſerved in this of Paolo Veroneſe? We ſhould deſire the critic to go and ſee the picture, and we ſhould rely on the uniform relation of thoſe that ſaw it, who proteſt it has charmed them notwithſtanding its defects. In fact, the uniform report of the ſenſes of other men, is the ſureſt way, next to the report of our own, to judge of things which fall under a ſenſitive perception. This we are ſufficiently convinced of, and it will be impoſſible ever to ſtagger human belief or opinion founded on the uniform report of other peoples ſenſes. A perſon cannot therefore, without an inexcuſable temerity, aſſert with confidence, when the queſtion relates to a poem he does not underſtand : That the opinion which men have of its excellence, *is only a prejudice of education founded on applauſes, which, upon tracing them to their firſt origin, we find for the moſt part to be no more than echoes to one another* [a] ; and 'tis ſtill a higher degree of raſhneſs to compoſe the imaginary hiſtory of this prejudice.

[a] *Diſcourſe on Homer, p. 122.*

C H A P. XXXVI.

Of the errors which persons are liable to, who judge of a poem by a translation, or by the remarks of critics.

WHAT should we think of an Englishman, supposing that any of them could be so indiscreet, who, without understanding a word of French, should attempt to arraign the Cid upon Rutter's translation [a], and pronounce judgment at length, that the fondness of the French for the original must be attributed to the prejudices of their infancy? We should tell him, that we are better acquainted than he is with the imperfections of the Cid, but that he cannot have our sensibility of the beauties which make us admire it, in spite of all its faults. In fine, we should say unto this presumptuous judge, whatever a persuasion founded on sense suggests, when we cannot readily recollect the proper reasons and terms for making a methodical refutation of propositions, whose error offends us. 'Tis difficult in such a case for the most moderate persons to contain themselves from breaking out into some harsh expressions. Now those who have learnt Greek and English are very sensible, that a Greek poet rendered into French, suffers a great deal more by the version, than a French poet translated into English.

[a] Printed in 1637.

All

All the judgments and parallels that can be made of thofe poems, which are underftood only by tranflations and critical differtations, lead us infallibly to falfe conclufions. Let us fuppofe, for inftance, the Maid of Orleans and the Cid to be tranflated into the Polifh tongue, and that one of the learned of Cracow, after having perufed thefe tranflations, paffes judgment on thofe poems by way of examen and difcuffion. Let us fuppofe, that after having made a methodical inquiry into the plan, the manners, the characters, and the probability of the events, whether in the natural or fupernatural order, he decides at length the value of thofe two poems ; he will certainly determine in favor of the Maid of Orleans, which in an operation of this nature will appear a more regular poem, and lefs defective in its kind, than the Cid. If we fhould likewife fuppofe, that this Polifh reafoner perfuades his countrymen, that a perfon is capable of judging of a poem written in a language he does not underftand, by reading the tranflation of it with critical remarks, they will certainly conclude, that Chapelain is a better poet than the great Corneille. They will treat us as people who are flaves to prejudices, for not fubmitting to their decifion. What fhall we therefore think of a proceeding which leads men naturally to this fort of judgments ?

C H A P. XXXVII.

Of the defects we imagine we see in the poems
of the ancients.

AS for those defects we fancy we see in the
poems of the ancients, and which we sometimes tell so dexterously at our fingers ends; 'tis possible we may be often and several ways mistaken.
Sometimes we may censure the poet, as defective in
his composition, for having inserted several things
which the time he lived in, and the respect due to
his cotemporaries, obliged him to mention. For
instance, when Homer composed his Iliad, he did
not write a fabulous story, that left him at liberty
to forge the characters of his heroes as he had a
mind, or to give the events what success he pleased,
and to imbellish certain facts with all the noble circumstances his imagination could suggest. He undertook to write in verse, a part of the events of a
war, which the Greeks his countrymen had waged
against the Trojans, whereof there was still a recent tradition remaining. Pursuant to the common
opinion, Homer flourished about a hundred and
fifty years after the siege of Troy, and according to
Sir Isaac Newton's chronology [a] he lived still nearer
to the time of that war, and might have seen several
persons, who knew Achilles, and the other illustrious
heroes of Agamemnon's army. I grant therefore
that Homer, as a poet, ought to have treated the
events in a different manner from that of a simple

[a] Chronolog. p 95. and p. 162.

historian.

hiſtorian. He ſhould have introduced the marvelous as much as it was reconcileable to probability,
according to the religion of thoſe times. He ought
to have imbelliſhed thoſe events with fictions, and to
have done, in ſhort, whatever Ariſtotle[a] commends
him for having performed. But Homer, in quality of a citizen and hiſtorian, and as a writer of
ballads or ſongs, that were deſtined chiefly to ſerve
as annals to the Greeks, was frequently obliged to
render his recitals conformable to the knowledge
the public had of thoſe facts.

We ſee by the example of our anceſtors, and by
the preſent practice in the North of Europe and ſome
parts of America, that the firſt hiſtorical monuments of nations, for preſerving the memory of paſt
events, as well as for exciting men to the moſt
neceſſary virtues in growing ſocieties, are drawn up
in verſe. The people therefore, tho' yet rude and
ignorant, compoſe a kind of ſongs to celebrate the
praiſes of ſuch of their countrymen as rendered
themſelves worthy of imitation, which they ſing on
ſeveral occaſions. Cicero[b] informs us, that juſt after Numa's time, the Romans were come into the
practice of ſinging ſongs at table in praiſe of
illuſtrious men.

The Greeks had their beginnings, like other people, and were an infant ſociety before they grew up
to be a poliſhed nation. Their firſt hiſtorians were
all poets ; wherefore Strabo[c] and other ancient writers inform us, that even Cadmus, Pherecides[d], and

---

[a] Poetic. cap. 24. [b] Tuſc. l. 4. [c] Geogr. lib. 1.

[d] *Verſuum nexu repudiato, conſcribere auſus paſſivis verbis Pherecides.* Apul. Flor. l. 4.

Heca-

Hecateus, the firſt who wrote in profe, made no alteration in their ſtyle but with regard to the meaſure of the verſe. Hiſtory preſerved for ſeveral ages among the Greeks ſome remains of its origin. Moſt of thofe who wrote afterwards in profe, retained the poetic ſtyle, and preſerved for a long while even the liberty of mixing the marvelous in their events. *The Greek hiſtorians,* ſays Quintilian[a], *aſſume a kind of liberty almoſt equal to that of poets.* Homer is not one of thofe firſt writers of fongs above-mentioned ; he did not appear till ſome time after them.

> ———— *Poſt hos inſignis Homerus,*
> *Tirtæuſque mares animos in Martia bella*
> *Verſibus exacuit.* —— HORAT. de arte.

Next Homer and Tyrtæus boldly dare
To whet brave minds, and lead the ſtout to war.
                    CREECH.

But people were accuſtomed in his time to look upon poems as hiſtorical monuments. Homer would have therefore been to blame, had he changed certain characters, or altered ſome known events, and eſpecially if he had omitted in the enumerations of his armies, the heroes who went upon that memorable expedition. We may eaſily imagine the complaints their deſcendants would have made againſt the poet.

Tacitus relates that the Germans uſed to ſing, at the time when he wrote his annals, the exploits of Arminius, who was dead fourſcore years before. Were the authors of thofe Cheruſcan fongs at liberty

_____
[a] *Græcis hiſtoriis plerumque poeticæ ſimilis ineſt licentia.* QUINT. Inſt. l. 2. cap. 4.

to contradict public and known facts, and to suppose, for example, in order to do more honor to their hero, that Arminius never took the oath of allegiance to the Roman eagles which he defeated? When those poets spake of the interview on the banks of the Wefer, between him and his brother Flavius, who ferved in the Roman army, was it poffible for them to finifh the conference with decency and gravity, when every body knew that the German general and the Roman officer abufed one another in prefence of the armies of both nations, and would have come to blows were it not for the river that was between them?

Let us take another example that will ftrike us better. Hiftory and poetry are in our days two very different profeffions. We have hiftorians to read when we are defirous of being informed with regard to the truth of facts; and we feek merely for amufement in the reading of poets. Chapelain wrote his Maid of Orleans at a much greater diftance of time from the event he fung, than that which was between the taking of Troy by the Greeks, and the time when Homer compofed his Iliad. And yet can we imagine that Chapelain was at liberty to treat and imbellifh the character of the principal characters as he pleafed? Could he reprefent Agnes Sorel as a violent and fanguinary maid, or as a perfon without any elevation of mind, and who had advifed Charles VII to live with her in obfcurity? Would he have been allowed to give this prince the known character of the count de Dunois? Would it have been right of him to change the events of combats and fieges according

C c 4

to

to his fancy? Was it poſſible for him to conceal ſome known circumſtances of his actions, which are not ſo much to the honor of Charles VII? Had he done any thing of all this, tradition would have ſtood up, and contradicted him. Beſides, as we have ſhewn in the firſt part of this work, nothing is a greater enemy to probability (which is the very ſoul of fiction) than to ſee the fiction contradicted by facts that are generally known.

If Homer's heroes do not draw their ſwords and fight as often as they quarrel, 'tis becauſe they had not the ſame notions with regard to point of honor, as the Goths and the like barbarous nations. The Greeks and Romans who lived before the general corruption of their countrymen, were leſs afraid of death than the Engliſh of our times; but it was their opinion, that a groundleſs contumely diſbonored only the perſon that pronounced it. If the contumely contained a juſt charge, their ſentiment was, that the perſon affronted had no other method of repairing his honor, than that of reforming his manners. Thoſe polite nations never dreamt, that a duel which is to be decided by chance, or at the moſt by a ſkill in fencing which they conſidered as the profeſſion of their ſlaves, was a proper method of juſtifying one's ſelf, with regard to a reproach, which frequently does not ſo much as concern a perſon's bravery. The advantage gained, proves only that one is a better gladiator than his adverſary, but not that he is exempt from the vice with which he is charged. Was it fear that hindered Cæſar and Cato from cutting one another's throats, after Cæſar expoſed in a full Senate-houſe a billet-doux

I

that

that had been sent him by Cato's sister? The manner in which they both encountred death, is a sufficient proof they were not afraid of it. I do not remember to have read either in the Greek or Roman history any thing that resembles the Gothic duels, except an accident that happened at the funeral games, which Scipio Africanus gave under the walls of new Carthage in honor of his uncle and father, who had both lost their lives in the Spanish wars. Livy [a] relates, that the champions were not common gladiators hired from the merchant, but barbarians, such as Scipio perhaps was very glad to get rid of, and who fought against one another thro' different motives. Some of them, says the historian, agreed to terminate their disputes by the sword. The Greeks and Romans, who were so passionately fond of glory, never imagined it a dishonorable thing for a subject to wait for satisfaction from public authority. It was reserved therefore for those people, whom misery drove from their northern snows, to believe that the best champion must of necessity be the honestest man, and that the name of government could with justice be given to a society, in which the rules of honor obliged fellow-citizens to revenge their real or pretended injuries by force of arms. If Quinault does not make Phaeton [b] draw his sword in the conversation between him and Epaphus, 'tis because he introduces two Ægyptians upon the stage, and not two Burgundians or Vandals.

The prejudice therefore which the greatest part of mankind have for their own times and country, is a

[a] Liv. hist. l. 28.   [b] Opera of Phaeton. act 3.

fertile

fertile source of false remarks as well as of wrong judgments. They take what is practised there for a rule of what ought to be always and every where observed. And yet there is only a small number of customs, or even of virtues and vices, that have been praised or condemned in all times and countries. Now poets are in the right to practise what Quintilian advises orators, which is to draw their advantages from the ideas of those for whom they compose, and to conform to them [a]. Wherefore we should transform ourselves, as it were, into those for whom the poem was written, if we intend to form a sound judgment of its images, figures and sentiments. The Parthian, who after being repulsed in the first charge, flies back full gallop, in order to take a better opportunity, and not to expose himself in vain to the enemy's darts, ought not to be looked upon as guilty of cowardice ; because this manner of fighting was authorized by the military discipline of that nation, founded on the idea they had of courage and real valour. The ancient Germans, so celebrated for their bravery, were also of opinion, that to retreat upon some occasions, in order to return with more vigor to the charge, was rather a prudent than cowardly action [b].

We have seen Homer condemned for giving an elegant description of the gardens of king Alcinoüs, not unlike, say some people, to those of an honest vine-dresser or gardener in the neighbourhood of Pa-

[a] *Plurimum refert qui sint audientium mores, quæ publicè recepta persuasio.* QUINT. Inst. l 3. cap. 9.
[b] *Cedere loco dum rursus instes, magis confilii quàm formidinis arbitrantur.* TAC. de mor. Germ.

ris,

ris. But allowing this to be true, that the defigning of a fine garden is the tafk of an architect, and to plant it at a very great expence, the merit of a prince ; ftill 'tis the poet's bufinefs to give a good defcription of fuch as are planted by the people of his time. Homer is as great an artift in the defcription he gives of the gardens of Alcinoüs, as if he had entertained us with that of the groves of Verfailles.

After reproaching the ancient poets for filling their verfes with common objects and ignoble images, feveral think themfelves very moderate, when they lay the fault they have not really committed, to the age they lived in, and pity them for having had the misfortune of appearing in a time of rufticity and ignorance.

The manner in which we live, if I may fay fo, with our horfes, prejudices us againft the fpeeches with which men addrefs thefe animals in the poems of the ancients. We cannot bear that their mafter fhould fpeak to them in the fame manner almoft, as a huntfman fpeaks to a hound. But thefe difcourfes were very fuitable in the Iliad, a poem written for a nation, among whom a horfe was, as it were, a fellow-boarder with his mafter. They muft have been agreable to a people, who fuppofed fuch a knowledge in horfes as we do not allow them, and who frequently ufed to talk in that manner to thofe creatures. Whether the opinion which admits beafts to have fome degree of reafon bordering upon that of man, be falfe or no, this is no bufinefs of the poet. His tafk is not to purge his age of its errors in phyfics, but to give a faithful defcription of the cuftoms

and

and manners of his country, in order to render his. imitation as likely as poſſible. Homer, in this very paſſage for which he has been ſo frequently cenſur-. ed, would ſtill have pleaſed ſeveral nations of A- ſia and Afric, who have not changed their ancient method of managing their horſes, no more than ſe-. veral other cuſtoms.

I ſhall give here an extract from Buſbequius, am- baſſador from the emperor Ferdinand I, to the Grand Signor Soliman II, concerning the manner of ma- naging their horſes in Bithynia, a country not far from the Greek colonies of Aſia, and bordering up- on Phrygia, where the great Hector was born, whom ſome of our critics would ſtrike ſpeechleſs for ſpeaking to his horſes. *I obſerved,* ſays he, [a] *in Bithynia, that every body, even the very peaſants, treat their colts with great tenderneſs ; that when they want them to do any thing, they careſs them as we do children ; and that they let them go to and fro about the houſe. Nay, they would be glad to make them ſit down to table. The grooms dreſs their horſes with the ſame gentleneſs, for 'tis by ſtroking and almoſt by perſuaſion they manage them, and they never beat them but in caſes of extremity. Wherefore they contract a kind of friendſhip for men, and 'tis very rare they kick up their heels, or grow vicious in any other manner. In our countries they are bred up in a very different way. The grooms never enter the ſtables without ſtorming againſt them, and ne- ver think they dreſs them well, unleſs they give them a hundred blows, a treatment which makes them fear and hate mankind. The Turks teach their horſes alſo*

[a] BUSBEQU. Legat. Turc. epiſt. 3.

to kneel down, that they may mount them with more ease. They teach them to pick up a stick or a sword from the ground with their teeth to present it to the rider, and they put silver rings in the nostrils of such as have been thus taught, as a kind of distinction, in recompence for their docility. I have seen some of them learn to stand in the same place, without being held by any body, after the rider had dismounted; and others go thro' their exercises of themselves, and obey all the commands of the riding masters, who stood at some distance. Mine, says Busbequius *some lines lower, give me a good deal of diversion every evening. They are led into the court, and the horse I call by his name, looks at me stedfastly and neighs. We have got acquainted by means of some slices of melon, which I myself put into their mouths.* 'Tis likely this was not effected, without the ambassador's making some of those speeches to his horses, which were capable of drawing upon him the censure of our critics.

There is no body in the republic of letters, but has heard of the chevalier d'Arvieux [a], a gentleman famous for his voyages, employments, and oriental learning. I shall not be charged with having cited exceptionable witnesses, to prove that a great many of the Asiatic inhabitants talk still to their horses, as Hector spoke to his in Asia. This gentleman after having discoursed at large, in the eleventh chapter of his relation, concerning the manners and customs of the Arabians, of the docility, and, if I may say so, of the good nature of their horses, and the tenderness and humanity with which their masters treat them, adds what follows. *A merchant of Marseilles*

[a] Deceased in 1702.

who

who lived at Rama, kept a mare in partnerſhip with an Arabian. This mare was called Touyſſe, and beſides her beauty, youth, and price of twelve hundred crowns, had the merit of being of the principal and nobleſt race. The merchant had her genealogy and all her lineal deſcents by father and mother, as high as five hundred years of ancientneſs, the whole proved by public acts drawn up in the abovementioned form. Abrahim (this is the name of the Arabian) uſed to go frequently to Rama [a] *to ſee how this mare did, whom he was moſt paſſionately fond of. I have had ſeveral times the pleaſure of ſeeing him weep with tenderneſs, while he was embracing and careſſing her. He uſed to kiſs her on theſe occaſions, and to wipe her eyes with his handkerchief. He rubbed her down with his ſhirt-ſleeves, and gave her a thouſand bleſſings during whole hours that he talked to her. My eyes, my ſoul, my heart,* ſaid he, *how hard is my fate to be obliged to let you out to ſo many maſters, without being able to maintain you myſelf? I am poor, my dear, thou knoweſt it well. My darling, I reared thee in my own houſe like my daughter, I never ſcolded or ſtruck thee, but always careſſed thee to the beſt of my power. God preſerve thee my beloved. Thou art handſome, ſoft, and amiable. God preſerve thee from the looks of the envious* ; and a thouſand ſuch like ſpeeches. *He uſed to embrace her then moſt tenderly, and to go away with his face ſtill towards her, giving her as he retired backward a thouſand tender adieus. This puts me in mind of an Arabian at Tunis, where I was ſent for the execution of a treaty of peace, who would not deliver up a mare we had*

[a] A village in Paleſtine.

bought

bought for the king's stud. When he put the money in
his bag, he cast his eyes upon the mare, and began
to weep. Is it possible, said he, that after having
bred thee in my house with so much care, and after
having had so many kind services of thee, in requital
I should deliver thee up in slavery to the Franks?
No, my darling, my life, I'll be guilty of no such
crime. Upon which he flung the money upon the table, and embracing and kissing his mare, he carried
her back with him. The relations of the oriental
countries are full of stories of this sort. But it is
not every where believed, neither has it been always
a received opinion, that brutes are nothing more
than mere machines. This we must own, is one of
the discoveries made by the new philosophy, without
the help of experiments, and by mere strength of reasoning. As for its progress, 'tis a thing that every
body knows, so that I shall say nothing concerning it.

'Tis not sufficient to know how to write well, in
order to be able to give a judicious criticism of
ancient and foreign poems, one must have also a
knowledge of the subjects they treat of. A thing that
might have been very usual in their time, and common in their country, may be contrary nevertheless
to probability and reason in the eyes of those censors,
who have no knowledge but of their own times and
country. Claudian is so surprized that the mules
should be obedient to the voice of the mule-driver,
that he thinks he can draw an argument from thence
to prove the truth of the history of Orpheus.

Miraris si voce feras placaverit Orpheus,
   Cum pronas pecudes Gallica verba regant.

'Tis

'Tis very probable that Claudian would have had some difficulty to give credit to a thing, which the inhabitants of Provence hardly take notice of, had he never quitted Ægypt, the country in which he is suppofed to have been born. Perhaps his countrymen cenfured him for tranfgreffing in this point againft the rules of probability.

C H A P. XXXVIII.

That the remarks of critics on particular poems do not give people a difrelifh of them ; and that when they lay them afide, 'tis only in order to read better performances of the fame kind.

BE it as it will with refpect to thofe faults, which paft and future critics have and fhall find in the writings of the ancients ; they will never be able to prejudice the public againft the reading of them. They will continue to be read and admired, 'till future poets produce fomething better. It was not our geometrical critics that gave our anceftors a diftafte for Ronfard's poems, and made them lay him afide ; but poems of a far more engaging nature than thofe of Ronfard's. It was Moliere's comedies that put us out of conceit with Scarron and other poets that preceded him ; and not the books that were wrote in order to detect the defects of thofe pieces. In cafe we fhould be entertained hereafter with better performances than thofe which are already

dy in the hands of the public, there will be no occafion
for critics to come and advife us to quit good for better.
People do not want to be inftructed with refpect to
the merit of two poems, as concerning that of two
fyftems of philofophy. They judge and form their
difcernments of poems by the help of their fenfes,
much better than critics with the affiftance of their
rules. Thofe who have a mind to diminifh the reputation which the public has for Virgil, and to deprive
him of his readers, muft favor us firft with a better
poem than the Æneid. They muft foar higher than
Virgil and his companions, not as the wren that
placed himfelf on the back of the eagle, to take his
flight when the bird of Jupiter grew tired, in order
to tell him infultingly that he had furpaffed him in
the heigth of his flight. Let them do it, with the
ftrength of their own wings.

Let them chufe therefore a new fubject from modern hiftory, in which they cannot borrow the inventions, nor the poetic phrafes of the ancients, but
muft draw the poetic ftyle and fiction from the fund
of their own genius. Let them write an epic poem
on the deftruction of the league by Henry IV, in
which the converfion of this prince, followed by
the reduction of Paris, would be naturally the un-
ravelling of the piece. A man that has a fufficient
ftrength of genius for poetry and is able to extract
from his own fund all the beauties neceffary for fuf-
taining a grand fiction, would find his account
much better in treating a fubject of this fort, in
which there would be no danger of clafhing with
any other writer, than in handling fubjects taken
from fable, or from the Greek and Roman hiftories.

Inftead of borrowing therefore their heroes from the Greeks and Latins, let them venture to take them from our kings and princes.

Homer did not fing the battles of the Æthiopians or the Ægyptians, but thofe of his countrymen. Virgil and Lucan took their fubjects from the Roman hiftory. Let our poets therefore attempt to fing thofe things we have before our eyes, fuch as our combats, feafts, and ceremonies. Let them entertain us with poetic defcriptions of the buildings, rivers, and countries we fee every day, and whofe originals we can compare, in a manner, with the imitation. With what grandeur and pathos would not Virgil have treated an apparition of St Lewis to Henry IV, the day before the battle of Yvri, when this prince, the honor of the defcendants of our holy king, made profeffion as yet of the faith of Geneva? With what elegance would he have defcribed the virtues in white robes, conducted by clemency, coming to open to this great prince the gates of Paris? The intereft which every body would find in this fubject from different motives, would be a fure pledge of the public attention to the work. But the reafons we have given in thefe reflections, together with paft experience, are fufficient to convince us, that the poffibility of writing a better epic poem in French than the Æneid, is only a metaphyfical poffibility, fuch as that of moving the earth by giving a fixt point without the globe.

As long as our modern writers do not excel, nor even equal the ancients, people will always continue to read and admire them, and this veneration

veneration will continually increase without any danger of being diminished by the malicious attempts of envy. We do not admire their works because of their having been produced in certain ages, but 'tis these ages we respect for giving birth to such great performances. We do not admire the Iliad, the Æneid, and some other writings, on account of their having been wrote a long time ago; but because we find them admirable when we peruse them, and those that understood them, have in all ages admired them; in fine, because a long series of ages is elapsed, and yet no succeeding rival has rose up to equal those authors in this kind of poetry.

C H A P. XXXIX.

That there are professions, in which success depends more upon genius, than upon the succour which may be received from art; and others on the contrary in which it depends more upon art than genius. We ought not to infer that one age surpasses another in professions of the first kind, because it excels them in the second.

WHAT has been above said with respect to poets, historians, and excellent orators, must not be understood of all the writers of antiquity. For example, the ancient writings on

those

thofe fciences, whofe merit confifts in extent of knowledge, are not fuperior to fuch as the moderns have wrote concerning thofe very fubjects. I fhould even be as little furprized at a man's fhewing no figns of admiration at the extent of the knowledge of the ancients, who had taken his idea of their merit from their works on phyfics, botany, geography, and aftronomy, becaufe his profeffion obliged him to make his principal ftudy of thofe fciences ; as at feeing a perfon who had formed his idea of the merit of the ancients from their works of hiftory, eloquence, and poetry, filled with admiration for thofe great originals. The ancients were ignorant in the abovementioned fciences, of a great many things which we are well acquainted with ; and led on by the natural itch, which men have of carrying their decifions beyond the limits of their certain knowledge, they fell, as I have already obferved, into an infinite number of errors.

Thus an aftronomer in our days underftands better than Ptolemy thofe very things which this mathematician knew, and befides he knows all the difcoveries which have been made fince the time of the Antoninus's, either by the help of voyages, or by the affiftance of the telefcope. Were Ptolemy to come back into the world, he would become a difciple to the obfervatory. The fame may be faid of anatomifts, navigators, botanifts, and of all fuch as profefs thofe fciences, whofe merit confifts more in knowing than in inventing and producing. But there are other profeffions, in which the laft comers have not the fame advantage over their predeceffors, by reafon that the progrefs they admit of, depends more on the talent

lent of inventing, and the natural genius of the
perſon that practiſes them, than on the ſtate of
perfection in which theſe profeſſions are, when the
perſon that exerciſes them, finiſhes his career.
Wherefore the man born with the happieſt genius, makes the greateſt progreſs in theſe profeſſions, independent of the degree of perfection in
which they are when he practiſes them.   'Tis
enough for him that the profeſſion he embraces
be reduced to art, and that the practice of this
art has ſome kind of method; nay, he may
invent the art, and digeſt the method himſelf.   The
ſtrength of his genius, which enables him to
gueſs and imagine an infinite number of things
above the reach of ordinary capacities, gives him
a greater advantage over men of common under-
ſtandings, who ſhall profeſs this very art after it
has been brought to perfection; than they can have
over him by the knowledge of new diſcoveries, and
by the new lights with which the art is inriched,
when they come to profeſs it in their turn.   The
aſſiſtance which may be derived from the perfection, to which one of the arts here mentioned has
attained, cannot lead ordinary capacities as far, as
the ſuperiority of natural lights is able to conduct
a man of genius.

Such are the profeſſions of a painter, a poet,
a general, a muſician, an orator, and even that
of a muſician. Men become great generals and
eminent orators, as ſoon as they practiſe theſe
profeſſions with a proper genius, let the ſtate of
the arts that inſtruct them be what it will. The

2   merit

merit of illuftrious artifts and of great men in all the profeffions abovementioned, depends principally on the portion of genius they have brought with them into the world ; whereas that of a botanift, a natural philofopher, an aftronomer, and a chemift, depends chiefly on the ftate of perfection, to which fortuitous difcoveries and other people's labor have advanced the fcience he intends to cultivate. Hiftory confirms what I have afferted here, with refpect to all thofe profeffions, which principally depend on genius.

Among the abovecited profeffions, that of phyfic feems to be the moft dependent on the ftate in which a perfon finds it, when he begins to profefs it. And yet when we enter into a ftrict inquiry concerning this art, we find that its operations depend more on the particular genius, in proportion to which every phyfician benefits by other people's knowledge as well as by his own experience, than on the ftate of phyfic, when he begins to profefs it.

The parts of phyfic are, the knowledge of the diftempers, the knowledge alfo of the remedies, and the application of the remedy fuitable to the diftemper. The difcoveries that have been made fince Hippocrates's time in anatomy and chemiftry, facilitate very much the knowledge of the difeafes. We are likewife acquainted in our days with an infinite multitude of remedies which Hippocrates never fo much as heard of, and the number of which confiderably furpaffes that of the remedies which he knew and we have loft. Chemiftry has fupplied us with

part

part of thefe new remedies, and for the other we
are indebted to the countries difcovered to the
Europeans within thefe two centuries. Our gentlemen of the faculty are agreed neverthelefs, that
Hippocrates's aphorifms are the work of a man,
who far furpaffes, taking him all together, any of
our modern phyficians. They do not pretend to
equal, but are fatisfied with admiring his practice and predictions with refpect to the courfe
and the conclufion of diforders, tho' he made
them with fewer fuccors than our prefent phyficians have for making their prognoftics. There
is not one of them that would fo much as hefitate, were he to be afked whether he fhould chufe
to be attended by Hippocrates in an acute diftemper, (even fuppofing the extent of Hippocrates's knowledge to be as limited as when he
wrote) than by the fkilfulleft phyfician of London
or Paris. They would all prefer to be in the
hands of Hippocrates. This is becaufe the talent
of difcerning the temperament of the patient, the
nature of the air, its prefent temperature, the
fymptoms of the diforder, as well as the inftinct
which makes a perfon hit upon a fuitable remedy,
and the critical moment of applying it, depend
upon genius. Hippocrates was born with a fuperior genius for phyfic, which gave him a greater
advantage in practice over modern phyficians, than
all the new difcoveries are able to give the latter
over Hippocrates.

'Tis vulgarly thought, that were Cæfar to
come back into the world, and to fee our fire-

I   arms

arms and modern fortifications, and in fhort all our offenfive and defenfive weapons, he would be exceedingly furprized. He would be obliged, fay they, to recommence his apprenticefhip, and even to make a very long one before he would be capable of leading two thoufand men into the field. Not at all, faid marfhal Vauban, who was fo much the more fenfible of the ftrength of Cæfar's genius, as he had a great fhare of it himfelf. Cæfar would be able to learn in lefs than fix months all that we know; and as foon as he would have learnt the ufe of our arms, and been acquainted, as it were, with the nature of our arrows and fhields, his genius would apply them perhaps to ufes which we do not fo much as think of.

The art of painting includes at prefent an infinite multitude of obfervations and experiments, which were unknown in Raphael's time; yet we do not fee that any of our painters have equalled that amiable genius. Thus, on fuppofition that we know fomething relating to the art of difpofing the plan of a poem, and of giving a decency of manners to the perfonages, which the ancients were ftrangers to; ftill they muft have excelled us, if it be true that they had a fuperior genius; and this fo much the more as 'tis certain that the languages in which they compofed, were more adapted to poetry than ours. We perhaps fhall commit lefs faults than they, but we fhall never be able to reach that degree of excellence which they attained. Our eleves will be better inftructed than theirs, but our mafters will have far inferior abilities.

Many

Many of thefe great natural genius's, fays one of the beft Englifh poets [a], *that were never difci-plined and broken by rules of art, are to be found among the ancients, and in particular among thofe of the more eaftern parts of the world.* Homer has *innumerable flights, that Virgil was not able to reach, and in the Old Teftament we find feveral paffages more elevated and fublime than any in Homer.*

In fact, Racine appears a greater poet in his Athalia, than in any of his other tragedies, on-ly becaufe his fubject being taken from the Old Teftament, it authorized him to imbellifh his ver-fes with the boldeft figures and the moft pom-pous images of fcripture; whereas he was allow-ed to make but a very fober ufe of them in his profane pieces. People liftened with refpect to the oriental ftyle when fpoken by the per-fonages of Athalia, and were infinitely charmed with it. In fine, fays the abovementioned Eng-lifh author in fome other place, we may be ex-acter than the ancients, but we cannot be fo fublime. I know not thro' what fatality all the great poets of the modern nations are agreed in preferring the compofitions of the ancients to any of their own. Indeed, 'tis acknowledging our in-capacity of writing in the tafte of the ancients, to endeavour to degrade them. Quintilian [d] obferves,

[a] Spectator. N°. 160. 3. Sept. 1711.

[b] *Quos ille non defliterat inceffere, cum diverfi fibi confcius generis, placere fe in dicendo poffit iis quibus illi placerent, dif-fideret.* QUINT. Inft. l. 10.

that Seneca continually difparaged thofe great men who had preceded him, becaufe he perceived that their writings and his were of fo different tafte, that either one or the other muft be difagreable to his cotemporaries. In fact, it was impoffible for them to have any value for the tinfel and pointed ftyle of Seneca's writings, which feemed to forebode a decline of genius; as long as they continued to admire the noble and fimple ftyle of the writers of the Auguftan age.

The End of the Second VOLUME.

BOOKS *printed for* J. NOURSE, *at the* Lamb, *againſt* Katherine-Street, *in the* Strand.

I. **A** New Method of learning, with great Facility, the GREEK TONGUE : containing Rules for the *Declenſions, Conjugations, Reſolution of Verbs, Syntax, Quantity, Accents, Dialeǫs,* and *Poetic Licence.* Digeſted in the cleareſt and con-ciſeſt Order, with Variety of uſeful Remarks, proper to the at-taining a compleat Knowledge of that Language, and a perfeǫ Underſtanding of the Authors who have writ in it. *Tranſlated from the French of Meſſieurs de* Port Royal. *In two Volumes* 8*vo.* Price bound 10 *s.*

II. The Conſtitution and Government of the *Germanick Body :* Shewing how this State has ſubſiſted for three hundred Years paſt under the Emperors of the Houſe of *Auſtria.* With an Account of, 1. The Dignity, Rights, Prerogatives, and Quali-fications, of the Emperor and the Electors. 2. The Election and Coronation of the Emperor, and the Articles he is obliged to ſwear to. 3. The Election of the King of the Romans. 4. The Ban of the Empire, and the Manner of depoſing an Emperor. 5. The Vicars of the Empire ; the Circles, Diets, Tribunals, and Councils. 6. The Evangelick Body ; and its Right to protect all thoſe of the Empire, who ſuffer for the Proteſtant Cauſe. Compiled from the fundamental Laws of *Germany,* the beſt Hiſtories of the Empire, and the authorities of its moſt celebrated Lawyers. By *M. NECKER, Profeſſor Juris Publici Germanici.* In Octavo. Price 4 *s.* ſewed.

III. A new Voyage to *Guinea :* deſcribing the Cuſtoms, Manners, Soil, Climate, Habits, Buildings, Education, Manual Arts, Agriculture, Trade, Employments, Languages, Ranks of Diſtinction, Habitations, Diverſions, Marriages, and whatever elſe is memorable among the Inhabitants. Likewiſe, an Ac-count of their Animals, Minerals, *&c.* with great Variety of entertaining Incidents, worthy of Obſervation, that happened during the Author's Travels in that large Country. With an alphabetical Index. By *William Smith,* Eſq; Appointed by the Royal African Company to ſurvey their Settlements, make Diſ-coveries, *&c.* The Second Edition. In 8*vo.* bound in Calf, Price

Price 4 s. Illustrated with Cutts, engraved from Drawings taken from the Life.

IV. Political Maxims of the State of *Holland*: comprehending a general View of the civil Government of that Republic, and the Principles on which it is founded; the Nature, Rise, and Progress of the Commerce of its Subjects, and of their true Interests with respect to all their Neighbours. By *John de Witt*, Penfionary of *Holland*. Translated from the *Dutch* Original, which contains many curious Paffages not to be found in any of the *French* Verfions. To which is prefixed, Hiftorical Memoirs of the two illuftrious Brothers *Cornelius* and *John de Witt*. Price 6 s.

V. The Elements of Natural Philofophy: Chiefly intended for the Students in the Univerfities. By *P. V. Muffchenbrock*, M. D. Profeffor of Mathematicks and Philofophy in the Univerfity of *Leyden*. Tranflated from the Latin, by *John Colfon*, M. A. F. R. S. Lucafian Profeffor of Mathematicks in the University of *Cambridge*. In two Volumes, 8vo. Price 10 s.

VI. The Philofophical Hiftory and Memoirs of the Royal Academy of Sciences at *Paris*: Or, An Abridgment of all the Papers relating to Natural Philofophy, which have been publifhed by the Members of that illuftrious Society. Illuftrated with Copper Plates. The whole tranflated and abridged by *John Martyn*, F. R. S. Profeffor of Botany in the Univerfity of *Cambridge*; and *Ephraim Chambers*, Author of the Univerfal Dictionary of Arts and Sciences. Five Volumes. 8vo.

VII. Travels into *Turkey*; containing the moft accurate Account of the Turks, and neighbouring Nations, their Manners, Cuftoms, Religion, Policy, Riches, &c. Tranflated from the Original *Latin* of the Learned *A. G. Bufbequius*. 12mo. Price 3 s. bound.

VIII. A General and Compleat Treatife on all the Difeafes incident to Children, from their Birth to the Age of Fifteen. By *John Aftruc*, M D Regius Profeffor of Medicine at *Paris*, and Chief Phyfician to his prefent Majefty the King of *France*, &c. 8vo. Price 3 s. 6d.

IX. An Appendix to the Doctrine of Annuities, containing fome Remarks on Mr *De Moivre's* Book on the fame Subject. In 8vo. Price 6 d.

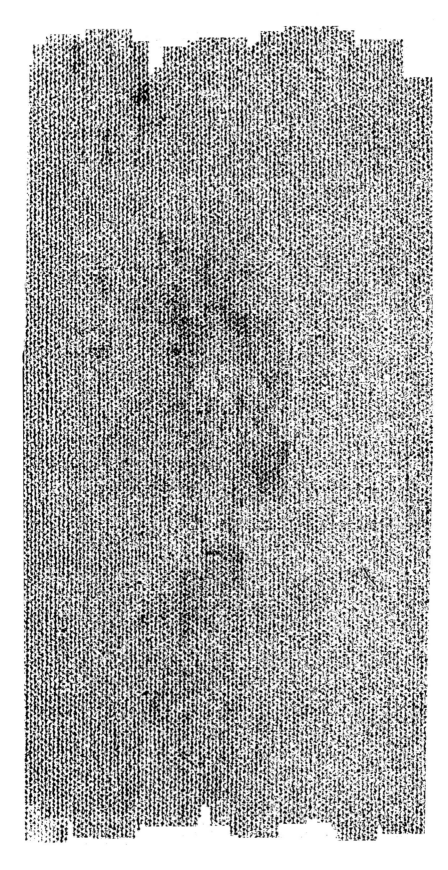